# A
# Cemetery
# Should
# Be
# Forever

# A
# Cemetery
# Should
# Be
# Forever

## The challenge to managers and directors

**John F. Llewellyn**

Tropico Press
Glendale, California

**Publisher's Cataloging-in-Publication**
*(Provided by Quality Books, Inc.)*

Llewellyn, John F., 1947-
    A cemetery should be forever : the challenge to
managers and directors / John F. Llewellyn. -- 1st ed.
    p. cm
    Includes bibliographical references and index
    Preassigned LCCN 98-96589
    ISBN 0–9665801–2–5


    1. Cemeteries--United States--Management.    I. Title.

RA629.L54  1998                        363.7'5'068
                                              QBI98-1310

To my wife, Linda, and daughter,
Sharon, for their love and support

and

To Hubert Eaton, Frederick Llewellyn,
and Forest Lawn's employees for their
unfaltering belief that a cemetery
should be forever.

# Contents

# Illustrations

## FIGURES

## TABLES

# Foreword

The time is right for this book. Not very long ago, a cemetery could be administered with a "caretaker" mentality and still survive. That is no longer the case. In this day of cemetery conglomerates, smart consumers, and a difficult labor market, administrators who manage their property like a park, rather than the tough business it is, simply will not survive. And as John Llewellyn says so well, "Cemeteries just don't go away when they fail...they become eyesores, nuisances, or financial burdens to their communities."

People are asked to join cemetery boards of directors for a variety of reasons: they may be friends with the CEO or another board member; they may have a talent that makes them particularly valuable; they may have been asked because of their diversity; they may have hinted to someone they would be interested if an opening ever came up. Regardless of how they came to be on the board, most members have little direct knowledge of the cemetery business, which is serious business indeed! It is a multi-billion dollar, ubiquitous, here to stay, international industry, but the majority of cemeteries remain relatively small businesses.

Likewise, newly-hired executives may come from backgrounds with some area of commonality—banking, sales, accounting, operations—but, generally, they have little understanding of the unique nature of the cemetery business. Certainly, this was true for me 21 years ago when I joined Spring

Grove Cemetery and Arboretum as an administrative and financial officer after several years in the commercial lending area of a large bank.

Our challenges are also our opportunities. All of us have the ability to serve customers better by providing superior service, improve the longevity of our cemeteries by creative master planning, strengthen our financial position by wise business practices, fund and manage our endowment funds effectively, and learn from those who are succeeding,

This book is a blessing to any person involved with managing a cemetery. Until now, there has not been a comprehensive, single source for all aspects of cemetery management; most of us "veterans" learned what we know piece-meal from a variety of different sources. Thanks to this book, newcomer and old-timer alike now have a reliable and thorough source of information, a compilation of information about the cemetery industry that would take an individual many, many years to learn on his or her own.

No one is more qualified to write such a book than John Llewellyn, CEO of Forest Lawn Memorial-Parks in Southern California. Since John's great uncle Dr. Hubert Eaton took the helm in 1916, Forest Lawn has been recognized as not only one of the country's premiere cemeteries, but also as the birthplace of many of the concepts that have driven the cemetery industry in the 20th century. John, like his father and great-uncle before him, has been an industry leader at both the national and state level. Forest Lawn is a success and has been for nearly 85 years. John has graciously shared much of what has made Forest Lawn a success.

This book is a tremendous contribution to the industry. Read, enjoy, and learn!

Andrew J. Conroy
President
Spring Grove Cemetery and Arboretum

# Introduction

After being exposed to a subject for a long time, it is easy to forget that the knowledge about it didn't come easily or overnight. I grew up in the shadow of Forest Lawn—all my life I've been steeped in the cemetery industry. Because of that, I sometimes forget that it takes time and exposure to understand the cemetery industry and to fully appreciate the complexity and challenge of cemeteries. I've come to realize that cemeteries are often not well understood—by those who use them as customers and by those who are new to the cemetery industry either in management positions or as members of governing boards.

The importance of educating new management personnel and board members was brought home to me when Forest Lawn had several new members join its various boards of directors. This is an outstanding group of people with rich experience and education. Over the years, we've had many dedicated directors, all highly intelligent, with backgrounds in business, finance, government, law, and education. Many have served on boards or in senior management positions with large publicly traded corporations and all have been community leaders. Despite their breadth of experience, none have had any previous exposure to cemetery management.

As I talked with other cemetery executives, I realized that nothing was available to help new directors understand cemeteries. Each person I talked to brought up the challenge of helping new board members become familiar with the cemetery industry. Several cemetery CEOs told me of attempts to educate board members by sending them to trade association meetings. While there is often a lot of good information at these meetings, the meetings don't provide an overview of cemeteries or the industry. They found little in print that helped develop a broad understanding of cemeteries. Trade periodicals offered information that was often too detailed and operations oriented to be of much value to new directors.

The cemetery industry is a specialized area of knowledge. I don't claim that I know everything about cemeteries, but I grew up with much of our family conversation dominated by Forest Lawn. At the tender age of twenty-four, I started working for Forest Lawn and have been there ever since. I followed my father, Frederick Llewellyn, as CEO of Forest Lawn, when he decided to step down in 1987. He had served as president of the National Association of Cemeteries, now the International Cemetery and Funeral Association (ICFA), and the Interment Association of California, as well as serving as a member of the California Cemetery Board. In 1966, he succeeded his uncle, Dr. Hubert Eaton, as CEO. Eaton was the man responsible for building Forest Lawn Memorial-Parks and for such innovations as the memorial-park plan and putting the first mortuary in a cemetery. I must credit my father and Hubert Eaton with setting the example and living the vision that a cemetery has a long-term responsibility that is unlike that of any other business.

Not only have I been steeped in cemeteries, I married into a cemetery family. My wife, Linda, has cemetery in her blood. Her family lived in a cemetery when she was born and her father, Bob Garrison, is a past president of the American Cemetery Association (now the ICFA) and is the respected president of Toledo Memorial Park in Ohio. Her grandfather, Stacy Leech, was also a president of the American Cemetery Association.

Since I grew up in a world dominated by Forest Lawn, it should not be surprising that Forest Lawn has had a heavy influence on my thinking about cemeteries. Doing business in

California also has had a great impact on my outlook. I use the term "Forest Lawn" in this book only to refer to the Forest Lawn Memorial-Parks that are located in Southern California. Although there are about twenty-seven cemeteries that use "Forest Lawn" in their name, Southern California's Forest Lawn is the one recognized as the origin of many cemetery and mortuary innovations as well as known for its outstanding art collection. Forest Lawn Memorial-Parks began with a single small location in 1906 and has grown to five locations with a total of almost 1,300 acres of dedicated cemetery property.

There are many different ways of running organizations. Although I express some specific views in this book, my hope is that this will be used as a beginning point for healthy discussions about philosophies, organizational structures, and operating policies of cemeteries. As pointed out in many places, much of what I've written will need to be considered in respect to specific laws and regulations that apply to a given cemetery because the statutory requirements vary substantially throughout the United States.

In the end, each cemetery must find its own way of operating and adapting. I hope this book helps readers understand cemeteries—an appreciation of why cemeteries are different from other businesses and a perspective of the special challenges and rewards of being involved in the cemetery industry.

The opinions expressed here are my own and should not be considered policy statements of any organization I am associated with. I admit to having a very protective view of cemeteries. I am committed to the responsibility cemeteries have to families through successive generations, and I believe cemeteries continue to have a valuable role in our changing society. In addition, I feel that those responsible for cemeteries should be held to high standards in managing those cemeteries—because a cemetery should be forever.

I'd like to thank Andy Conroy, president of Spring Grove Cemetery and Arboretum in Cincinnati, Ohio, who was a catalyst for this book, and was willing to be a litmus test for some of my ideas. I count myself as fortunate to have many friends, in and out of the cemetery industry, who helped by giving me general and specific advice on various subjects. Many people helped give me ideas and different perspectives. Others made a great contribution by giving positive feedback about the project. I would like to thank Larry Anspach, Bill Conway, Arlie Davenport, Gordon Ewig, Bob Fells, Fred Miller, Keith Renken, Ken Siegel, and Greg Williamson for their thoughts and encouragement. I'd also like to thank the people who were willing to share their perspectives "off the record." All of these people helped correct inaccuracies and challenged me to refine some of my thoughts. In the process of writing this book, I've found that my own perception of cemeteries changed; I'm even more committed to the importance of what cemeteries represent to the families who use them and the communities where they are located.

My assistant, Kim Young, deserves special recognition for her efforts in reviewing, proofing, and correcting the many drafts of this material.

Finally, this book wouldn't have been completed without the countless hours of review and many suggestions made by my wife, Linda. Thanks, Linda, for your help in making this become reality.

Since I didn't always take the advice given me, blame me for any shortcomings of this book. Whatever may be said, the objective of this book is to reinforce the concept that a cemetery should be forever.

## ACKNOWLEDGMENTS:

Thank you to the following cemeteries for providing photographs that have been used in this book:

Allegheny Cemetery, Pittsburgh, Pennsylvania
Crown Hill Cemetery, Indianapolis, Indiana
Forest Lawn Memorial-Parks, Glendale, California
Greenwood Memorial Park and Mount Olivet
    Cemetery, Fort Worth, Texas
Jefferson Memorial Cemetery, Pittsburgh,
    Pennsylvania
Metairie Cemetery, New Orleans, Louisiana
Spring Grove Cemetery and Arboretum,
    Cincinnati, Ohio
Swan Point Cemetery, Providence, Rhode Island
Toledo Memorial Park, Sylvania, Ohio
Woodlawn Memorial Park, Orlando, Florida

Thanks also to the International Cemetery and Funeral Association which graciously allowed inclusion of their summary of state laws and regulations in Appendix B.

## DISCLAIMER

*History of Mourning*

*Figure 1–1 Egyptian pyramids are an example of ancient memorial architecture.*

# What is a cemetery?

Will it always be a cemetery?

EVENTUALLY, EVERYONE encounters a cemetery. It may be by attending the funeral and burial of a family member or close friend or from visiting a cemetery because of its historical importance. However, not many people think about the role of cemeteries or how they operate. To them, the simple answer to the question "What is a cemetery?" is the one found in a dictionary: it is a place for the burial of the dead. That dramatically understates the role of cemeteries, for they embody the history of nations and families; they hold treasurers of art and architecture; they are places that reflect religious and spiritual thought; and they challenge us philosophically. Whether in a role of day-to-day management or as part of a policy setting governing body, it is important that those responsible for cemeteries understand cemeteries' importance to society.

## History of Cemeteries

Cemeteries have been around since before the beginning of recorded history. While burial solves a practical hygienic problem, the role of burial has been far greater than just that practical act. Burial practices have provided a way of expressing ideas about human nature and destiny. From the earliest times, the disposition of the dead has been related to rituals that celebrate the miracle of life and cause reflection on the meaning of the end of life.

Prehistoric burial grounds have been found in Asia, Europe, and most other parts of the world. Archeologists have opined that inhumation (burial) began as a natural and simple way of disposal but evolved into an important ritual. One of the principal ways archeologists have learned about old civilizations is from their burial practices, such as the tombs of the pharaohs of Egypt and the burial mounds of the Anasazi Indians here in America.

Throughout the world, leaders and heroes are memorialized. Europe is filled with monuments and memorials erected to honor individuals. Washington, D.C., is the home of many memorials. Each year thousands journey to the city to visit the Lincoln Memorial, Washington Monument, Jefferson Memorial, and the eternal flame at John F. Kennedy's interment in Arlington National Cemetery. The Taj Mahal in India and the Tomb of Ranjit Singh in Pakistan are examples of Eastern Hemisphere memorials built in honor of specific individuals.

The details of burial have been varied. Bodies have been laid directly in the ground, with and without household or other items. Burials from Paleolithic times included food and various implements indicating a belief that these things would be needed in the grave. The use of coffins appears to have stemmed from as early as the third millennium B.C.

As humankind has tried to understand the cycle of life and death, burial has played a central role in the culture of virtually every society. This quest for understanding the meaning of life is reflected in all religions and an explanation of the cycle of life and death is central to the philosophical and ritualistic dogmas of most religions. Thus, it is not at all surprising that cemeteries are important for religious as well as for practical reasons.

In the Western world, we often think of cemeteries and their evolution in terms of their relationship with Christianity. The word "cemetery," which means a sleeping place, was what the early Christians called the places set apart for the burial of their dead. At first, these were outside city walls and weren't adjacent to churches. In the third century A.D. burial for Chris-

A History of Mourning

*Figure 1–2 Père Lachaise Cemetery, Paris, France c. 1888.*

tians moved to catacombs beneath cities. In medieval times, interment in church crypts or churchyards became prevalent.

By the mid-1700s, many of the churchyard burial facilities were running out of space. Burial within city limits was increasingly a space problem. The burial spaces under the pavement of the churches and the small open space around the churches had often become packed with burials. Inside many of the buildings, the air was foul and became a source of disease to those who visited them. Outside, coffins were buried in tiers in the graves, until the burials had very little dirt covering them. The space was so limited that the sextons had to furtively remove bones and partially decayed remains to make room for new burials.

Although all large cities experienced these problems in some measure, London, because of its size and related death rate, forced the issues of burial space on its populace. After several failed attempts at corrective action, almost all the churchyard cemeteries were closed in 1855. The Burial Act of 1855 marked the beginning of cemetery development in Great

Britain although several cemeteries had been established earlier in London by private enterprise.

In America, we had a combination of church cemeteries and country cemeteries. When the colonists were clustered in their first settlements, the cemeteries were clustered with them—often in conjunction with the church. But as the population spread out, it became impractical to transport the dead to a consecrated churchyard cemetery. The solution was to have a family burial yard as part of the farm. This same pattern held throughout the westward expansion of the country.

Poems, like Longfellow's "God's-Acre," have confirmed and strengthened the view of cemeteries as special places:

> I like that ancient Saxon phrase, which calls
> The burial ground God's-Acre! It is just;
> It consecrates each grave within its walls,...

In a scholarly work on cemeteries, David Charles Sloan identified eight types of cemetery development in the United States—frontier, domestic, churchyard, Potter's fields, town or city cemeteries, rural cemeteries, lawn-park cemeteries, and memorial parks.[1] The first five types originated in the early settlement of the country and continue to exist today.

Frontier graves were practical burials where the location was dictated by the site of death. The graves were either unmarked or had only a simple memorial of wood or stone that indicated the deceased's name and date of death.

Domestic homestead graveyards were designed for more than one burial and generally would be in a farm field. They were small, family owned, and functional.

Churchyard cemeteries, patterned after the churchyard cemeteries of England, were generally the first ones to have any care, and the church would often appoint at least a part-time sexton to manage it. Two examples of these are Trinity in New York and St. Philip's in Charleston, South Carolina.

Potter's fields for burial of indigents, exemplified by New York City burial grounds, arose from practical need. They were designed in geometric functional patterns and had only plain monuments, if any. Parallel to the Potter's fields were town or city cemeteries. These were designed more like formal gardens and had three dimensional markers, monuments, and sculpture to mark interment sites. Although Potter's fields were publicly owned, these cemeteries could be either family or government owned.

The rural cemeteries of the mid-1800s marked the beginning of changes in cemeteries. Suburban in location, these were designed with aesthetics in mind—picturesque, natural gardens. They were managed by a trustee or superintendent and were privately owned. Memorialization was broadened from only marble and granite monuments, some having sculpture on top, to include private mausoleums. Père Lachaise in Paris and Mount Auburn in Cambridge, Massachusetts, were influenced by their designs.

Lawn-park cemeteries followed the rural cemeteries. These pastoral, park-like places were an evolutionary step from the rural cemeteries. They continued to have large monuments and sculpture but also had close-to-the-ground markers. The

*Figure 1–3 Spring Grove Cemetery and Arboretum is one of the best examples of lawn-park cemeteries.*

Photo courtesy of Spring Grove Cemetery and Arboretum

management of these was either entrepreneurial or trustee. Sloan lists Spring Grove Cemetery and Arboretum in Cincinnati as the archetype for this type of cemetery.

Memorial-parks, which are covered in the next section, were the last type Sloan identified. According to Sloan, Forest Lawn Memorial-Park in Glendale, California, is the paradigm for all cemeteries of this type.

## Memorial-Parks

When Hubert Eaton conceived his "memorial-park plan" in 1917, he transformed the way cemeteries were operated and viewed by society. Up to that point, changes in cemeteries had been slow—evolutionary.

Eaton had some radical thoughts. He envisioned a park-like appearance of sweeping vistas dotted with trees, flowers, and landscaping. Although many have focused on what Eaton described as the physical characteristics of a memorial-park, the important part of Eaton's vision was the philosophy of a memorial-park.

Eaton outlined his vision in a 1936 speech to the American Cemetery Owners Association which was titled "Who Wants to be Forgotten?" The central thought was spiritual rather than physical. Eaton believed that cemeteries should be inspirational and play an important role in the active day-to-day life of their communities. The speech was reprised several decades later at a National Association of Cemeteries meeting and eventually became a book titled *The Comemoral*, in which Eaton described what he called the "memorial impulse"—a universal desire to be remembered.

In the following years, many cemeterians came and viewed Eaton's dream as it developed. They saw the open space of Forest Lawn and went home and built something that they thought was similar. For them, that was a big transition. Many of them even began to call their cemeteries "memorial parks." But, they only copied the physical changes they thought they saw, building cemeteries without monuments. They had seen, but not understood.

Courtesy of Jefferson Memorial Cemetery

*Figure 1-4 The open spaces of Jefferson Memorial Cemetery are typical of memorial park type cemeteries.*

Eaton had written what he called The Builder's Creed as a statement of his vision of what Forest Lawn should be (Figure 1-5). It described a vision that was much broader than creating park-like grounds and avoiding becoming an "unsightly stoneyard." He had a view of a cemetery as being part of a religious experience. Heavily influenced by his Baptist upbringing, his Christian point of view was that death was a positive thing—"...that those gone before who believed in Him, have entered into that happier life." He viewed cemeteries as places of affirmation of this statement and his vision of cemeteries was that they should also be places that were positive cultural assets.

## Life Cycle

In Figure 1-6, a chart of the theoretical life cycle of a cemetery is presented, however there are so many variables that this must be seen only as a conceptual framework. The actual pattern for any given cemetery will be governed by long-term trends

*Figure 1-5 The Builder's Creed—The Vision of a Memorial-Park*

On New Year's Day, 1917, a man stood on a hilltop overlooking the small country cemetery of some fifty-five acres which had just been placed in his charge. He saw no buildings-only a patch of lawn with a few straggling headstones. Beyond the scant dozen acres of developed ground, the hillsides rose, sere and brown.
In that moment, a vision came to the man of what this...might become....When he reached home, he put this promise into words and called it The Builder's Creed.

From the 1944 edition of
the *Pictorial Forest Lawn*

## THE BUILDER'S CREED

I believe in a happy eternal life.

I believe those of us left behind should be glad in the certain belief that those gone before have entered into that happier life.

I believe, most of all, in a Christ that smiles and loves you and me.

I therefore know the cemeteries of today are wrong because they depict an end, not a beginning. They have consequently become unsightly stoneyards, full of inartistic symbols and depressing customs; places that do nothing for humanity save a practical act, and that not well.

I therefore prayerfully resolve on this New Year's Day, 1917, that I shall endeavor to build Forest Lawn as different, as unlike other cemeteries as sunshine is unlike darkness, as eternal life is unlike death. I shall try to build at Forest Lawn a great park, devoid of misshapen monuments and

other customary signs of earthly death, but
filled with towering trees, sweeping lawns,
splashing fountains, singing birds, beautiful
statuary, cheerful flowers, noble memorial
architecture, with interiors full of light and
color, and redolent of the world's best
history and romances.

I believe these things educate and uplift
a community.

Forest Lawn shall become a place where
lovers new and old shall love to stroll and
watch the sunset's glow, planning for the
future or reminiscing of the past; a place
where artists study and sketch; where school
teachers bring happy children to see the
things they read of in books; where little
churches invite, triumphant in the
knowledge that from their pulpits only
words of love can be spoken; where
memorialization of loved ones in sculptured
marble and pictorial glass shall be
encouraged but controlled by acknowledged
artists; a place where the sorrowing will be
soothed and strengthened because it will be
God's garden. A place that shall be protected
by an immense Endowment Care Fund, the
principal of which can never be expended—
only the income therefrom used to care for
and perpetuate this Garden of Memory.

This is the Builder's Dream; this is the
Builder's Creed.

in population, competition, management competency, original size, and economic conditions. Understanding the life cycle of a given cemetery is clearly a responsibility of management and the board of directors—more will be said on this subject in later chapters.

Unit sales of cemeteries are not the same throughout the selling years. Sales rates may vary substantially over short periods, sometimes masking longer-term trends. The short-term, year-to-year variations are not reflected in the smooth curve of Figure 1–6. Sales usually begin slowly, often driven by practical need. Although the cemetery may begin a preneed sales program early in its existence, it takes some time for that program to gain momentum and for the cemetery to gain recognition and acceptance in the community. The cemetery then enters a growth phase that is a function of the quality of cemetery management and the growth of the surrounding community. As the community stabilizes, so do the cemetery's at need sales.

Eventually, as the cemetery has less property available for sale, sales trail off due to a more limited selection of types of interment property. As time goes on, virtually all property is sold. Even after the cemetery has sold the last piece of property, it still will have an economic life, for it still will be able to sell interment services and memorials. The "sold out" condition occurs when most of the activity at the cemetery is related to maintenance of sold property.

At some point, though, the revenue stream from sales won't support the cemetery. The cemetery doesn't go away just because no property remains to sell and the revenue produced from sales of services is insufficient to care for the cemetery. Even after it is sold out, the cemetery remains a cemetery. Whether or not it remains a community asset and a place of positive remembrance for families is closely related to how much money was put into the endowment care fund during its active life. Chapter 7 discusses the principles of endowment care funds and Chapter 13 includes a case study about the Metropolitan Cemetery's effort to determine if income from its

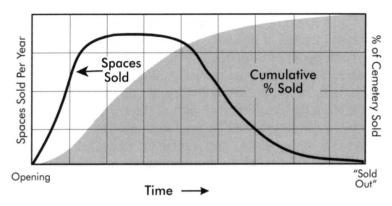

*Figure 1-6 Cemetery life cycle.*

endowment care fund will be sufficient to care for the cemetery when it is sold out.

Of course, not all cemeteries will follow this exact pattern of unit sales, for the life cycle of cemeteries is not unlike the lives of people. No two individuals lead their lives in exactly the same way, and no two cemeteries will have exactly the same life cycle. Many cemeteries which are still in their growth phase and are not close to the decline or "sold out" phases have not put much effort into consideration of the inevitability of running out of space.

### More Complex Than A Simple Model

With people, life is more than just the passing of years. Similarly, life cycles of cemeteries are more complicated than indicated by a simple theoretical model of unit sales. A cemetery will have its ups and downs depending upon ownership, economic conditions, and personnel. A positive public image will always help, but lawsuits or other highly visible problems may cause setbacks. If ownership changes, the cemetery may face a change in priorities.

Perhaps a new owner will want to build an impressive mausoleum to make a statement of the stability to the community. Or, perhaps an owner did build that impressive mausoleum and spent so much money on its construction that the cemetery needed to be sold to get more capital.

Each generation of management will have a somewhat different outlook on how things should be done. One generation might focus on sales dollars, another on profits, another on building the cemetery as a part of the community, and still another on building through the future by stressing unit sales rather than dollar sales. Each course change takes time for an organization to assimilate and will have an influence on the life of the cemetery.

Although it is counter-intuitive to most people, cemeteries are affected by economic conditions. While it is true that deaths occur in all kinds of economic times, consumers can cut back on the amount spent on cemetery property and services when they are feeling pressure or economic uncertainty. Somewhat related to this is the principle that deaths do not occur at a steady rate. There is randomness along with factors such as weather and diseases that make it almost impossible to predict the short-term death rate for a single cemetery's market area. Add to that any shift in market share, and the equation for forecasting units becomes quite complicated.

The model puts the end of the life cycle as the point when a cemetery is substantially sold out. The question faced at that time is: "Will the cemetery still be a cemetery or should the land be put to some other use?" Most people, indeed most societies, don't like the notion that a cemetery will be torn up when it is full. Generally, interment spaces are not re-used and little thought is given to converting a cemetery to something else.[2] Whether one views this as a continuation of a primitive taboo or an act of respect for those gone before, there seems to be some universality of respect for burials and the reluctance to turn a cemetery into anything else.

So, once a cemetery is a cemetery, it will most likely always be a cemetery. While no one can promise that value systems and legal restrictions will always protect a cemetery and those interred within it, it seems likely that any given cemetery is going to remain a cemetery for a very long time.

Later in this book, there is a discussion of some of the problems associated with cemeteries that are sold out and the potential for them becoming a blight or liability to a community rather than an asset.

## Endowment Care

Although many states have adopted the term "endowment care," others have kept the older term "perpetual care." The word "perpetual" is used as a statement of intent. The goal is to allow the cemetery to be maintained forever—in perpetuity. This reflects the premise of "once a cemetery, always a cemetery." In some states, the lawyers and semanticists have successfully lobbied against the word "perpetual" and have mandated the use of "endowment" instead.

Regardless of whether the term is "perpetual care" or "endowment care," the goal of these funds is to provide for the care of the cemetery for as long as possible after the cemetery is sold out.

Some cemeteries have specific areas that are not covered by endowment care. Usually, these are older areas that were sold before the cemetery had a requirement for money to be put in an endowment care fund from each sale of cemetery property.

The existence of an endowment care fund is different from the issue of the level of maintenance provided. The mere existence of a care fund doesn't promise a high level of care. The size of the fund has a direct bearing on the amount of income available for maintenance. The size of the fund is dependent upon how much is contributed to the fund with each purchase, how much is kept in the fund, and how much growth comes from the investment of the fund.

It is hard to make a cemetery go away. A cemetery may fall upon hard economic times, but it is still a cemetery. Even when the income from a cemetery's endowment care fund isn't big enough to provide a reasonable level of maintenance, it is still a cemetery. Although these events are sad, the permanence of cemeteries is important because they reflect an important part of the human condition.

## Cemeteries Should Be Forever

Cemeteries fulfill a practical role, but that is not why they are valued. Cemeteries link us with the past—with memories of loved ones who are no longer with us as well as the events that bind us to them. We use cemeteries to honor people and as part of the healing process from the grief caused by the loss of a loved one.

Cemeteries are also a connection to people we never knew and events we may not have been part of. Cemeteries encourage these memories and provide this connection with history. Through memorialization in cemeteries, everyone is given a chance to leave a "footprint" that shows they passed through life.

Cemeteries challenge our spirituality. For some, they provide reinforcement of religious beliefs and for others, a place to contemplate the meaning of life. Cemeteries remind us of our mortality. For some people, they provide the inspiration to live their lives differently, to do things that they will be remembered for.

Cemeterians often use the following quotation attributed to William E. Gladstone:

> Show me the manner in which a nation or community cares for its dead and I will measure with mathematical exactness the tender sympathies of its people, their respect for the laws of the land and their loyalty to high ideals.[3]

We count on cemeteries to last because we expect our memories of the past to last. We hope that these memories, as enshrined in cemeteries, will carry on through countless generations. We derive strength, understanding, and hope from the past as well as a sense of challenge for the future. And, because of all this, we expect that cemeteries will be forever.

1. David Charles Sloan, *The Last Great Necessity: Cemeteries in American History*.

2. Although not a common practice in the United States, a few cemeteries do limit the time a space may be used.

3. Although attributed to Gladstone, the original source for the quote is uncertain. *Respectfully Quoted: A Dictionary of Quotations Requested* from the Congressional Research Service lists the quote as "unverified" from an article titled "Successful Cemetery Advertising" in The American Cemetery, March 1938. The quotation is similar to the opening sentence of an article by W. Lloyd Warner, "The City of the Dead," *in Death and Identity* by Robert Fulton. Warner footnoted it with a reference to J. W. Swain's 1915 translation of *The Elementary Forms of Religious Life* by Emile Durkheim:

   > cemeteries are collective representations which reflect and express many of the community's basic beliefs and values about what kind of society it is, what the persons of men are, and where each fits into the secular world of the living and the spiritual society of the dead.

*God's Acre Beautiful*

*Figure 1–7 The cemetery of the future as envisioned in 1883.*

# Cemetery Organizations

Chapter 2

The similarity is only on the surface

CEMETERY ORGANIZATIONS may be divided into three broad classifications: private, religious, and government. Private cemeteries may be for-profit or not-for-profit.

The for-profit and not-for-profit firms share many common characteristics. This isn't surprising as both must make burials and maintain grounds. Each must develop interment property and generate revenue to cover expenses. Each also should be concerned about developing trust funds that will be large enough to adequately maintain the cemeteries in the future.

There is considerable diversity in how cemeteries operate. Some have developed mortuaries. Some have opened flower shops. Many have preneed programs of various sorts. Some are part of large publicly traded corporations. Some are single location operations (often called "independents"). Some are very small and make only a few interments each year. Others are very large and make thousands of interments each year. All share the general responsibilities and challenges of being cemeteries.

## For-Profit Cemeteries

Cemeteries operated for-profit seem to have originated about 1860. Generally, they are a regular for-profit corporation that can do just about anything they want that is legal. However, in most jurisdictions, they also may be sole proprietorships or partnerships.

There are five publicly traded firms: Service Corporation International (SCI), Houston, Texas; the Loewen Group, Inc., Burnaby, British Columbia; Stewart Enterprises, New Orleans, Louisiana; Equity Corporation International, Lufkin, Texas; and Carriage Services, Inc., Houston, Texas. Table 2–1 shows a comparison of key financial information about these firms.

SCI is by far the largest of these firms in terms of revenue and locations. Robert Waltrip, son of a Texas funeral director, founded the firm in 1962. By 1975, SCI was the largest provider of funeral services in the United States. About 27% of its revenue and 23% of its profit comes from cemetery operations. Funeral operations dominate the company with 72% of revenue and 76% of profits. About a third of SCI's revenue is from outside the United States. SCI has facilities in most states of the United States and boasts of having "affiliates" on five continents. Their Internet WebPage (www.sci-corp.com) shows a motto of "Serving the world one family at a time."

The Loewen Group follows SCI in size. Like Waltrip, Ray Loewen grew up in the funeral business. His father was a funeral director in Manitoba. In 1985, he founded the Loewen Group. According to the company, over 90% of its revenue is from the United States. There was a great deal of friction between SCI and Loewen in 1996 when SCI made a hostile tender offer for Loewen. Although the take-over attempt was dropped, it left a great deal of animosity between these two fiercely competitive companies. Loewen successfully fought off SCI's $45 per share takeover bid, but in early October 1998 its stock price dropped to under $8 a share. At that time Ray Loewen stepped down as CEO and became a non-executive co-chairman. Loewen's cemetery operations account for about 32% of its revenue. Although it is a Canadian company, the majority of Loewen's properties are in the United States. Loewen can be found on the Internet at: www.loewenacquisitions.com and www.loewengroup.com.

Founded in 1910, Stewart Enterprises has its roots in the cemetery business and is the oldest of the publicly traded firms.

| Company | Sales | Net Income | Share-holder's Equity | Public Since |
|---|---|---|---|---|
| Service Corporation International (SRV) | $2,468.4 | $333.8 | $2,726.0 | 1969 |
| Loewen Group (LWN) | 1,114.1 | 28.2 | 1,540.2 | 1987 |
| Stewart Enterprises (STEI) (Oct. 31, 1997) | 535.5 | 67.4 | 819.6 | 1991 |
| Equity Corp. (EQU) | 135.1 | 14.7 | 226.5 | 1994 |
| Carriage Services (CSV) | 77.4 | 4.5 | 112.5 | 1996 |

*Table 2-1 Financial size of publicly traded firms at December 31, 1997 (dollars in thousands).*

About 55% of its revenues are from funeral operations. Although it went public in 1991, control is still held in the hands of the Stewart family. Stewart's operations cover almost half of the United States as well as Australia, Argentina, Canada, Mexico, New Zealand, Puerto Rico, and Spain.

Equity Corporation International began operations in 1990 with the acquisition of 71 funeral homes and 3 cemeteries from SCI. It focuses its operations and acquisitions in non-metropolitan areas. As this book was going into production, it was announced that SCI planned to acquire Equity Corporation for about $594 million in stock.

Carriage Services has its headquarters in Texas like SCI and Equity Corporation and was incorporated in 1993. When this was written, the company said that slightly less than half of the total cemetery acreage it owned could be developed in the future.

Table 2-2 shows the number of cemetery and funeral operating units each of the companies owned at the end of 1997. It is clear that these companies focus on the funeral home business rather than the cemetery business. There are probably a number of reasons for this. First, there are many more funeral homes than cemeteries. For example, Los Angeles County has more than two hundred funeral homes, but less

| Company | Cemeteries | Mortuaries |
|---|---|---|
| Service Corporation International | 392 | 3,127 |
| Loewen Group | 497 | 1,101 |
| Stewart Enterprises (Oct. 31, 1997) | 132 | 428 |
| Equity Corp. | 76 | 282 |
| Carriage Services | 20 | 120 |

*Table 2–2 Operating units of publicly traded firms at December 31, 1997.*

than fifty cemeteries. Second, with the exception of Stewart, the companies began with a focus on funeral homes—the primary business was selling funerals. Third, the financial rewards appear to be higher—better margins and faster returns on the investment. The information about the number of cemeteries and funeral homes each company owns are frequently published, but this can be misleading since the sales and profit volume may vary significantly between locations.

## Consolidation

A wave of consolidation has hit the cemetery industry, much the same as in other industries. The cemetery and funeral industries have been particularly good targets because the industries have been primarily composed of small, single location operators. Consolidation of small units has enabled more efficient operations by combining back office support operations like accounting and allowing equipment sharing between multiple locations. Also, consolidation has created the opportunity for many relatively small operators to gain liquidity by selling their businesses.

The main drivers of the consolidation movement have been the publicly traded companies that now own many cemeteries and mortuaries. Although the firms discussed here are in the cemetery business, it was interesting that in searching an online investment database, these firms show up as having a primary Standard Industrial Code (SIC number) for the funeral service business.[1] There were no firms listed as being primarily in the cemetery business.

Some have wondered when the consolidation of the industry in the United States would end. Were there still many acquisition opportunities? Although it sometimes seems as though "everyone" has sold out, the acquisitions keep going. According to Steve Saltzman, an analyst with ABN-AMRO Chicago Corporation who follows the publicly traded firms, "acquisition opportunities remain even in the most consolidated markets."

This isn't intended to be a treatise on the publicly traded firms. A call to a stockbroker will bring reams of information on each, including information about their acquisition programs, earnings, historical stock prices, and more.

## Impact of Acquisitions

The acquisition firms now own about 15% of the mortuaries in the United States, but no reliable figures are available regarding what percentage of cemeteries have been acquired. There is a wide spread belief, aimed primarily at the mortuary business, that prices rise dramatically after an acquisition. *Money* magazine opined that the chain ownership should bring efficiency that should result in lower prices but said, "under pressure from corporate management, most newly acquired funeral homes *raise* prices."[2] Bill Heiligbrodt, president and chief operating officer of SCI, is credited with saying that SCI's firms are among the priciest in any market because, "It's like the difference between a Cadillac and a Ford."[3]

Not everyone agrees that the acquisitions drive up prices. Of course, some of the big firms say it isn't so. Others support their position. According to Berkeley professor Dwayne Banks, when funeral prices are adjusted for inflation the price of an average funeral has risen only a few percentage points in the last twenty-five years. He maintains that it is the creative introduction of all sorts of new products and services, which has increased prices.[4]

On February 1, 1998, CBS' "60 Minutes" aired a program that was critical of the funeral industry, particularly SCI. I'm not a fan of "60 Minutes," but I do respect the fact that many people watch the program and form opinions from it. SCI reacted by issuing a statement that called the report "irresponsible, biased, and a totally inaccurate representation of the industry or SCI....As the industry knows, you cannot run a successful business by gouging the American public....SCI provided comprehensive background information to CBS, including in-depth discussions with senior executives of the company, none of which was used."[5]

The downside of consolidation is less choice of providers for consumers. Many consumer advocates feel particularly strong about this because none of the consolidators put their names on firms they acquire. The practice is to continue to do business under the image of the prior ownership. Someone once told me that the goal of one of the listed companies was to be widely known on Wall Street but remain unknown to consumers.

With the American pastime of knocking big business, the press has certainly taken its licks at the large funeral and cemetery firms. This seems to have created a negative image for the rest of the firms in those industries as well, because many who are exposed to the media coverage don't, or can't, differentiate between the publicly traded firms and the independent firms.

The consolidation movement has changed the business environment for cemetery suppliers. As the big firms get bigger, so does their negotiating power. Not only does this put pressure on the suppliers, but it also has a ripple effect on independent cemeteries. The consolidation of cemeteries and mortuaries puts pressure on the suppliers to consolidate also. Although an acquisition of a cemetery doesn't decrease the number of cemeteries, to the extent a large company uses its consolidated buying power, it does decrease the number of firms making buying decisions. Suppliers who lose blocks of business from consolidation risk becoming extinct. For example, if a company is selling special computer software to cemeteries, it will probably lose a customer when an existing client is sold—the acquiring company wants its systems to be used.

Not all things about consolidation are bad, however. Large firms have the resources to understand compliance with the many laws and regulations related to OSHA, labor, environmental, and other issues that all businesses face today. Indeed, most large firms have people or departments whose primary responsibility is compliance with government laws and regulations. So, to the extent that the governmental requirements are good, better compliance should also be beneficial.

The large firms are certainly competitive, but they also have a tendency to improve the professionalism of management within the industries by adopting progressive methods of doing business. An organization with thousands of employees just can't operate well with inefficient methods of operations.

Bob Waltrip, chairman of SCI, has been sensitive regarding comments made about his company and its acquisitions. Waltrip and SCI filed a lawsuit against Darryl Roberts and his publisher, Five Star Publications, for allegedly defaming them claiming they falsely accused Waltrip of stating that it was his goal to turn SCI into "the True Value Hardware of the funeral-service industry."[6] A Texas district court didn't agree that it was defamation and dismissed the suit.[7] Roberts' book, *Profits of Death: An Insider Exposes the Death Care Industries*, criticizes the sales methods of funeral homes and cemeteries.

A final upside of acquisitions is that the very existence of multiple firms in the acquisition business has given many owners an opportunity to turn businesses they've built into cash for estate planning purposes. And, many investors have made good financial returns from investing in the stocks of the better performing corporations.

## Not-For-Profit Cemeteries

Not-for-profit cemeteries are exempt from taxation under Section 501(c)(13) of the Internal Revenue Code.[8] Most states allow the same tax exemption. The theory behind exemption has generally been that cemeteries provide a needed service—aiding society in disposition of its dead in an orderly manner. Lawmakers created the tax exemption for cemeteries, as they realized that cemeteries needed to be encouraged.

Not-for-profit cemeteries may vary in size from those that have no employees and make only a few interments a year to large cemeteries with hundreds of employees and thousands of interments a year. Just as they differ in size, they also differ in complexity. Some serve families only "at need," others have aggressive preneed sales programs, and some operate mortuaries or flower shops in wholly owned taxable subsidiaries. The variations reflect the history and management of each organization as well as the needs of the communities they serve.

## Religious Cemeteries

Cemeteries operated by recognized churches generally are exempt under the exemption for the church. However, different states have different views of how religious cemeteries should be regulated. Some states regulate these cemeteries just like any other cemetery. Other states exempt all or part of church owned cemeteries operations from regulations and reporting. The theory for the exemption seems to be based on the constitutional concept of separation of church and state—some states have determined that since burial may be seen as a religious rite, religious cemeteries should be exempt from regulation.

Looking at the same arguments from another perspective, other states have determined that burial is, in part, a public health issue. From that viewpoint, they conclude that the sale of goods (cemetery property and related merchandise) to consumers requires the government to protect society and consumers by the regulation of all cemeteries. Some cemeteries that compete, or would like to compete, with religious cemeteries feel that the exemption is an unfair advantage for what should be viewed as a business enterprise rather than part of religious rites.

Regardless of which approach a state takes to the regulation of religious cemeteries, it seems to be rather static. Once a

Courtesy of Woodlawn Memorial Park

*Figure 2-1 Many non-denominational cemeteries feature
religious art like this depiction of Jesus in the Temple at
Woodlawn Memorial Park, Orlando, Florida.*

pattern is established, no group seems to want to expend the
political energy necessary to change it. Periodically, the issue
will be raised as some of the religious cemeteries change their
methods of operation from an accommodation of members of
the faith to aggressive preneed sales programs. This has been
done by actually operating funeral homes or by leasing a portion of the cemetery property to an operator of funeral homes.
In 1998, the Archdiocese of Los Angeles announced that it had
entered into an agreement with Stewart Enterprises to operate
mortuaries within its cemeteries. Other publicly traded firms
have scrambled to try to get a piece of that action in other
parts of the country. As church owned cemeteries find ways to
enter the funeral home business, new questions probably will
be raised.

## Municipal and District Cemeteries

Most states have some sort of municipal or district cemeteries.
Many district cemeteries were formed because there were no

other cemeteries to serve an area. In the absence of private cemeteries, government stepped in to provide a place for burial. Many times the laws that apply to these cemeteries restrict their activities, because they may compete with private cemeteries and it is generally against public policy to have government compete with private industry. Private cemeteries object not only to competition from government owned cemeteries, but also to government owned cemeteries being exempt from the regulations that apply to private cemeteries—disclosures, licensing, annual filings, inspections and audits, and required endowment care funds.

These restrictions are frustrating to those responsible for these cemeteries, because the rules often limit what can be sold. This then limits revenues (except from whatever allocation of tax revenues they might get) which limits upkeep. Poor upkeep hurts sales, which limits upkeep even more. A downward spiral is created which just keeps feeding itself, unless there is financial aid from the outside.

Although municipal and district cemeteries are very important to the areas they serve, there doesn't appear to be an accurate count of how many are actually in operation currently. In California, we believe there are about 25% more government operated cemeteries than licensed cemeteries (approximately 237 district cemeteries vs. 190 licensed cemeteries—religious cemeteries are exempt from licensing requirements).

## Veterans Cemeteries

Veterans cemeteries are a category of cemetery that is somewhat related to the district and municipal cemeteries, because they are run by government agencies. These are operated either by an individual state or by the U.S. Department of Veterans Affairs. The national veterans cemetery system began 1862 with fourteen cemeteries. The system has expanded to a network of 115 cemeteries in 39 states. More than two million interments have been made the government reports that it currently has over 300,000 full-sized ground interment spaces and almost 60,000 places for cremated remains. With 10,900 acres of land within the system, just over half the acreage has been developed. The size ranges from the 902 acre Calverton National Cemetery in New York to the .03 acre Hampton National Cemetery in Virginia. The most famous of them is Arlington National Cemetery outside of Washington, D.C.[9]

Veterans organizations have historically liked the idea of these cemeteries. However, more recently other veteran benefits, like healthcare, have been threatened during congressional budget negotiations, so veterans cemeteries have not had as high a priority on veterans groups' legislative agendas. The fiscal year 1999 budget request for the National Cemetery System which operates these cemeteries was $92 million, about two-tenths of one percent of the budget of the Department of Veterans Affairs.

Private sector cemeteries often have opposed veterans cemeteries because they have viewed them as government com-

*Figure 2–2 Arlington National Cemetery outside Washington, D.C., is known for honoring those who served in the United States military as well as being the resting place of national leaders like John F. Kennedy.*

peting with private enterprise. Veterans cemeteries are expensive to create and expensive to run. The existence of a cemetery for veterans creates an on-going maintenance obligation and expense for the responsible government agency, and cemetery maintenance must compete in the annual budgetary competition for available tax dollars. Although most private cemeteries are required to have endowment care funds, the concept of setting aside money for care doesn't fit with the fund accounting used by government, even if government would have the discipline to set aside endowment care funds.

Non-government cemeteries have argued that a burial allowance was more cost effective than developing new veterans cemeteries because it allowed a veteran to choose a cemetery close to where they live and to put the burden for the cost of long-term care on the private cemetery. The private sector has maintained that it could provide the same services at a cost lower than the government could render the service itself. However, the burial allowance felt the ax of budget cutting. From 1973 to 1990, there was a $150 plot allowance for wartime veterans who were not otherwise receiving Veterans Administration benefits. At the same time the plot allowance was cut in 1990, a reimbursement for memorials purchased by veterans also was eliminated.

The burial benefit in a Department of Veterans Affairs cemetery includes the interment space, burial, and, according to the government, "perpetual care." The reason for putting it in quotes is that it is not the same as perpetual or endowment care in a private cemetery where money is placed in a trust for future care of the cemetery. Rather, it is an obligation that must be allocated by Congress from future general tax revenues. Veterans who die on active duty are eligible for burial in a national cemetery. An eligible veteran must have been discharged or separated from active duty under conditions other than dishonorable and have completed the required period of service. Spouses and minor children of eligible veterans and service members may also be buried in a national cemetery.

The Veterans Administration provides memorials for the

interment spaces of veterans anywhere in the world and for eligible dependents of veterans buried in military post, national, or state veterans cemeteries. While the government will pay the cost of installation of the memorial in a national cemetery, the family of the deceased must pay the cost of placing it if the memorial is being placed in a private cemetery. Some families choose not to use memorials supplied by the Veterans Administration because of the small size and restrictions on what the government will put on the memorials.[10]

## Cremation Societies

Cremation societies often provide disposition of remains, but they are not cemeteries. The usual services they provide involve practical disposition of a body through cremation. The cremated remains are often scattered. Cremation is discussed more in Chapter 3, Philosophy.

Although many cremation societies have "members" and even charge a membership fee, they are usually for-profit utilitarian disposers rather than not-for-profit associations. Several of the publicly traded companies operate cremation societies. Because cremation societies do not have the investment in a facility that is typical of a cemetery that provides cremation services, they may be able to offer lower prices. They work hard at achieving operating economies and may not pay the same attention to detail and respect for the deceased that a cemetery might. Although they provide disposition, cremation societies serve a different market than do cemeteries.

Sometimes the effort to cut costs at cremation facilities leads to unpleasant results. There have been a number of reported problems with how some cremation societies have handled remains, before and after cremation. However, because the cremation societies are not alone in being the target of allegations of wrongdoing, I've put the discussion of problems within the cremation section of Chapter 3.

It should also be noted that states are not consistent with how crematories are licensed. Some license them as cemeteries, license them as funeral homes, and others have separate licenses for them. In California, a cemetery may operate a crematory but there is also a separate license for a crematory that is not part of a cemetery.

## Beyond Form of Organization

The preceding discussion of types of cemeteries deals with the superficial side of the organizations—their legal structure. Although the legal structures do put a certain set of boundaries on an organization, there are probably as many ways to deal with those boundaries as there are organizations.

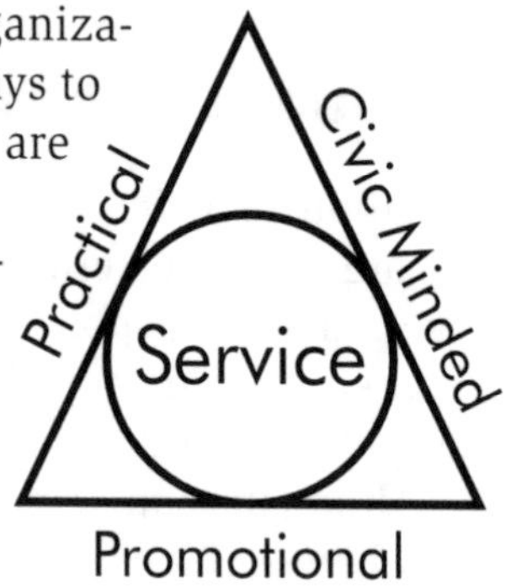

Figure 2-3 Types of cemeteries.

Another way of classifying cemeteries is to view their motivation and philosophy. Some possible categories for classifying the orientation of cemeteries would be: Promotional, Civic Minded, Practical, and Service.

These categories are much like personality types. Being in a particular classification or another isn't good or bad, just like having certain personality traits isn't necessarily good or bad. Like people, organizations will have one dominant type, but may well exhibit some traits of other personality types. For many, different personality strengths will dominate at different times. Some organizations will deliberately adopt a certain style to accomplish objectives. Indeed, organizations will sometimes deliberately try to change their personalities to meet changing needs.

### Practical Cemeteries

The Practical Cemetery is what most people would envision as a "traditional" cemetery—a cemetery that just buries the dead of a community. They do it with little fanfare, don't have aggressive sales programs, and get the job done in a conservative way. This organization is orderly and efficient and has probably been around for a long time. It will tend to have stable management and directors. It doesn't worry about much more than practical disposition, although it has a sense of its importance to the community.

## Civic Minded Cemeteries

The Civic Minded Cemetery often shows that its ancestors were Practical Cemeteries. The Civic Minded Cemetery efficiently takes care of the disposition of the community's dead, but it seeks to be more than that. Examples that come to mind are Spring Grove and Mount Auburn. Each of these was founded as a place for burials and as an arboretum for the community to enjoy. An early illustration of Mount Auburn shows a couple strolling through the manicured grounds on a Sunday afternoon—a clear indication that this was something more than just a place for burial.

Cemeteries may display the Civic Minded side of their personalities with events for the community such as choral presentations, Easter sunrise services, or Veterans Day ceremonies. Others might display artworks, make their facilities available to community groups, or find other innovative ways to serve their communities.

## Promotional Cemeteries

The Promotional Cemetery is quite sales oriented. Maximizing sales and current profits drives this organization. It tends to be something of a chameleon. If better service will help accomplish the goals, then service will be what is stressed. If something else will do a better job of accomplishing the goals, then that will be given priority. This type will run the gamut from cemeteries that just want to build themselves financially to those that will do almost anything for financial gain.

The cemeteries that fall into this group are often borderline Service Cemeteries. While they definitely have a profit motive, they have a long-term view of things. They realize that a cemetery isn't a shoe store—you can't start or end one very easily. They may appear to be like Service Cemeteries, because they will adopt a service posture to help their promotional and sales programs. However, for them, service is a means to achieving a profit goal rather than a primary goal sought for its own sake.

Promotional Cemeteries at the extreme end of the spectrum are current-bottom-line, improve-revenues-at-any-cost organizations. These organizations don't worry about high turnover rates of salespeople or high cancellation rates as long as they don't lose money from either. These organizations are more likely to have aggressive programs for selling services in advance of need that may overshadow at need sales of cemetery property and services.

## Service Cemeteries

Service Cemeteries define themselves as being a community resource and as having a primary goal of providing service to client families. They are also chameleons and have aspects of every category. Although the group will tend to be dominated by the larger not-for-profit cemeteries, size alone is not a criterion for admission to the club.

These organizations are Practical, Civic Minded, and Promotional all at once. Just like the other types, these organizations have the economic pressure to break even but they have given themselves more flexibility in how they achieve that end. They realize that their culture is a composite of the other types of cemeteries.

Seldom are these cemeteries owned by government agencies or publicly traded companies because the very nature of each of these puts constraints on what can be done. Government and district cemeteries often have statutory limitations imposed on how they operate. Publicly traded firms must put a high priority on profits—return to shareholders. This isn't to imply that they cannot be service organizations, but rather that service is not their primary mission—it is a means to an end.

Sometimes the word "service" is misused by organizations to imply that sales and service are synonymous. While good service may result in sales, selling by itself isn't necessarily service.

## Constituencies

No matter what form of organization a cemetery takes or what type of cemetery it wants to be, it must serve a number of masters—property owners, the community, religious organizations, employees, and owners or shareholders in the case of for-profit cemeteries.[11] Each of the groups has different needs, and all must be satisfied for the cemetery to be successful.

Property owners represent past users of the cemetery as well as current ties to the community and are a most likely source for future business. Since their loved ones are interred there, they often have passionate feelings about how the cemetery is maintained. This group has an emotional tie to the cemetery that is closely related to the very reason for the existence of the cemetery. For most not-for-profit cemeteries, management and boards of directors feel the most responsibility to this group.

Communities care about cemeteries for different reasons. When cemetery employees are active in the community, the effect is often that the cemetery is viewed as a positive asset to the community. The public events that some cemeteries hold become an important part of the culture of a community. Other times, the community only thinks about the cemetery when there is a need for it—perhaps the death of a prominent citizen or someone who lost their life trying to save or protect someone else. Occasionally cemeteries come into the community spotlight because they have become a problem—perhaps the cemetery has become unsightly because there isn't enough money for maintenance.

Cemeteries, as pointed out earlier, have a strong link to all religions. Whether a cemetery is owned by a church or is a non-denominational for-profit institution, most burials are still treated as a religious function. Hence, cemeteries, by their very nature, have an on-going relationship with the religious community. A number of people like to describe cemeteries as quasi-religious organizations.

Employees take pride in their association with the cemetery and what it does for the community. The cemetery also has the employer/employee bond. Because cemetery employees tend to have a positive attitude about the cemetery itself, relations within the cemetery's organizational family—employees and management—tend to be better than for many other industries.

Lastly, there is the ownership function. This doesn't include only the for-profit cemeteries. Whatever organization owns the cemetery needs to focus on it as an economic unit. It needs to be efficient in its use of capital and provide a return on the amount invested. This perspective is necessary whether a cemetery is trying to maximize the profits for its shareholders, meet the needs of members/parishioners, provide a service to citizens of a municipality, or operate as a not-for-profit non-denominational cemetery. Even if a not-for-profit cemetery were organized to give interment rights away, it should still have some measure of how effective that program is from an economic standpoint.

## Does it matter?

Over the years, I've had countless conversations with cemeterians about how they view their cemeteries and about their various business philosophies. My conclusion is that there is so much diversity that it is futile to try to put organizations in neat little boxes. Not only do they not fit into simple classifications, but they often change with circumstances. A shift in priorities will usually be reflected in the character of an organization.

I remember a conversation I had with a group of self-described small cemetery operators. We were discussing sales—a common topic among cemetery managers. I asked why they didn't do something to increase their sales and grow the organization. One of them replied, "We don't want to become a big organization." Whether he was saying that out of fear of failure (or fear of success), I don't know. He was obviously very comfortable with running a Practical Cemetery and didn't want to venture far from that. Although I didn't share his view, I respect the fact that he understood his own motivations and wanted to be true to his vision of his cemetery.

Sometimes these philosophical issues show up in how an organization spends its money. Not too long ago I was talking with a prominent cemetery manager, and we were lamenting the problems of creeping increases in overhead. He said rather proudly that he wouldn't accept collect calls at the cemetery. I recoiled and asked, "Do you mean if people want to call, you won't talk to them?" He replied that there were just too many collect calls from "people who wanted to know when the gates close." He knew that we had installed an "800" number at Forest Lawn, and he thought that was a wasteful extravagance.

Who was right? Should a business accept collect calls? Callers might want "frivolous" things like finding out the cemetery's hours or they might want to buy something. I suppose each of us was right for our respective organizations. He was doing a good job as a Practical Cemetery manager—not allowing a dime to be wasted. As he puts it, he runs a "tight ship"—I sometimes wish I had such a hands-on grasp of where all the money goes. On the other hand, I think our "800" number helps fulfill Forest Lawn's goal of being a Service Cemetery. I want Forest Lawn to project a friendly, responsive image to everyone who has contact with us and view the costs of service as something essential to our organization's success.

## Summary

When it's all said and done, is it better to be one of these types than another? Probably not. Although all cemeteries perform a common function, their methods of fulfilling their self-defined role and their vision of individual purpose will vary greatly. The important thing is for an organization, particularly its management and board of directors, to understand what the organization is and what it aspires to be and, then, to manage it accordingly.

1. Standard Industrial Classification 7261 is for Funeral Service and Crematories; 6553 is for Cemeteries and Cemetery Developers.

2. Marlys Harris, "The Final Payment," *Money*, September 1997, p. 88.

3. Miriam Horn, "The Deathcare Business," *U.S. News & World Report*, March 23, 1998, p. 55.

4. Judith Newman, "At Your Disposal," *Harpers Magazine*, November 1997, p. 66.

5. "Industry Reacts to '60 Minutes' Segment—Same Old Story," *American Funeral Director*, March 1998.

6. "SCI, Waltrip Expand Roberts Lawsuit," *Funeral and Cemetery Today*, vol. IV, no. 4, April 1998, p. 5.

7. "SCI Defamation Suit Dismissed," *International Cemetery & Funeral Management*, International Cemetery and Funeral Association, September, 1998, p. 52.

8. Internal Revenue Service Code Section 501(c)(13) includes as organizations exempt from income taxes "Cemetery companies owned and operated exclusively for the benefit of their members or which are not operated for profit; and any corporation chartered solely for the purpose of the disposal of bodies by burial or cremation which is not permitted by its charter to engage in any business not necessarily incident to that purpose and no part of the net earnings of which inures to the benefit of any private shareholder or individual."

9. "National Cemetery System History," and "Facts and Statistics," National Cemetery System, www.cem.va.gov.

10. According to the Veterans Administration, memorials are "inscribed with the name of the deceased, the years of birth and death, and branch of service. Optional items which may be supplied at VA expense include military grade, rank, or rate, war service such as 'World War II'; months and days of birth and death, an emblem reflecting one's religion beliefs; valor awards; and the Purple Heart."

11. Most cemeteries sell consumers a right of interment rather than fee title to property. Although purchasers are often referred to as "property owners," the rights conveyed are more like those of easement holders than those of fee title owners. Although many cemeteries issue "deeds" to property, these usually restrict the rights of the buyer to a right of interment. Also, the documents include other restrictions on the use of that specific property and generally reaffirm the cemetery's right to adopt and modify rules and regulations.

# 3 Philosophy
Objectives may differ

MOST PEOPLE can look back to a handful of conversations that stand out as being important in developing an understanding of their careers. For me, one of those was a conversation I had with the then Director of Cemeteries for the Archdiocese of Los Angeles, Jerry McAdams. Jerry had passionate feelings about the role that cemeteries play. Our discussion took place in the early days of the acquisition movement. Although most of the acquisition activity was aimed at funeral homes, we were talking about the impact of consolidation on the cemetery industry. Specifically, we both wondered about the impact of the consolidation of so many cemeteries into the hands of publicly traded firms. During this discussion, Jerry posed the question about the philosophy of running a cemetery: "Is it a business?"

Good question.

Jerry wondered whether it was proper for cemeteries to be pulled into the arena of big business. As an executive who ran a group of church owned and operated cemeteries, Jerry wasn't sure that big business had the sensitivity and long-term perspective necessary for cemeteries. His question was really about values and mission. From his point of view, a cemetery exists to fulfill a higher purpose, in his case a religious purpose, rather than to make profits. The essence of Jerry's question was whether a quest for profits meant lower levels of caring service and a lack of commitment to the "forever" nature

© Crown Hill Cemetery and Funeral Home

*Figure 3–1 The skyline of Indianapolis as seen from Crown Hill Cemetery,
Indianapolis*

of cemeteries. Although the answer is "no," the question is a valid one for everyone involved in the management or governance of cemeteries.

Profits and returns on investment are essential for businesses; however, the measurement of return on investment may differ for various cemeteries. A publicly traded firm will be judged on financial return, but a church owned cemetery might judge itself on how well its parishioners are served—each can be a valid method of measuring return.

No matter what method of measurement is appropriate, a cemetery operation must look beyond the short-term if it is going to survive and be successful over the long haul. Regardless of the current criteria for assessing performance, cemetery management must address the long-term financial aspects of a cemetery. While a cemetery has a finite financial life from sales, it has an endless life for maintenance expenses.

Running a cemetery calls for a unique set of values because of the long-term nature of the business. It has often been said that a cemetery is the only business that sells something once and takes care of it forever. This is the challenge to those responsible for cemeteries.

## Why cemeteries?

The reasons cemeteries exist are quite varied. They may exist for philosophical, practical, mystical, spiritual, and other very human purposes.

Cemeteries take care of the practical act of disposition of the human dead. Although that is important, it is probably secondary to cemeteries' role in the continuum of life. Humankind has long sought the "meaning of life." This quest for the answer to the mystery of life has occupied the minds of scientists, religious scholars, philosophers, writers, and artists throughout the ages.

While different, each of the great religions of the world deals with death in a manner that usually incorporates a vision of an afterlife. The Egyptian pharaohs were carefully laid to rest with food, household implements, and other things to help them in their next life. Many other cultures also have buried various items with their dead. I suppose that it would be fair to say that they couldn't accept "that's all there is" as the answer to the timeless question of the mystery of life.

Part of Christianity's appeal is the belief that one will be rewarded for living a virtuous life upon reaching heaven. When Hubert Eaton was dreaming about what cemeteries should be and wrote the Builder's Creed, he was heavily influenced by his Baptist upbringing. He began his vision with "I believe in a Christ that smiles and loves you and me. I believe that those gone before, who believed in Him, have entered into a happier life."

Eaton reflected Christianity's teaching that death of our mortal bodies is not the end. Death is a transition—a step on the road to being with God. This is an important point, because it is central to Western ideas about funerals and burial. It represents the dichotomy of how society views cemeteries.

On the one hand, cemeteries represent sorrow. People look at cemeteries and are challenged by their own mortality. They think of loved ones they have lost to "the great beyond." Hence, cemeteries are linked to sadness, and they are often described as depressing.[1]

On the other hand, cemeteries also challenge us to think about what we believe: Is there some grand scheme to life, and if there is, how do we fit into it? Some choose answers steeped in religion and others accept secular explanations. But no matter what explanation is accepted, the universality of questions about the mystery of life and death cut across nations, religions, and cultures.

Additionally, cemeteries rekindle warm memories for many. An interment space is a place to remember someone who was special. Some have characterized the burial spot as a "footprint" left behind—a touch of immortality.

## Practical Disposition

Cemeteries have a practical and spiritual reason for existence. Early societies realized that for health reasons something had to be done with members of the tribe who had died. Burial was generally the answer.

From a pragmatic standpoint, there are a variety of ways to dispose of human remains. Remains can be buried in the ground or above ground. Cremated remains can be interred just like bodies or may be scattered (at sea or in other places) subject to restrictions of federal, state, and local laws. And, needless to say, within each of these possibilities are many other options.

Donation of organs is a noble offer and certainly can leave the gift of life to another. However, the donation of organs still requires a decision about the final disposition of the deceased and what type of service, if any, to have.

Some people still consider donating their bodies to science, but most medical schools are offered more bodies than can be used. For those who are able to donate their bodies to medical schools, the donation resolves the question of what to do with the body (generally, the parts are cremated after dissection in medical schools). But, even under these circumstances, a family may still want to hold a memorial service for friends and relatives to honor the deceased.

Each of these methods fulfills the need for disposition of the remains. Consumers choose among the options using many different criteria—cost, religious beliefs, family traditions, accessibility, guilt, and ego.

Costs can vary widely, not only from cemetery to cemetery but also within a cemetery. Mausoleum property is usually more expensive than property for ground burial. Even with a single type of property, like ground interment property, there will often be a range of prices. Location and the amount of embellishments in an area are factors that affect price. Scattering gardens for cremated remains are formalized common graves and are often lower priced than single interment spaces.

Religious beliefs, too, may have an important impact on the method of disposition. Some religious groups believe it is only proper to be buried in church property. Others prohibit or discourage cremation and still others view cremation as the "norm."

Likewise, family traditions are an important consideration when deciding upon final disposition. Families often gain solace from continuing their traditions—following what has been done in prior generations, whether burial in the ground, entombment in a mausoleum, or cremation with scattering.

Accessibility and convenience are also factors in making decisions. Some families of veterans choose local cemeteries rather than a free space in a veterans cemetery simply because the nearest veterans cemetery is usually quite a long distance away. Similarly, although a family might desire a religious cemetery, there also might not be one within a reasonable distance.

Furthermore, guilt and ego are emotional factors that may have a bearing on the disposition of a loved one. Guilt may come from a variety of causes. The best way to help guilt ridden and vulnerable survivors from overspending is through preneed arrangements. Whether a family makes a prearrange-

ment by buying ahead of time or just writing down prefer-
ences, the documentation of what to do when death occurs
helps the survivors make the necessary decisions with confidence. (Chapter 6 discusses prearrangements in more detail.)

Ego often manifests itself in pride of ownership. This isn't
a phenomenon unique to cemeteries. A small sub-compact car
may get you there, but many derive pleasure from making the
same trip in a Mercedes or Cadillac. Smart cemetery managers
who realize that not everyone wants the same thing, will develop products to match consumers' desires.

## Community Asset

Although cemeteries have a significant practical role, it is important to remember that they are far more than just places for
utilitarian disposition. When Hubert Eaton wrote his Builder's
Creed, he said, in a rather derisive way, that old style cemeteries performed a "practical act, and that not well." Even though
his statement may seem harsh, his intent was to explain how
different he wanted Forest Lawn to be from other cemeteries.

Cemeteries are an important part of the community because of their longevity and ties to the citizenry. Cemeteries
embody the history and memories of the community. In the
large urban areas, they provide peaceful greenbelts that are a
welcome relief from the clamor of big cities.

Most cemeteries are active participants in their communities. Members of management belong to local service clubs,
churches, and other civic organizations. The cemeteries often
have programs for the community—the most popular is a ceremony in conjunction with a major holiday such as Memorial
Day or Veterans Day. Others have extensive community programs for children, speakers' bureaus, religious services, or
museums.

These activities make cemeteries an asset to the community. They are employers, fulfill a community need, act as a
stable community institution, and, in most cases, part of the
social fabric that defines a community.

Forest Lawn Memorial-Park Association

*Figure 3–2 Easter Sunrise Service at Forest Lawn–Glendale, c. 1940.*

## Cremation

Very often when people talk about "cremation," they are using the word as shorthand for practical, no-frills, no-service disposition. In coastal areas, including Southern California, "cremation" often means cremation with disposal at sea. What many consumers don't understand is that cremation is only a process; it is not a form of disposition of the remains. Having a body cremated doesn't dispose of it; it merely alters its form. Although cremation may sometimes be linked to low cost, "practical" disposition, there is no requirement that this be the case.

A 1995 study by The Wirthlin Group showed that Americans are increasingly likely to choose cremation.[2] The interesting thing is that people were more likely to accept cremation for themselves than for a loved one.

## The Cremation Process

Many consumers have a romantic notion of cremation resulting in fluffy ashes that can be lifted to the skies by a gust of wind. That picture is entirely wrong. Cremated remains are not ashes and they are not fluffy. To correct the popular misconception and avoid consumers being surprised when they find out they are wrong, California now requires the following statement on all cremation authorizations:

> The human body burns with the casket, container or other material in the cremation chamber. During the cremation, the contents of the chamber may be moved to facilitate incineration. The chamber is composed of ceramic or other material which disintegrates slightly during each cremation and the product of that disintegration is commingled with the cremated remains. Nearly all of the contents of the cremation chamber, consisting of the cremated remains, disintegrated chamber material, and small amounts of residue from previous cremations, are removed together and crushed, pulverized, or ground to facilitate inurnment or scattering. Some residue remains in the cracks and uneven places in the chamber. Periodically, the accumulation of this residue is removed and interred in a dedicated cemetery property, or scattered at sea.[3]

## Disposition

When the process is over, the remains still must be disposed of in some manner, the common methods being burial, placement in a niche in a columbarium, scattering in a cemetery, scattering at sea, and taking the remains home. Each state has its own laws about what may be done with cremated remains outside of cemeteries, including scattering cremated remains on public as well as private land. In some cases, local zoning laws add an additional level of restrictions to state laws. Although niches in columbaria are specifically designed to hold urns for cremated remains, most cemeteries allow urns to be placed anywhere a burial may take place—in the ground or in a mausoleum crypt.

Jim Lahey, former executive director of the California Cemetery Board and later executive vice president of the Interment Association of California, has told a number of people about a time when his daughter and her friend had been bicycling in a public park in California. They were on a bike path that was next to a stream. As they went under a bridge, they were showered with cremated remains being dumped from the bridge into the stream, but which had been caught by the wind! Not a pleasant experience. If Jim hadn't been associated with the cemetery industry, the girls wouldn't even have known what was happening. Several years later, due to an incident involving the dumping of thousands of cremated remains on public property, the California legislature re-instituted the law prohibiting the scattering of cremated remains on public property and only allowing scattering on private property with the owner's permission.

## Cremation Rate

Many people ask cemetery operators, "Isn't cremation having a big impact on your business?" They've been exposed to media reports about the rise in cremation rates and have some notion that cremation is going to put cemeteries out of business. Although the cremation rate is rising, it isn't always linked to low cost disposition. Part of the problem with the media approach to cremation is that it is treated as being uniform throughout the country. Nothing could be further from the truth.

Cremation rates vary tremendously by area. While the cremation rate for the United States as a whole rose from 13.9% in 1985 to 21.1% in 1995, there was still a large variation by state. In 1995, the cremation rate in Alabama and Mississippi was just under 4%, while it was over 50% in Nevada, Alaska, Hawaii, and Washington.[4] In addition, while the rate in California was about 41% in 1995, there still are large variations within geographical areas of the state.

Several types of organizations perform cremations: cemeteries, funeral homes, and crematories. This sometimes depends upon state licensing laws, and sometimes it is simply a business decision. For instance, in California, cremations only may be done by a crematory licensed under the Cemetery Act or a cemetery. Although it is common practice for mortuaries and others who are not licensed to perform cremations to advertise cremation services, the state has chosen not to worry about whether those advertising cremation services are licensed to perform those services. Businesses that only provide cremation services often promote themselves as providing low cost disposition, while cemeteries or funeral homes that provide cremations make cremations available to give consumers more choices.

The low cost cremation business has attracted some operators who have cut corners in providing services. Figure 3–3 shows a few samples of headlines involving cremation providers and gives some indication of the types of trouble they've been in. Note that the headlines cover a decade and many parts of the country. The most common allegations have been that cremated remains of more than one person were mixed illegally and that bodies weren't treated properly before cremation took place. I suspect that part of the reason these firms have been in trouble is that they have incorrectly presumed that families who choose low cost disposition or scattering without a service care less about their loved ones than families who had a traditional funeral service and burial. A funeral director develops a relationship with a family in the process of making arrangements and holding the service. A cemetery expects an on-going relationship with all families with loved ones interred in the cemetery. These relationships are based upon a commitment to respect the deceased and handle all details with dignity.

Not all cremation providers cut corners or perform illegal acts. Some of the newspaper articles are reports of allegations not findings of fact. However, the headlines show that when things aren't done right, or even just alleged to have been done wrong, bad publicity will follow. The majority of firms per-

*Figure 3–3 Sample cremation-related news headlines.*

*San Jose Mercury News,* January 17, 1987

## Suit Accuses Crematory of Mixing Human Ashes, Seek Punitive

A report that a letter from one crematory about possible illegal practices at another prompted filing a class action suit alleging mixing of cremated remains.

*Charlotte Observer,* April 21, 1990

## N.C. Probes Raleigh Mortuary Former Workers Allege Bodies Mishandled

Story of a funeral home operator being fined $110,000 and accused of dumping cremated remains in vacant lots and delivering cremated remains of unknown humans and animals to families.

*Arizona Republic,* November 27, 1991

## Mortuary Penalized—Stacked Decaying Bodies, Mixed Human Remains, Animals

An account of a state mortuary board investigation of a funeral home. Allegations were made of cremated remains being misplaced, substitution of animal bones for human bones, and improper disposition of cremated remains.

*San Jose Mercury News,* February 20, 1992

## Crematory Suit Settled for $15.4 Million

Reported $15.4 million settlement of a class action suit that had accused a crematory of mixing cremated remains, plundering dental gold from corpses, and secretly selling body parts.

*Los Angeles Daily News,* January 26, 1997

## County Sues Crematory

A story about Kern County suing a crematory after authorities found cremated remains in a creek.

forming cremations do so with dignity and conformance to the law. Note that the Neptune Society operates through franchises, so a negative report about one location should not be seen as a reflection on all Neptune operators.

## Scattering

Many incorrectly presume that cremation implies scattering of the remains. This isn't so. As indicated earlier, cremated remains usually can be placed anywhere designated for a regular interment within a cemetery. And as mentioned earlier, some cemeteries have established "scattering gardens." In scattering gardens, cremated remains are spread out on the grounds rather than contained in an urn. These scattering gardens vary significantly from cemetery to cemetery. In one the scattering may be done in an actual garden setting, while in another scattering might done by peeling back the sod and scattering the cremated remains under a grass area. Still another variation would be to have scattering done in a natural area of native foliage. There are many different approaches.

Cemeteries often remind consumers that scattering is an irreversible process. Once cremated remains are poured out of their container into the ocean or onto the land, it is impossible to retrieve all of them. Families should be cautioned to wait to act if they are not certain about making or living with a decision to scatter cremated remains.

Almost every cemetery can tell stories of families that made hasty decisions to scatter cremated remains and later regretted it. To help overcome the lack of a specific place to go and honor or remember a relative, some cemeteries permit memorialization next to scattering gardens. When the scattering is done at sea or in some place other than a cemetery, families sometimes will purchase a cenotaph as a memorial to the loved one whose remains were scattered elsewhere. The crux of this is that cemetery operators have an obligation to fully inform families of the irreversible nature of scattering, so each family can make a decision that is appropriate for it.

Although the general public seems to accept scattering, not all religions endorse the practice. Roman Catholic Arch-

Courtesy of Woodlawn Memorial Park

*Figure 3–4 Woodlawn Memorial Park offers a variety of options for disposition in its Cremation "Garden of Memories."*

bishop Michael Shehan of Santa Fe, New Mexico, wrote a pastoral letter warning members that the church teaches respect for human life and for the body after the soul leaves it in death. He said that the body or its "ashes" must be buried or placed in a mausoleum blessed by a priest. According to a newspaper report, he became alarmed when he learned that cremated remains were being divided among family members or mixed with clay to make memorial pots.[5]

## Death Care—What's in a name?

The investment community has embraced the term "death care" to describe what the publicly traded acquisition firms do. Personally, I take offense at the term but, certainly, defend the right of those organizations to position themselves as being in the "death care" business if it fits their corporate strategies and self images.

Nevertheless, just as we should be tolerant of those who wish to use death care to describe what they do, they should be tolerant of those who do not feel the term describes their missions. I put Forest Lawn and myself in this latter category. "Death care" does not describe our organization.

"Death" refers to the act of dying or the ending of life. Death is an event, the moment life ceases; it does not include anything that precedes or follows it. The word "care" means to look after or provide for. Therefore, death care is simply providing for the moment life ends. This rather limited focus is part of my objection to the term.

I certainly see Forest Lawn as having a much broader scope than the term "death care" indicates. Death care is what funeral directors do. There is nothing wrong with that—Forest Lawn does operate five mortuaries. But, while the services funeral directors provide are necessary and are certainly incidental to memorialization, those services are limited to what is done over a short period. It is the permanence of the memorialization in cemeteries that carries on for future generations.

The public wants more than death care. History is filled with examples of societies that believed in something beyond death. Even people who have rejected religion have developed their own rituals to cope with death—some as simple as getting together with friends to share memories, and some more elaborate than any traditional funeral service.

I object to the use of the term "death care," because it is limiting. I want Forest Lawn to do more than just a practical act. We must be able to serve the living while being a sacred repository for the dead.

Forest Lawn has positioned itself as a positive part of the community, not because it is good business (it is) but because it is an important part of why we exist. As Eaton described it, it is our mission to "educate and uplift the community," to serve the living.

In part, we serve the living by helping them cope with death, but there is far more to our relationships with families and the community. We want to build relationships that last through time and cover many generations. This sentiment has been adopted by the International Cemetery and Funeral Association which describes its members as "guardians of a nation's heritage"—a true and powerful statement—and not "death care."

We changed our name from Forest Lawn Cemetery to Forest Lawn Memorial-Park more than 75 years ago, because we wanted to be more than just a cemetery. In the process of expanding our thinking, we opened our first flower shop and a mortuary, developed an extensive art collection, and sought ways to serve our community.

Forest Lawn's million visitors a year don't come here searching for death care. Some come to look at the art, some come because we are guarding some of their family's heritage, and some come as part of religious or patriotic observances. Tens of thousands of school children come for an educational experience, and still others come simply to experience the tranquillity of a great park in the midst of a busy urban area.

I expressed my concerns about the term "death care" in a letter to the editor of *Cemetery Management* magazine.[6] Frank Stewart, chairman of Stewart Enterprises, wrote a rebuttal to my letter saying, in part:

> I am convinced that until someone finds a way to truthfully and adequately label our industry, the correct and fair terminology is "death care."…
>
> The public respects truthful, honest people, not people who play games in facing reality. It's time we all face reality and understand why we do what we do the way we do it, and why all people do what they do the way they do it. I don't like the term "death care" either, but until someone finds a better way to tell the public the truth about why our businesses exist, there's no reason to disguise the truth.[7]

Several years after my letter to the editor of *Cemetery Management*, Ronald G. E. Smith wrote a book about the death care industries. While I fundamentally dislike the term "death care," I believe Smith was right in talking about related industries rather than a single industry. Smith proposed a Standard

Industrial Classification (SIC) which would recognize the separate but related industries of funeral homes, crematories, cemeteries, and monument dealers.[8]

It may seem that the issue of whether or not the term "death care" is appropriate is primarily an academic exercise. While it might be viewed that way, discussion of the term's applicability also can be viewed as the starting point for each organization to consciously define itself—not for purposes of assigning a label, but for the purpose of illustrating its individual mission. It is meaningful for every organization to define and understand its values and philosophy of doing business. This understanding is critical to effective operations and planning.

## So, is it a business?

Whether or not a cemetery is a business is in the eye of the beholder. However, regardless of how one chooses to characterize it, administration of a cemetery requires a different kind of thinking than running other organizations.

The role of a cemetery is both broad and lasting. Society realizes this and expects high standards of conduct from those who run them. When things do go wrong, public outrage follows. Few things incite a community as much as malfeasance in running a cemetery, particularly when the bad deeds can be attributed to greed.

Dealing with something as personal as the death of loved ones is far more sensitive than most interactions between consumers and a typical business. The emotions are deep and powerful. This relationship is more akin to that between a patient and a psychologist than that between a consumer and a business. Cemeteries end up holding the intangible memories of the deceased as well as the physical body. Their impact isn't just for today or for those few days between the time of death and the actual burial—it is for generations.

Throughout the world, people visit places of interment to honor those gone before. In many instances, the visitors never knew these people. People may visit the burial place of a famous political leader like Abraham Lincoln, a movie star, or perhaps a great grandfather who is only known from stories passed from generation to generation.

Therefore, while a cemetery can be a business, it is not an ordinary business. As shown by the publicly traded companies and many smaller private companies, the economic rewards of cemetery operation can be good. The public accepts private cemeteries as for-profit enterprises, but that doesn't lower their expectations about a cemetery's upkeep, ethical standards, or responsibility to the community. A cemetery can be a very good business, but it also has some large far-reaching, unique obligations. The objective of taking care of something forever is a huge responsibility.

## Summary

Although cemeteries perform the practical act of disposition of the dead, they are valued by society not as a pragmatic necessity but rather for the memories they enshrine. Cemeteries are perceived to be community assets because they are entrusted with honoring the past and for the open space they represent in many urban communities.

As more consumers choose cremation as part of their decision about the ultimate disposition of a loved one, cemeteries are challenged to give consumers complete information so that customers can make enlightened decisions. The biggest challenge is to overcome the perception that cremation is disposition of the remains rather than just a process that can be used as a step in disposition.

Because of the personal nature of a cemetery, those responsible for cemeteries must realize that they have a responsibility that lasts for generations.

---

[1] Hubert Eaton described them as becoming "unsightly stoneyards, full of inartistic symbols and depressing customs; places that do nothing for humanity save a practical act, and that not well."

[2] Wirthlin Group, 1995, *Study of American Attitudes Toward Ritualization and Memorialization*, September 1995.

3. California Health & Safety Code section 7054.7(b).

4. Cremation Association of North America, *State Percent Cremations Predictions 2000 and 2010,* undated.

5. "Archdiocese Warns of Disposal of Ashes," *Los Angeles Times*, November 29, 1997.

6. *Cemetery Management*, American Cemetery Association, November 1994, p. 6.

7. *Cemetery Management*, December 1994, p. 7.

8. Ronald G. E. Smith, *The Death Care Industries in the United States.*

Forest Lawn Memorial-Park Association

*Figure 3–5 An actor portraying Montezuma teaches schoolchildren about the early history of Mexico at the* Plaza of Mexican Heritage *at Forest Lawn–Hollywood Hills.*

# 4 Cemeteries and Mortuaries
Related, but quite different

TO UNDERSTAND the relationship between cemeteries and mortuaries, it is helpful to understand the evolution of the funeral provider as a business, what a mortuary actually does, and some of the business challenges of the mortuary business. The term "mortuary" is synonymous with "funeral home" and "funeral establishment." A "funeral director" and an "undertaker" perform the same function.

## The Beginning of Mortuaries

The evolution of mortuaries parallels the evolution of cemeteries—both evolved as society changed.

When the country was largely rural and agrarian, multiple generations of a family would often live together in one home. New family members were born there, and older family members died there. When a death occurred, the men would go out to the barn and make a coffin, while the women would wash and dress the body. A visitation or wake would be held in the parlor, and the burial would take place in the family cemetery or, perhaps, in a churchyard cemetery.

For city dwellers, the pattern was much the same, although they might have called upon a cabinetmaker to build the coffin, rather than making it themselves. Burial would most likely be in a churchyard cemetery.

© Crown Hill Cemetery and Funeral Home

*Figure 4–1 Crown Hill Funeral Home and cemetery office.*

As the country grew and urbanization began, families sought others to do the things family members had done earlier. Like private cemeteries, the funeral directing profession filled a need. Local morticians took over the job of preparing the body and had a selection of caskets to choose from. The societal shift represented by families beginning to live some distance apart encouraged the growth of the practice of embalming. The purpose of embalming then, as now, was to allow a delay before the time of the funeral to allow family and friends to travel to the service. Embalming became an accepted and widely practiced procedure.

At least one study suggests that many consumers don't understand the difference between a mortuary and a cemetery. Research done for Forest Lawn suggests this is often due to the confusion between the terms "funeral home" and "funeral director." Because a funeral often culminates with a burial in a cemetery, many consumers are confused about where the funeral directing stops and the cemetery operations begin. This isn't too surprising, because the process of holding the funeral, the part the funeral director is in charge of, is just a step leading to final disposition of the remains, the role of the cemetery. Despite this confusion, there is a vast difference between what mortuaries and cemeteries do as covered in the section on "Death Care" in Chapter 3. It is incumbent on practitioners in both fields to be very careful to explain to consumers what services they will render and what services others will render.

There has been a lot of tension between mortuaries and cemeteries over the years. Most of this is economic in nature, as illustrated in a September 1936 "Religion" column in *Time* magazine titled "Business of Death." This article stated that, at the annual conventions of the Cremation Association of America and the American Cemetery Owners Association, it was reported that "Out of every Death dollar which they divide, undertakers get 90 cents, cemetery owners ten cents."

## Mortuary Functions

Many people think that a mortuary is primarily the place the undertaker prepares a body for burial. While this is true, it is an incidental part of a mortuary. A mortuary's primary function is to help a family with the observance of the death of a loved one. This might be done by holding a traditional funeral service or arranging for a direct, no service cremation with scattering at sea. The closest analogy to what a mortuary does probably would be a planner for special functions who is ready, with almost no notice, to plan and execute a one-time event that must go well and is packed with emotion.

In the process of planning the service the family wants, the mortuary helps the family move from the initial numbness at the loss of a loved one and begin the process of healing.

A mortuary is operated by a funeral director. The funeral director, or member of his staff, meets with the family to determine the details of the funeral service. The mortuary staff provides the professional care related to the funeral which includes removing the deceased from the home or hospital, embalming (more on this in a later section), bathing, and dressing. Beyond the professional care, the mortuary assists in executing the funeral service—transporting the deceased to the service location, sometimes helping the family find a clergy person to officiate, actually conducting the funeral service, and conducting the committal service at the cemetery.

A mortuary's revenue comes from three sources: rendering services, selling funeral goods, and commissions on prefinanced sales (the latter depending on the actual funding method and individual state law). What is often not understood about the financial side of mortuary operations is the heavy overhead involved. According to the National Funeral Directors Association, their average member conducts 160 services per year.[1] With people dying 365 days per year, a mortuary must be ready to act every day. But with only 160 funerals per year, the mortuary's staff and facilities—autos, buildings, and other equipment—are only involved in providing funerals every other day. This results in a great amount of idle time which must be covered in a typical mortuary's prices.

## Mortuaries in Cemeteries

Before 1934, common ownership of cemeteries and mortuaries existed; however, they were not combined within the cemetery grounds. Additionally, the cemetery was secondary to the funeral business conducted by the mortuary.

The rise of mortuaries as part of cemeteries has taken some time to take hold. Around 1930, Hubert Eaton was faced with a dilemma. He could either give in to the demands of local undertakers by giving them illegal kickbacks to refer business to Forest Lawn, or he would have to find some other method of stemming the drop in Forest Lawn's business. As he thought about this, he decided that the best way of dealing with the problem was to hit it head on—have Forest Lawn enter the funeral business.

Eaton forged ahead and built a mortuary, the first mortuary within dedicated cemetery grounds in the world. This was

Forest Lawn Memorial-Park Association

*Figure 4–2 Forest Lawn Mortuary under construction in 1933.*

an idea the undertakers found threatening, and they fought it every step of the way.

The undertakers put pressure on casket manufacturers not to sell caskets to Forest Lawn. This was a big obstacle, because California law required a mortuary to have an inventory of caskets before it could get a license. The casket manufacturers contributed to a fund to fight the mortuary/cemetery combination and collected $1 per casket sold which is roughly equivalent to $11.50 in 1995 dollars. Eventually, Forest Lawn found a funeral director who disapproved of the methods being used to fight the new mortuary. He bought caskets and re-sold them to Forest Lawn.

The licensing agency, the California Board of Funeral Directors and Embalmers, fought Forest Lawn's license application in every way it could. Finally, when it could find nothing else to object to, it simply refused to issue the license. Forest

Lawn then sought a legal remedy and got a court order to compel the Board to issue a license. But, no license was issued. Things wound up back in court, and the license was issued only after the Appeals Court served notice that the Board would be held in contempt if the license wasn't issued immediately.

After Forest Lawn opened the first mortuary within cemetery grounds in 1934, it was twelve years before the next mortuary/cemetery "combination" was opened in Chapel Hill Cemetery in Dixon, Illinois. Two years later, the mortuary opened at Greenwood Memorial Park in San Diego, and in 1950, Rose Hills in Whittier, California, opened its mortuary. When I began attending national trade association meetings in the early 1970s, combinations were still uncommon. My recollection is that the association only counted about thirty combination operations out of a membership of more than a thousand.[2]

Today, the picture is far different. The leading national association for cemeteries, the ICFA, reported about 1,800 cemeteries as members at the beginning of 1997, and hundreds of these are combination operations.[3]

## Stifling Competition

A number of states still have laws that prohibit or make it difficult for a cemetery to own or operate a mortuary. Indeed, many of the laws are aimed at protecting the turf of those who currently hold funeral directors licenses. The effect of these statutes is to create barriers to competition from new funeral firms.

These obstacles to combination operations consist of outright explicit bans of common ownership, requirements for a licensed funeral director to own a majority of the business, and mandates that the licensed funeral director's name be the name of the establishment. As far as I know, none of these laws do anything except stifle competition. Most were sponsored by funeral directors who were motivated by fear of competition from cemeteries.

The result is that the consumers lose. Competition usually leads to lower prices and the business combination of a cemetery and a mortuary creates efficiencies and economies of scale that allow the operator to compete on a price basis if they so choose. These laws, which are passed under the guise of consumer protection, are actually laws to keep out competitors and stifle competition. In my opinion, the rationale behind these restrictive laws is simply outdated and wrong.

However, cemeteries need to carefully contemplate how to expand into the mortuary business, for it is different from running a cemetery. Not-for-profit cemeteries should be particularly careful about how they open a mortuary. The Internal Revenue Service has taken the position that preparation of the dead for burial (what a mortuary does) is not incidental to burial. In other words, running a mortuary may well cause the IRS to question the cemetery's tax exemption if the new operation is not structured properly. Some not-for-profit cemeteries have started mortuaries but only with a formal separation between the mortuary and cemetery operations. Any not-for-profit cemetery contemplating a combination operation should make sure it obtains good legal and tax advice.

## Storefront Casket Sellers

Recently, there has been a lot of publicity about storefront casket sellers. They bill themselves as "discount" sellers and are clearly trying to compete with mortuaries on a price basis. The usual pitch criticizes the mortuaries for their markups on caskets, and of course, the ads represent that the discount seller has much lower markups.

This isn't a new phenomenon. Some twenty years ago, certain Southern California firms tried to sell caskets directly to consumers, bypassing the "normal" distribution channel, the local mortuary. These firms generally were undercapitalized and failed. The more recent entrants into this business seem to be better financed. Despite this, only time will tell if a significant number of consumers will opt to buy caskets from discount sellers rather than from mortuaries. Although many have criticized the prices of funeral providers, historically, few consumers have made decisions about where to buy cemetery or funeral goods and services based on competitive price shopping.

The statements made about casket markups may be somewhat inflated, but it is a financial reality that mortuaries cover some of their overhead through the markups on caskets. At one time, funeral services and caskets were bundled—a single price was quoted which included the service and casket. However, over time, some states required separation of casket and service prices. In order to keep the service fees down, mortuaries used two or three times markups on caskets. The theory was that those who were buying higher priced merchandise would pay more of the overhead—somewhat like a progressive tax.

With the advent of the Federal Trade Commission (FTC) Funeral Trade Rule, separation of casket and service prices became mandatory. The Funeral Trade Rule did not change firms' prices; it simply required full disclosure of the prices and options that were available. If casket retail operations begin to make significant inroads on the sales volume of mortuaries, there undoubtedly will be a shift in mortuaries' pricing strategies. To the extent that casket prices contribute to covering overhead, unless the mortuary can become more efficient (cut expenses), a reduction in casket prices would be offset only by other price increases. More price-driven decision-making on the part of consumers also might result in lower overall prices.

On an anecdotal basis, consumers generally appear to be buying caskets from the storefront operations because they believe that the storefront operations are discounters. In the Los Angeles area, at least, the decision to use an alternate source doesn't seem to be based on price comparison shopping, but on representations and impressions from advertising. At least one observer has likened buying from a storefront casket retailer to purchasing at a discount store or factory outlet mall. Some consumers buy at these types of facilities because they believe the prices will be lower. They don't actually make any price comparisons. In other words, they believe the claim of "discount" without checking it, thus illustrating that image is the more important factor.

## A New Regulatory Challenge

The rise of retail casket sellers has created a regulatory problem in some states. In California, for instance, a funeral establishment is defined as someone who sells funeral services and merchandise. Since the retail stores only sell merchandise, caskets, they are not funeral directors and not subject to regulation by the state's Department of Consumer Affairs. A problem arises because state law requires mortuaries to make certain disclosures about caskets and, for preneed sales, to place 100% of the retail casket price in trust. Because the retail stores are not mortuaries, they do not have to comply with any of the state laws.

The California legislature realized that this was an anomaly. It reasoned that if consumers needed the disclosures from mortuaries, then all casket sellers should provide the disclosures. Also, if consumers needed the protection of having 100% of the price of the caskets placed in trust when a casket was sold preneed, then all preneed sellers should be required to put the preneed casket sales revenue in trust. A bill was passed to put the retail stores on the same basis as the regulated mortuaries. However, when the bill reached the governor's desk, it was vetoed upon recommendation of the Department of Consumer Affairs. In his veto message, Governor Wilson said that he vetoed the bill realizing that some of its principles were valid, but that it would have placed an undue burden on small business. Of course, many mortuaries are small businesses, and no one has suggested that they should be excused from compliance. Most mortuaries just wanted to have the same rules apply to all businesses doing the same thing—to have a level playing field.

The battle over who sells caskets and how they are sold isn't unique to California. In 1992 in Georgia, the funeral directors were successful in getting a law passed that made it illegal for anyone other than a mortuary to sell a casket. On a national basis, the trade association for casket retailers tried unsuccessfully to get a court injunction to stop mortuaries from offering package prices which provided substantial discounts on mortuary services to consumers who also bought a casket from the mortuary.

Clearly, the challenge to government is to uniformly protect consumers while encouraging competition, avoiding putting undue burdens on business, or giving one group of competitors an advantage over another group.

## Funerals

I believe in the value of holding a funeral.

All through history, friends and family have gathered to say goodbye to those they have loved and known. The funeral ritual is the time for remembering and honoring human life. At the time of the funeral, the family is just beginning to realize its loss, and a sense of loneliness sets in. When friends show their concern through their presence and comforting words, the family's loneliness is lessened, and the loss may become easier to bear.

The funeral also helps those who attend. It is recognition of the passing of someone who touched others' lives, and it is a way of showing support for those who are left behind.

A funeral has value to everyone present. A contact with the end of a life may cause each person to reexamine the meaning of life. Funerals offer people an opportunity to reflect on the deceased's life, thus often causing them to renew their beliefs, faith, and spiritual values. According to University of Minnesota sociologist Robert Fulton, a funeral is not only a declaration of a death that has occurred but also a testimony to a life that has been lived.

The details of a funeral are a matter of personal choice.

These include where the funeral will be held, whether the service will be public or private, who will officiate, what music will be played or sung, whether to have flowers, and so on. The job of the mortuary is to make sure each family has the type of funeral service it wants.

## Embalming

Until approximately 1860, bodies usually were packed in ice as soon as they had been bathed in order to allow time for friends and families to gather for the funeral. When arterial embalming was developed, refrigeration as a way to preserve the body became uncommon.

In arterial embalming, a small incision is made, one or two tubes are inserted into blood vessels, and body fluids are replaced with disinfectant liquids. This provides temporary preservation for a few days to a few weeks. For best results, embalming should be done as soon as possible after death.

Until fairly recently, almost all mortuaries routinely embalmed decedents unless specifically asked not to. Some consumer groups felt embalming was too expensive and lobbied for laws requiring mortuaries to obtain permission before embalming. Consequently, instances where embalming is not done have increased, and many mortuaries have installed special refrigerators or enlarged ones they had. Refrigeration may cost less than embalming if the body is held for only two or three days. However, in many mortuaries, the refrigeration charges are based on amounts per day, so refrigeration actually has the potential to cost more than embalming.

Although mortuaries generally may not require embalming, there are some special conditions where some jurisdictions mandate embalming—for example, when a deceased is to be shipped across state lines or out of the country. The FTC Funeral Trade Rule requires a statement about embalming generally not being required but acknowledges that embalming may be required "if you select certain funeral arrangements, such as a funeral with viewing."[4]

## Memorial Societies

Memorial societies are difficult to classify. Technically, they are neither cemeteries nor mortuaries. Although they are primarily funeral oriented, many also dispense information about burial.

The trade association for memorial societies is the Funeral and Memorial Societies of America (FAMSA) which is located in Hinesburg, Vermont. It says, "FAMSA is dedicated to a consumer's right to choose a meaningful and dedicated funeral." Although their stated primary purpose is to disseminate information, the FAMSA states that "most societies have agreements with one or more undertakers in the community who will provide dignified, inexpensive services for a predetermined cost." The FAMSA unsuccessfully petitioned the FTC to accelerate the planned date of the review of the Funeral Trade Rule from 1999 to 1998. It wanted the FTC to eliminate any non-declinable fee charged by mortuaries.[5]

Actually, memorial societies are competitors with traditional mortuaries. Although they don't actually render the services themselves, the arrangement they have with local mortuaries is a form of brokering services. Many memorial societies have chosen a "knock-the-competition" strategy rather than just competing on merits. A number of people have opined that a memorial society that makes funeral arrangements, even though they actually aren't rendering the services, should be required to be licensed as funeral directors. The memorial societies, not surprisingly, recoil from that notion and say that they are really "consumer organizations."

The FAMSA makes a point of separating memorial societies from cremation societies. It points out, as mentioned in a previous section, that the use of the word "society" doesn't necessarily mean that an organization is not-for-profit. The notion that an organization is preferable just because it is exempt from income taxes may only be a theoretical advantage. The tax status actually may not make any difference. A for-profit firm is not intrinsically bad, nor is a not-for-profit firm destined to be full of virtue and perfection. Consumers should be more concerned with how they are treated and the value they get for their money rather than be worried about the form of organization of the seller. Here are a few of the things that should be considered:

- ✦ Are the prices clearly disclosed?
- ✦ Does the consumer get to make meaningful choices about what is purchased?
- ✦ Does the seller make clear what services and merchandise are available?
- ✦ Is good value received for the price charged for the services?

Although mortuaries' prices have been criticized as being too high, consumers have not encouraged price competition. Few consumers make price comparisons before making cemetery or mortuary buying decisions. A statement by Ray Loewen, then CEO of the Loewen Group, is an indication of the perceived lack of importance of price to consumers in selecting a mortuary:

> Despite some who say differently, research indicates that a vast majority of consumers—some 80 per cent—choose their [mortuary] or cemetery because of its reputation....Approximately 20 per cent consider price a primary factor.[6]

If consumers made cemetery and funeral decisions based on prices, it would undoubtedly have an impact on the competitive price structure.

## Summary

Mortuaries and cemeteries have a close relationship. Mortuaries prepare the deceased for burial and usually conduct the funeral service. Because many funeral services conclude with a committal service in a cemetery, there usually is a seamless transition from mortuary functions to cemetery responsibilities. Many cemeteries have recognized this continuum and have entered the mortuary business. They did this because they believed that it was a good extension of their business and provided better service to their customers by offering "everything in one place" convenience.

The rise of storefront casket sellers is the first major change in the mortuary business in decades. The casket retailers are attempting to carve out a niche in the funeral goods market. To the degree that they are successful, this most likely will cause increases in funeral service prices as mortuaries attempt to recapture the margin lost on casket sales made by these new sellers. If mortuaries cannot gain consumer acceptance of price increases that try to regain the lost margin, the total cost of funerals will decrease.

Although some are critical of the prices of funerals, this should not be confused with the demonstrated value of having a service of some kind. The practice of embalming was originated to improve convenience to families in scheduling services although it is often erroneously cited as one of the reasons for high costs of funerals. State laws and the FTC Funeral Trade Rule have required disclosures about embalming and prices that should make it easier for consumers to shop and compare before choosing a mortuary or deciding what services to buy. Despite the availability of price information, consumers have been slow to adopt price shopping as a major factor in deciding which mortuary to patronize.

---

1. National Funeral Directors Association, "About NFDA," *NFDA Online*, www.nfda.org, March 1998.

2. These mortuary opening dates were gleaned from correspondence in Forest Lawn's archives. It is possible that others may have opened earlier, but I have not found any good source for information on the early history of mortuaries opening within dedicated cemeteries.

3. The ICFA now admits mortuaries, monument retailers, florists, and cremationists as well as cemeteries to membership. The ICFA's records only reflect common ownership of cemeteries and mortuaries, but this does not mean the mortuary is on the cemetery grounds.

4. FTC Funeral Trade Rule, Sec. 453.3 (a)(2)(ii) *See Appendix G.*

5. Fells, Robert M., Esq., "Consumer Group Urges FTC to Accelerate Review Date of Funeral Rule to 1998; Include Cemeteries, Other Sellers," *International Cemetery & Funeral Management*, January 1998, p. 6.

6. Ray Loewen, "Corporations in Funeral Service—Does This Trend Serve Consumer Interests?" *The Loewen Group Inc., Corporate Comment,* www.loewengroup.com, January 1998.

*A History of Mourning*

*Figure 4–3 Funeral of St. Edward the Confessor, 1066. The body, covered with a pall adorned by crosses is carried by eight men, and followed by many priests, to Westminster Abbey, which he had founded.*

Forest Lawn Memorial-Park Association

*Figure 4–3 First wedding at Forest Lawn, 1923.*

# 5 Related Operations

## Serving all needs

THE TRADITIONAL concept of a cemetery has been that a cemetery is a burial ground and nothing more. However, with time, this notion has changed. The expansion of cemeteries into the mortuary business was discussed in the prior chapter. It is quite common today for cemeteries to be involved in many other activities that are incidental or related to the function of burial: flower shops, vault manufacturing, insurance sales, and so on.

There is no "right" mix of activities; each cemetery must determine what works for it in the context of its resources, community served (market), competition, and business philosophy. While there is certainly a possibility of synergy in some of these activities, there is also risk. Some organizations may not have the depth or strength of management to take on a broader business challenge, while other organizations simply will be forced to take on the additional activities in order to survive. And still others will find that they have a talented management team that needs more of a challenge, and that the best way to use those talents is expansion into related fields.

Many cemeteries have found it desirable to offer a broad range of products and services. They have discovered that it is in the consumer's best interest to offer convenient one-stop shopping at a difficult time. The consumer has only one firm to deal with and only one bill to pay. Since a single firm is being dealt with, the consumer need only look to one organization to ensure their needs are met. This should prevent anything falling between the cracks in their dealings with the cemetery, mortuary, and flower shops. Many times this everything-in-one-place concept will mean lower prices, because the overhead burden is spread over a larger base. Also, a broad offering of goods and services is often a solid business decision. By having more opportunities to serve families, there are more opportunities for revenue. Having related businesses allows spreading "back office" overhead over a larger enterprise, making operations more efficient.

## Flower Shops

While many cemeteries have opened or acquired mortuaries, not all of them have gone into the flower business. This is often a missed opportunity, because it is such an appropriate combination. Flowers are used both for placement on interment spaces and funeral services. Thus, a flower shop provides a needed service and convenience for people coming to the cemetery as well as additional business opportunities for the cemetery/mortuary. The risks and challenges of opening a flower shop are similar to any type of business expansion and vary with the implementation. Opening a flower shop in an existing part of a facility may reduce the needed amount of construction and investment. And, evaluation of market size and competitive conditions should be a part of the decision.

The flower shop business, although complementary to a cemetery or mortuary, is different—specialized skills are needed to make flower arrangements, and the principle product, flowers, is perishable. Part of the success of operating a flower shop is having enough flowers on hand to fill orders, but not so many that they wilt before being used.

One of the things which the floral networks like Teleflora and Florist Transworld Delivery, now known as "FTD," bring to the floral industry is quality control in the form of inspection programs to make sure members maintain quality stan-

Forest Lawn Memorial-Park Association

*Figure 5–1 Delivery truck in front of The Flower
Shop in Forest Lawn, c. 1927.*

dards. However, these organizations appear to be experiencing increased competition from flower sellers with "800" numbers.

Some florists cut corners when making funeral flower arrangements by using flowers of borderline quality to enhance current profits. Flower shops that are part of a mortuary/cemetery combination cannot afford to do this, because the poor quality perception eventually will spill over to the core businesses—the cemetery or mortuary. Flowers are one of the few things sold by a cemetery or mortuary which the customer is familiar with—they buy flowers at stand-alone florists, grocery stores, street vendors, and many other places. So, skimping on quality when it comes to selling flowers can be a big mistake.

Although a consumer may only be exposed to mortuary or cemetery services every ten years or so, most have occasion to buy flowers more frequently. Consequently, consumers may reach conclusions about the pricing and quality of the cemetery or mortuary primarily based on the level of satisfaction with the price and quality of a flower purchase. Therefore, an on-site flower shop also can have an impact on the organization's image.

Some organizations are aware of the benefit of having a flower shop on their premises but don't want to risk entering a new line of business. They've found creative ways to joint venture with local flower shops or even lease space to a local florist as a way to enhance their revenue and offer more complete service to consumers while limiting the amount of risk to the cemetery.

## Monuments and Memorials

For decades, tension existed between monument builders and cemeteries. This tension was caused primarily by economics. Each wanted to be the sole source for selling memorials or monuments to consumers, and each sale one made took away a potential customer of the other.

A few cemeteries were so engrossed in their quest for sales dollars that they adopted their own rules and regulations that restricted consumers' options. The most restrictive of these provided that consumers could only purchase memorials or monuments from the cemetery itself, an "exclusive sales" rule.

Other cemeteries realized that such a rule wasn't going to pass antitrust tests and adopted a rule that only they could install the memorials and monuments in their cemeteries. The rationale behind these "exclusive installation rules" was both economic and practical. Financially, the cemetery wanted to at least get the revenue from the installation if it couldn't get any revenue from selling the merchandise. On the practical side, an outside installer didn't have to cope with installation problems that might crop up years in the future. Since the cemetery had the responsibility for the care of the grounds, the cemetery reasoned it had an incentive to do it right and not cut corners for short-term profits. If the cemetery installed a memorial poorly, then it would be proper for it to bear the cost for correcting it. Cemeteries did not want any risk of having to bear the expense of correcting problems caused by installations done by others.

## Litigation Followed

It was inevitable that litigation would follow in the battle for customers. Monument dealer Mack Moore filed the first of the antitrust suits in Oregon.[1] Not only did the defendant cemeteries want the exclusive right to install the memorials, but a few went so far as to require that the memorials be purchased from the cemetery. Thus, the litigation issues involved both exclusive installation rules and exclusive sales rules relative to antitrust laws. The case went back and forth between the trial court and the appellate court; however ultimately, Mr. Moore prevailed, and the court ruled that the practices of exclusive sales rules and exclusive installation rules were per se violations of the Sherman Act. The decision also held that the reasonableness of the restrictions didn't matter.[2]

A similar case, commonly referred to as Rosebrough, was tried in the 8th Circuit Court of Appeals.[3] In this instance, the allegation was that the cemeteries had conspired to limit trade by adopting the same set of rules and regulations–rules that provided for exclusive installation of memorials by the cemeteries. This case also went through the appellate process. When the dust settled, the court had found that the defendant cemeteries' exclusive installation rules were illegal tie-ins, but it did allow consideration of the reasonableness of the restrictions.[4]

While the Moore and Rosebrough cases were winding their way through the judicial system, a number of copycat suits were filed around the country. These suits only fanned the flames of acrimony between the two industries. Each side collected money for "legal defense funds," and the attorneys prospered.

## Installation Guidelines Adopted

With the final appellate decision in Rosebrough, the issues seemed to be settled. Cemeteries clearly defined installation requirements in their rules and regulations that applied to themselves and outside installers. In some cases, inspection fees were charged for the cemetery to oversee the installation pro-

Forest Lawn Memorial-Park Association

*Figure 5–2  A cemetery section with both monuments and flush memorials.*

cess. Again, a few cemeteries got carried away and tried to levy huge fees for supervision, but this was squelched rather quickly. A few cemeteries began to charge fees for the monument dealers to come on their property—so called "gate fees." These practices were short lived due to a joint effort by the ICFA and the Monument Builders of North America. These two trade associations adopted guidelines for memorial installation and formed a joint committee that has been successful in mediating disputes between monument companies and cemeteries.[5] And peace followed—it's been more than ten years since there was any federal antitrust litigation on memorial installation issues.

However, there was litigation in Indiana questioning whether cemeteries must allow outside firms to make burials within the cemetery grounds. This is a sensitive issue with cemetery operators, as making interments usually involves correctly identifying the interment space, driving heavy equipment such as backhoes over cemetery sections, opening the space without damaging anything, and backfilling the space properly to minimize future subsidence. The litigation was ul-

Forest Lawn Memorial-Park Association

*Figure 5–3 Memorial parks use flush memorials to create sweeping vistas.*

timately settled, but by agreement rather than a judicial opinion which could be cited in other cases.

## Monuments vs. Flush Memorials

Why would some cemeteries only have monuments, some only allow flush memorials, and still others allow both? The answer involves money and philosophy.

Revenue is derived from the sale of monuments that vary tremendously in size and selling price. A twenty-foot tall obelisk will produce a fair chunk of revenue for whoever sells it. In some areas, monuments are easier to sell, because consumers view monuments as the customary means of memorialization. In other areas, consumers have embraced the memorial-park concept and expect flush memorials. Forest Lawn, the originator of the memorial-park concept, has allowed only flush memorials for decades because of a desire to achieve a more open, park-like setting.

Beyond the sales revenue issue, cemetery operators also worry about the cost of caring for the grounds. An area filled with monuments is a lot more complicated (and expensive) to mow and irrigate than an area with flush memorials. It has been estimated that it may take as much as five times longer to mow an acre of grass with monuments than to mow the same sized area with flush memorials.[6] Some of the monument manufacturers have tried to produce statistics showing grounds maintenance expenses in monument areas aren't any greater than maintenance costs in flush memorial areas. Although this conclusion seems counter-intuitive to me, each cemetery needs to reach its own conclusions about costs. The on-going cost of maintenance related to memorials is an important issue in planning for the financial future of any cemetery.

Some cemeteries haven't wanted to choose between traditional monuments and flush memorials. Continuing to develop monument sections is often the result of wishing to match existing monument sections and believing that families will not accept change. Additionally, area monument dealers may promote the idea that flush memorials are not "proper" and create additional pressure to keep making new areas for monuments.

Cemeteries should be sensitive to consumer needs. With the Edsel, Ford Motor Company provided the consummate demonstration of the principle that consumers can't be pushed to buy something they don't want. However, consumers need to have information before they make decisions. The success of the memorial-park plan in most areas of the country suggests that there is an appeal to the broad vistas it creates while still allowing highly individualized memorialization.

## Other Services

Cemeteries are thinking beyond obvious related businesses like flower shops and monument sales and are expanding their offerings of services and goods. Just as mortuaries have increasingly sold cemetery merchandise, cemeteries have introduced funeral merchandise where allowed without regulatory prohibitions. In states without legal constraints, cemeteries sell caskets and preneed funerals.

Many mortuaries have explored grief counseling in various forms as well as new options for memorialization. "Family service" programs are designed as a form of support and counseling for families who have recently had a loss. The firms usually view this type of program as part of their public relations efforts. It has become common to refer to these as "aftercare" programs. Sherry L. Williams, president of Accord Aftercare Services, has written that "[Aftercare] is not a great profit generator, but it will add to [a mortuary's] bottom line and [its] community image over time."[7] She views aftercare as a service, but some firms think of it as a sales lead generation tool.

Technology also is becoming a factor in memorialization. Several firms have begun to offer ways of recording pictures, still and video, and audio remembrances. One of the firms that sells this service puts the audio and pictures on a compact disk that is accessed via a computer. The computer is in a kiosk that is located in the cemetery. Although there is some risk of changes in technology making this obsolete, it is an indication of the innovations that are being explored. It is also an indication of the problem of change for cemeteries. Once a cemetery offers a hi-tech service like this, there is an implied message that the service will always be available. Even if the cemetery stops selling new recorded remembrances, it must address the issue of how it will continue to service what has already been sold. Customers will expect these recordings to be available as long as the cemetery is there. If the cemetery comes close to the goal of being forever, that is a promise with far-reaching implications.

## A Note of Caution

While most for-profit cemeteries have a wide range of latitude regarding the products and services they sell, not-for-profit cemeteries need constantly to be aware of the limitations of their tax exemption. The Internal Revenue Service generally has taken a narrow interpretation of code section 501(c)(13).[8] Not-for-profit cemeteries should work closely with their tax advisors when expanding offerings of goods and services to make sure they don't inadvertently cross the line and risk losing their tax exemption.

Although for-profit cemeteries may not need to worry about the IRS, some states do have restrictive laws about what cemeteries can or cannot sell. For example, as noted in Chapter 4, in some states, only mortuaries can sell caskets. Furthermore, in California, anyone can sell a casket, but only mortuaries have required disclosures and trusting requirements on preneed sales. Awareness of all restrictions is essential in order to avoid disciplinary action by a regulatory agency that can result in fines or even threaten the cemetery's license to operate.

## Summary

As cemeteries have sought to improve service to customers and enhance revenue they have expanded their offerings to the public. Many entered the mortuary business. Others have opened flower shops. Although many cemeteries have sold memorials for a long time, improvements in technology have encouraged others to manufacture their own flush granite memorials. It is likely that cemeteries will continue to look for service and revenue enhancements.

[1] Moore v. Jas. H. Matthews & Co., 550 F.2d 1107 (9th Cir. 1977).

[2] After years of battle, many cemeterians were delighted to learn that Mr. Moore sold his cemeteries and used the proceeds to buy a brothel, which is legal in parts of Nevada. Rich Thurlow, "Cemetery Owners Enter Lively New Field—Brothels," *Pahrump Valley Times*, April 4, 1997, Page C4.

[3] Rosebrough Monument Co. v. Memorial Park Cemetery Association, 666 F.2d 1130 (8th Cir. 1981).

[4] A second case in the 8th Circuit involved practices similar to Rosebrough. It didn't change the law from Rosebrough, which allowed consideration of the reasonableness of restrictions, but it did find the plaintiffs had not shown that defendants had the market power required for a Sherman Act violation. Baxley DeLamar Monuments, Inc. v. American Cemetery Assn., 938 F.2d 846 (8th Cir. 1991).

[5] "Memorandum of Understanding Between the American Cemetery Association and The Monument Builders of North America," November 7, 1986.

6.   G. J. Klupar, *Modern Cemetery Management*, p. 239.

7.   Sherry L. Williams, "Aftercare Issues," *Today in Deathcare*, April 1998, vol X, no. iv.

8.   However, regarding cemeteries exempt under 501(c)(13), the IRS held, in a private letter ruling in 1998 (LTR 9814051), that the act of selling caskets wouldn't put the cemetery's exemption in jeopardy or make it subject to unrelated business income taxes as long as the caskets were only for the purpose of burying bodies in that cemetery and that proceeds from the sale of the caskets were only used for maintenance of the cemetery.

Courtesy of Jefferson Memorial Cemetery

*Figure 5–4 This 1782 settler's log cabin was rebuilt on its original site, now part of Jefferson Memorial Cemetery, with some original logs and all original rafters as a way of preserving the history of the area.*

Courtesy of Greenwood Memorial Park

*Figure 5–5 The entrance to Greenwood Memorial Park, Fort Worth, Texas, features full-sized reproductions of four bronze horses from St. Mark's Square, Venice, Italy.*

# 6 Prearrangement

## Not as simple as it seems

IT ALL STARTED with the concept of selling something before a death produced a need. The sales were referred to as "before need" or "preneed." At first, sales were only of interment property. Later, the concept was gradually expanded to cover services and merchandise which would be delivered "at need"—when a death had occurred. As the concept expanded, it came to involve not just cemetery property but also cemetery and funeral related services and merchandise. Additionally, terms like "prearrangement," "prefinancing," "prefunding," "preplanning," and "prepaid contract" were added to the original terms "before need" and "preneed," creating a lexicon which is often unclear—even to practitioners in the industry.

## Confusing Terminology

The cemetery industry most commonly uses the term "preneed" in referring to interment property sales and "prearrangement" to refer to a much broader scope of sales. Although the terms "preneed" and "before need" are interchangeable, Forest Lawn has continued to use Eaton's term, "before need."

Within the cemetery and funeral industries, there is a lot of talk about prearrangement. It is not always clear whether preplanning or a prepaid sale is intended, since the terms are used rather loosely. As a generalization, though, people within the industries are most often talking about selling things in advance of a need caused by a death.

To help keep things straight, a distinction should be made between prearrangement, preplanning, and prepaid sales. Prearrangement is the umbrella term and encompasses both preplanning and prepaid sales (Figure 6–1).

The term "prearrangement" encompasses the preneed planning or purchase of cemetery property as well as cemetery or funeral merchandise and services.

Preplanning is the non-financial side of prearrangement. It entails specifying what kind of funeral and burial a consumer wants. There is a wide range of the amount of detail in preplanning documents. The simplest form is a very general statement like "throw a great big party in my memory." Preplanning often includes many details of the service: specifying who will officiate at the service, listing what music will be played, describing what kind of casket should be used, where burial will take place, and so on. Depending on the form preplanning takes and the laws of the state of residence, preplanning can be binding on the heirs whether or not it involved a purchase.

Figure 6–1 Components of prearrangement.

Although the terms "prefinancing," "prefunding," and "prepaid purchase" are often used interchangeably, some effort is being made by the ICFA to more uniformly use just "prepaid purchase" or "prepaid contract." Often the prepayment is on an installment basis, and the interest earned on these installment accounts can be an important source of revenue. When the product isn't delivered to the consumer in some fashion—actual delivery, delivery to a qualified storage program, or a deed to property—usually, some form of financial instrument is used to guarantee performance. This can be either a trust or insurance.

In most instances, prepaid prearrangements include a price guarantee—pay this amount and the consumer won't have to pay any additional amount later. However, some prepaid sales do not include a price guarantee on all or a portion of the purchase. To avoid future conflicts, sellers are well advised to make sure that contracts state plainly any limitations on price guarantees.

Although a cemetery's decision to sell preneed may seem simple, it may be more complex than it would appear at first look. Given the many items and services which are now sold in advance of death occurring, it is helpful to think about these in terms of what can be delivered in the present versus what can be delivered or performed only at time of death.

## Deliverables

Those items that can be given to the consumer immediately are "deliverables." This includes developed cemetery property that can be deeded to the consumer when it is paid for and both parties have fulfilled their part of the contract. The customer paid for it, and the cemetery delivered a deed giving title to the property (in most instances, the customer is only granted a right of interment).

"Non-deliverables" are all those things which a consumer might purchase but actually won't (often can't) receive until sometime in the future. Some non-deliverable items may have a known or "not-later-than" delivery date. The best example of this would be the purchase of a predeveloped mausoleum crypt. The purchaser puts up the money knowing that the building hasn't been built yet. It is common, even required in some states, for the contract to provide an outside date for completion of construction. If the construction is not done by this date, the customers can get their money back.

Then, there are those items that cannot be delivered at a known time, as delivery is conditioned upon someone's death.

It has been suggested that these non-deliverable items are really a form of life insurance. Here, the principal cemetery service sold is the burial itself and is often called an "interment charge" or "opening and closing charge." Although this category primarily is comprised of services, it may also include merchandise like vaults or outer burial containers that cannot be used until the interment takes place.

State laws about requirements for placing some of the sales proceeds in trust often govern the delivery of products sold preneed, including products that relate to burial, such as the burial vault and memorial. Sellers will often try to find some way to "deliver" the goods by having a third party store the merchandise. This may increase their cash flow and avoid trusting requirements, because they have delivered the goods to a third party. Some of these programs have been legitimate and have included a high level of integrity to protect consumers; others have been scams to avoid putting money in trust.

It is important for new cemetery managers and board members to understand past problems that have occurred in the industry in order to avoid them for their cemeteries. It has been my experience that the vast majority of cemetery operators want to do the right thing and support efforts to curb poor selling practices.

It is difficult to discuss preneed sales on anything but a general basis, because the laws of each state vary considerably and are often complex. Each cemetery must be aware of and comply with the regulations and laws where they do business.

## Preneed Cemetery Sales History

The idea of selling cemetery property before time of death has been around since close to the beginning of the century. No one seems to be sure who had the idea first.

While in St. Louis, Hubert Eaton had been exposed to the idea of selling cemetery property preneed by a college fraternity brother, Charles Marsh. Eaton's biography tells about a meeting with Marsh and how Eaton then spent several weeks going door to door in St. Louis trying to sell cemetery property.[1] However, in 1912, Eaton and C. B. Simms, who had been at Valhalla Cemetery in St. Louis, were attempting to get a sales contract with Forest Lawn. Obviously, Eaton made a success of preneed selling at Forest Lawn, but it isn't clear from Forest Lawn's records what role, if any, Simms played in the early sales efforts.

Apparently, Simms' before need cemetery property sales were based largely on an investment motivation—there was only so much cemetery property available; everyone was going to need it; and the price of property will increase in the future. Eaton wasn't comfortable with the heavy emphasis on selling cemetery property as an investment. However, he saw that stressing other benefits to the consumer might result in a more enlightened sales program. Today, we would say that Eaton had a "value" based sales philosophy similar to that used for life insurance sales. He realized that families were far better off deciding upon a purchase of cemetery property when they could do it together rather than waiting for death of a spouse or other loved one to force them to deal with the issue. He understood that just making the decision would give peace of mind. Furthermore, long before consumerism had been thought of, he realized that making the financial decision without the emotional stress and pressure of the recent death of a spouse was a big benefit of a before need purchase. Women, realizing that they statistically outlive their mates, were particularly drawn to the idea.

Eaton sold the directors of the little Forest Lawn Cemetery on the idea and went on to build one of the first successful before need sales forces, perhaps the first sales force that wasn't primarily based on an investment rationale. He was successful, and his methods inspired other cemetery operators.

## Why sell cemetery property preneed?

Most of the reasons cemeteries sell interment property before need are financial (even for Service Cemeteries). For example, a preneed sale can provide cash flow for development. When preneed sales proceeds can be used for development, borrowing for construction usually isn't necessary, thus eliminating additional interest expense. It also can produce profits. Additionally, preneed sales often lead to other sales, and in many cases, the sales are financed over time with the interest charged being another source of revenue. Sales of prepaid plans, using either insurance or trust vehicles, can provide not only some current income, but also provide a bond to the seller for the future.

Cemetery property is the most obvious item in the deliverable class. It physically exists (if it has been developed), and generally, it cannot be moved. As long as the cemetery records are properly maintained, there is little risk to the consumer. Even if, heaven forbid, the organization operating the cemetery were to go bankrupt, the cemetery property is still there. The caveat about properly keeping records may seem unnecessary. However, while it is true that in most cases there is little risk associated with how records are kept, there have been instances of a cemetery getting into financial problems and reselling spaces that had already been sold. Their records were a mess, and it was very hard to determine who had rights to what. Although a recurrence of this unfortunate situation seems unlikely, it is prudent to remember that it did occur at least once.

Development of ground property is completed when the grass, landscaping, irrigation system, and access roads are in place.[2] For other types of property—mausoleum and garden crypts, lawn crypts, or other constructed property—all of the foregoing items must be finished as well as construction of any structures involved.

If the property is being sold "predeveloped" or "preconstruction," the consumer is somewhat at risk until the development occurs. The mitigation of this risk is accomplished in different ways in various jurisdictions. In some cases, there is no protection. In other instances, as mentioned earlier, a requirement is imposed to complete development within some specified period of time. Yet, in others, the protection is from a performance bond or placing a portion of the sale proceeds in a trust. Most cemeteries, either because of state law or recognition of a potential problem, have a contractual provision for providing a substitute in the event that a death occurs before completion of construction of the predeveloped property. The most common practice is to provide property of comparable value as a substitute or provide property for temporary use until the development is completed.

Although cemeterians often talk about selling "property," in most cases, they actually are selling a right of interment or burial, and there are usually restrictions on those rights. Conceptually, the burial right is more like a specialized easement than conveyance of a fee interest. As with most easements, the rights of the fee holder also are limited by the granting of the easement. Thus, when the cemetery conveys the right of interment, broad limitations apply to what individuals can do with the property. This is accomplished through conditions on the deed and by the cemetery's rules and regulations.

As time passed, before need sales of cemetery property were expanded, and some cemeteries began to make preneed sales of other cemetery related items, such as vaults and memorials, and services such as interment charges. With this expanded selling by an increasing number of cemeteries, came some unethical sales programs by a few promoters which prompted various regulations and restrictions on sales and uses of the sales' proceeds. Many of the cemetery trade associations recognized that the industry needed to keep itself clean and drafted or supported laws and regulations to protect consumers. They also adopted codes of ethics as symbols of their belief in sound selling practices.

## Preneed Services

The subject of preneed sales of services can generate heightened levels of emotion from consumers and cemeterians, because a preneed sale of services is a promise to deliver something in the future based upon present day prices. The preneed sale of services fits a classic definition of life insurance—a customer pays now to receive a benefit (service) upon someone's death. Although most states have complex and stringent laws to protect consumers in insurance transactions, states generally do not use the insurance statutes to regulate preneed sales of services. Instead, they have come up with various other regulatory strategies for consumer protection. A later portion of this chapter discusses some of the principles involved in these regulatory plans.

Despite what critics say, the practice of selling services preneed is well entrenched throughout the country. Many cemetery operators see selling services preneed as a means of survival, of locking-in future business, or at least committing it, and it is often a way of producing current income.

The biggest business issue with respect to the preneed sale of services is one of whether or not to guarantee prices. This isn't a simple "yes" or "no" decision, because even when the answer is "no," it may be "yes!" The reason that a "no" may be "yes" has to do with consumer perceptions. When a sales person sits down with a family and sells them preneed cemetery property and funeral services, the family often sees this as a complete, everything-is-taken-care-of package. Even when that is not the case, over time buyers forget the details and parents tell their kids everything is taken care of.

When a death has just occurred and the children come in to make arrangements for their parents, they often react negatively when told that there wasn't a price guarantee and that more money must be paid. They suspect the seller is trying to take advantage of them—even trying to be paid a second time for the same thing.

Although strong legal grounds may exist to prove that there isn't a price guarantee, practical sellers realize that consumers' perception is often reality. Image is everything to a cemetery, and tarnishing that image with stories of taking advantage of widows or other survivors is something most cemeteries shun. Therefore, the seller may very well find that they must treat the preneed sale as though there was a price guarantee, even when there wasn't.

Does the preneed sale of services make financial sense? In some cases, the answer is an unequivocal "yes." However, it takes some very careful analysis to find out whether or not this is true for an individual seller. Often the determination of financial benefit rests on the concept of "marginal" business.

A marginal unit is one that can be delivered with little additional cost. For the marginal unit, any revenue generated over the direct cost helps to defray overhead and contributes to profit. In the case of a cemetery making 1,000 burials a year and working six days a week, the cemetery would average just over three burials per day. The cemetery already has the equipment necessary for its current volume. It owns a backhoe, dirt hauling equipment, lowering device, and so on and has a trained staff. If the cemetery could make one additional burial per week, it wouldn't need any more equipment, it wouldn't need to hire more people to do the job or to supervise it, and it would have very little increase in overhead. More fuel would be used to make the burial and the cemetery might have to pay the staff overtime, but these incremental costs would still be far less than the revenue generated by the cemetery's current interment price. These additional costs are the marginal cost, and the amount paid by the consumer is the marginal revenue. As long as the marginal revenue exceeds the marginal cost, the additional interment is financially valuable.

This simple model doesn't reflect reality except for small shifts in volume. Actually, there tends to be a stair-step pattern to the fixed expenses, as shown in Figure 6–2. A cemetery can't buy half a backhoe, and employees tend to be added in even increments. Yes, it is possible to add part timers in some positions, but this is a simple model. So, over a wide range of volumes, the fixed expenses tend to rise in jumps, and the variable expenses continue their upward march as volume increases.

Although it is relatively easy to explain the concept of marginal expenses, it is far more difficult to translate the theory into a live financial model for an individual organization. Despite that difficulty, a marginal cost analysis is an important exercise for organizations that sell things preneed that are not delivered. Delivered goods and services are a definite, immediate, and determinable fixed expense rather than a promise to deliver in the future at a cost which can be difficult—even impossible—to determine at the time of sale.

Among cost considerations for the seller, the first issue is usually "selling" costs. In some states, these expenses cannot be recovered initially from what the consumer pays in. Some states don't allow recovery of these expenses from income generated from amounts paid in. In other states, the selling expenses are only recoverable from income generated above a certain amount. Still other states are more liberal in allowing recovery of selling costs. This is done by requiring less than 100% of the retail price to go into the trust or by specifying an increment over the wholesale cost that must go into the trust. The foregoing assumes that the prepaid sale is under some form of trust arrangement (covered later in the chapter). If the sale is based on an insurance product, a different set of rules will apply.

Calculation of the amount of overhead and other expenses applicable to a prepaid sale requires many judgment calls. Some determination needs to be made about the direct expenses of performing under the contract. Although discussions about prepaid contract trusting requirements often focus on wholesale costs of goods, some direct expenses must be incurred in addition to the purchase price of the good.

For example, take the case of a bronze memorial purchased on a trusted prepaid basis, but not delivered until death occurs. Someone needs to process the paper work to place the order for the memorial, make the claim against the trust for payment, create a work order for placement of the memorial, and pay the foundry for the memorial. This is in addition to the obvious direct cost of the purchase price of the memorial and the labor and material cost of placing it.

The preceding example doesn't address the issues of overall business overhead. This could include fringe benefit costs of the employees doing the paperwork, occupancy costs for the office staff (rent, lighting, heating and air conditioning, water, etc.), supervisory salaries, general insurance, and so on. When a prepaid sale is viewed as a marginal unit, most of these costs are not relevant. The people doing the paperwork and making the memorial placement are already on staff, the occupancy expense isn't any higher, and there is no material

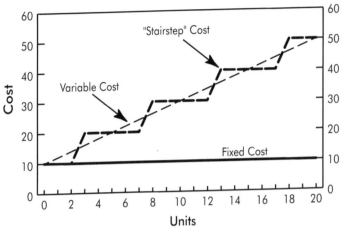

*Figure 6–2 Fixed, variable, and "stairstep" expenses.*

impact on other overhead. However, the marginal cost view is only appropriate when the volume of the prepaid sales is small relative to the whole picture. As the prepaid sales become a larger percentage of the whole, more and more of the overhead costs do have some relationship to the level of prepaid activity.

It is easy to see the two extremes. When there is a very small percentage of prepaid related transactions, most of the overhead issues can be ignored. On the other hand, if the entire sales volume were related to prepaid transactions, then the entire amount of overhead would need to be included as a cost of the prepaid sale in any realistic analysis. Although it is unlikely that any cemetery would reach this latter point, the vast gray area between the two extremes suggests that some overhead should be applied as the prepaid contract volume increases. The judgment call is determining how much of that additional expense needs to be included in reaching a conclusion about the financial viability of prepaid sales for a given organization.

The most rigorous form of analysis would involve having an actuary evaluate the likely life of a preneed account and apply various economic scenarios to arrive at an estimate of the financial impact of the decision to sell preneed with a guaranteed price.

## Commodities

The commodities that are sold preneed include such things as memorials, vaults, urns, and vases. The vaults, vases, and most urns are functionally fungible—any vault of a given type and specification performs the same function as another. However, memorials are, by definition, personalized. Although a memorial could be manufactured as soon as it was sold preneed with the name and date of birth, the date of death cannot be filled in preneed. Sometimes, commodities can be installed, rendering them as "delivered." As with services, there are many variations from state to state about what is permissible.

Preneed sales of commodities have been in and out of the spotlight of criticism. Often, this has centered on the question of delivery, as the cemetery can receive all the funds paid into a trust upon performance of the contract—delivery of the goods purchased. There were tales of vaults (outer burial containers) being stacked by the hundreds in open fields with the cemetery claiming that "constructive" delivery had been made because a consumer's name was identified with each one. At one point, questions were raised about memorials that were manufactured without a date of death but were held in a storage facility. Publicity attached to investigations regarding these types of issues has always been uncomfortable for the industry, because the delivery stories included an innuendo of high-pressure selling tactics and often raised the question of whether or not the consumer would get the goods they paid for. The image painted was not complimentary to cemeteries.

## Consumer Needs

As with any transaction, the seller needs to understand what the consumer is trying to accomplish. Only by understanding the consumer's needs can a transaction result that fulfills those needs and leaves both the buyer and seller happy with the bargain.

The consumer wants the "peace of mind" of having made "final arrangements." They've seen many stories about how unscrupulous people, mostly funeral directors, took advantage of people in grief. Thus, most realize that if a couple can make a decision together there is little opportunity for doubt later—the dilemma of "what would he (she) have wanted?"

Consumers have become better informed about most purchases. They want to know what they are buying and what conditions or restrictions are placed on the purchase. Much of this consumer awareness has come from media reports about how businesses of all types take advantage of people. Although the impression created is probably an overstatement of reality, the by-product of that impression has been an increased consumer wariness. Buyers often recoil from slick or high-pressure sales situations.

The objective of consumers is to transfer as much risk as possible to the seller. Thus, if the seller is willing to sell something now at a fixed price, it is seen as a better deal for the buyer, who transfers the risk of price inflation to the seller. Consumers don't always understand that the seller may compensate for taking that risk by charging a higher current price or putting other restrictions on the sale. Consumers can protect themselves by making sure the seller will be around to make good on the promises made in the sales contract. A wonderful promise from someone who has gone out of business is worthless.

Consumers also may be concerned with portability of their prepaid purchase—if they move out of the area, will another provider be willing to deliver under the contract. This is a direct conflict between the needs of sellers and consumers' desires. Since many of the trust based funding mechanisms for prepaid sales require only some portion of the amount of the sale to be placed in trust, the amount available to another seller is something less than 100%. Consequently, many sellers are unwilling to accept assignment of the trust proceeds as payment-in-full for their services. Although insurance based funding mechanisms are more likely to have some portability, if a consumer moves to another area it might be difficult to find a seller willing to provide the goods and services for the amount of the insurance proceeds. This is very likely to occur when the new market has significantly higher prices.

Some consumer groups have advocated laws allowing consumers to cancel prepaid sales and receive refunds of all money paid. This ignores the fact that the seller incurred current expenses in making the sale. Under some of the regulatory mechanisms, the seller may not recover these expenses, unless it receives the revenue from delivering the goods or services called for under the contract. Overhead issues also come into play when determining what is fair upon a request for cancellation or refund. The economic reality is that if consumers have a right to a full refund a cemetery will either charge higher prices overall to cover losses from those refunds or it will not make prepaid sales available to consumers.

## Seller Needs

The seller's motivations for selling everything possible preneed is both financial and strategic.

The financial motivation is to secure future business and generate current income. The general accounting treatment is to defer recognition of the revenue until the services are actually rendered. When death occurs, the funds are received—from insurance proceeds or from a trust—and the sales revenue is recorded. Depending upon the method of financing used (and state laws) a preneed sale may generate some current income, although the services have not been rendered. In the case of insurance products, the current income is commissions from the sale of the policies—sometimes these can be more than 20%. Some states do not require that 100% of the retail amount of the sale be put in trust, which leaves proceeds from the sale that don't go in trust and can be used for any purpose. When a trust is created from a prepaid sale, the amount of the trust is generally an asset and the service price is a liability. The sum of the two balances is zero.

Companies seem to have several ways to account for prepaid transactions. The specifics have to do with how state laws regulate prepaid contracts, tax considerations, and generally accepted accounting principles. A look at the notes to the financial statements of publicly traded companies can provide an indication of the variety of ways which these transactions may be recorded, but each cemetery will ultimately need to determine what requirements apply to it and what options, if any, fit it best.

The strategic motivation for the preneed sale of services is to create a backlog of committed business. Although no one can know when an individual will die and receive at-need services, each preneed service sale does create a bond for future use of the cemetery or funeral home. The risk to the seller is that the consumer may move out of the market area and not use the seller's services. If this occurs, the seller will usually recover the selling expenses, but not the profits from performance of the services or delivery of the goods included in the contract. The annual reports of the publicly traded companies often discuss the importance of this "backlog" of business.

The most important risk to the seller is that the funds received from the prefinancing method will not cover the actual expenses of rendering the services or delivering the goods. As discussed earlier, determination of whether the expenses are covered or not requires some study and judgment on the part of the seller.

Another issue that concerns both buyer and seller is how much of the prepaid contract proceeds does the seller receive at the time services are rendered. For example, suppose that a prepaid burial is sold for $1,000 which includes both the burial and an outer burial container. The purchase is secured by an insurance policy for $1,000. The policy has a provision that it increases in value according to some economic index so that at the time of death of the buyer the amount due from the policy is $1,600. If the price of the burial service and outer burial container is only $1,500 at the time of the buyer's death, who should get the "extra" $100. The seller took the inflation risk, but prices didn't go up as fast as the index used for the policy. If the seller gets its full current list price at the time of delivery of the goods and services, should the estate of the buyer get the excess? Not too surprisingly, sellers usually take the position that they should get it all, because they would have to accept a lower amount if prices had gone up faster than whatever the policy was indexed to. The same questions also can be raised about proceeds from trusts used in prepaid arrangements.

## Assuring Performance

The preneed sale of services or merchandise that isn't delivered until death occurs is only part of the transaction between the consumer and the cemetery.

From the consumer's standpoint, the assurance that the goods and services specified in the contract will actually be delivered is an important part of any prepaid transaction. Fundamentally, there are two primary methods of protecting preneed sales of services: trusts and insurance products. In addition to those methods of providing funds at need, other methods attempt to protect the consumer. Although there are many variations depending upon the jurisdiction, I will try to cover the most common arrangements for each.

For the cemetery, the concern is primarily financial. The cemetery is concerned with whether or not the money received upon delivery of the goods and services will be sufficient to pay the costs of delivery, overhead, and the expected profit margin. Because some of the consumer protection laws severely limit the types of permitted investments, the issue is often a question of whether the total return on the investments can exceed the increased costs of delivery. To the extent that a large amount of revenue comes from preneed sales of services, the cemetery can be betting its future on its ability to have investment returns exceed cost increases.

Whether a prepaid arrangement depends on a trust or an insurance policy, the buyer and seller have some common concerns. Both want to make sure that an adequate amount of money will be available to render the services and deliver the products. Sellers, particularly smaller firms, want the amounts of money they receive to keep pace with their prices.

One proxy for price increases would be the consumer price index (CPI). To make a very gross snapshot of investment return relative to increases in prices, a single comparison was prepared of what would happen to $1,000 if it were invested in (1) the CPI, (2) a 5% increasing insurance product, and (3) in one year U.S. Treasury Bills. For the CPI, the All-Urban Consumers figures from the Bureau of Labor Statistics of the U.S. Department of Commerce were used. The one-year treasury rate was based on the average daily rate for December as reported by the Federal Reserve.

The results are shown in Figure 6-3. This chart must be qualified by pointing out that it is just one way of looking at this and is only for a single time period: 1970 to 1996. Different results would come from studying other periods and using other investment instruments. This is intended to only illustrate the principles that need to be analyzed. Each company needs to reach its own conclusions about the risks it wishes to take given its individual circumstances, regulatory environment, and beliefs about future rates of inflation and interest rates. The national CPI doesn't necessarily reflect what happens to price increases regionally, let alone for a single cemetery or the various products a cemetery may choose to sell. Most business operators can point to expenses that have risen faster than the CPI as well as those which have had far more moderate price increases. Also, the so-called "basket of goods" used to calculate the CPI has many components that have no relationship to costs of providing cemetery merchandise or services.

The heavy line in Figure 6-3 is the hypothetical increase in expenses from the CPI. The thin solid line below it is the growth in value of a $1,000 investment that earns 5% compounded annually. The dashed line is that same $1,000 invested in one-year treasury notes. Comments follow about each of these options.

## Trusts

To ensure the delivery of the goods and services promised by the seller, funds received from prepaid sales are usually required to be put into a trust. The two main variables among the types of trust arrangements are the amount which must be

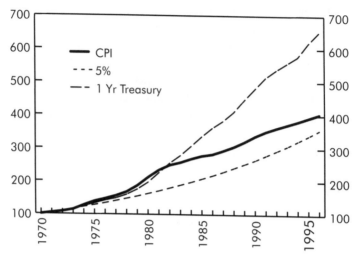

*Figure 6–3 Consumer Price Index increases vs. selected investment options.*

put in trust and the amount which may be taken out prior to the trust being revoked or used.

Generally, the amount that must be put in trust is based on a percentage of the sales price or a percentage of the whole-sale cost of the sale. In states where proceeds from prepaid sales must be put in trust, the amounts placed in trust will run from a high of 100% of the retail sales price to a low of 100% of the wholesale cost of the merchandise.

There are as many variations in laws about how income may be removed from trusts as there are variations in the amounts required for deposits into trusts. Some states allow withdrawal of a portion of the income for administrative ex-penses and recovery of selling expenses, and some states al-low withdrawal of capital gains while others don't. When the issue of cost recovery arises in discussing legislation, there is generally an attempt by sellers to at least recover overhead costs in addition to direct selling expenses.

Often the funds received as payments on prepaid sales based on trusts must be transferred to the trust within 30 days of receipt. Individual state laws dictate how this applies to installment contracts.

The amount of income or capital gains that may be taken out also may vary according to who bears the inflation risk. If the trust is just a means of putting money away for a future service but the customer is expected to pay the prices in effect at the time the services are used, then the consumer has the risk of inflation. On the other hand, some prepaid sales guarantee the price arrangement—once the customer has paid the entire amount of the contract the seller has the responsibility for providing all the goods and services specified in the contract with no additional cost to the consumer. This puts the inflation risk on the seller.

As the laws on this have developed, sellers have argued that they should be able to remove more from the trust fund if they have the investment risk. Consumer advocates generally understand this but are concerned that the service provider either might not be around when the services are to be rendered or might not be in a financial condition to render the services. Although the primary reason for requiring money to be put into a trust is to ensure performance, part of this assurance is having a pool of money large enough that another service provider could use it if the seller were to fail.

If the $1,000 hypothetical investment shown in Figure 6-3 had actually been a prepaid sale made in late 1970 and the proceeds had been invested in one year treasuries, the seller would have achieved inflation protection if the trust had remained active for more than twenty years. Before that, the amount in the fund would not have grown as fast as the CPI. This is assuming that no income was paid out to defray selling costs or administration of the trust. After twenty-one years, the amount in the trust would have exceeded the growth of the CPI.

## Insurance

The insurance products used in prepaid sales also have quite a bit of variability. Products can be used to just have money available for services, or insurance policies can be used as part of price guaranteed sales.

Generally, two types of policies are used for preneed sales of service: policies that increase at a constant rate and policies that are indexed to some economic measure. An example of the first type would be a policy that increases in value by 5% per year. The second type of policy might be a policy where the proceeds increase the same amount as the Implicit Price Deflator of the Gross Domestic Product of the United States (IPD). Although the latter is a mouthful, the IPD is one measure of inflation for the entire United States economy. The IPD doesn't exactly track the consumer price index. The recent controversy about whether or not the consumer price index is a valid measure of inflation is one of the reasons for choosing the IPD as an escalator.

Figure 6–3 shows that compared to the CPI for this particular period, a 5% policy didn't fair too well in producing investment results that at least met inflation.

From a consumer's standpoint, the quality of the insurance company is key to the policy proceeds being there when needed. The most common ratings quoted are those of the A.M. Best & Co.

There is a saying that "If a deal looks too good to be true, it probably is." This holds with insurance policies. There should be an explanation for one insurance company offering a big yield or earnings advantage over another. Often, that explanation has to do with the amount of risk the consumer takes in buying the product. Each consumer must make an individual decision about how much risk to take in selecting an insurance company for a preneed purchase. It is often a quality versus return issue. Sellers are concerned with the same issue when they guarantee prices. While the seller wants to get the most proceeds possible, if the insurance company can't deliver as promised in the policy, it's a bad deal for the purchaser and seller.

Although I've spoken in terms of return on an insurance policy, it is actually a little more complicated and depends on the specific insurance product. The important issues are how fast cash value builds up (if applicable), how much is paid in, what the proceeds will be upon death, and what happens in the event the buyer chooses to cancel the policy.

Some cemeteries will defer the expense of a preneed sale of services and undelivered merchandise to match the revenue with the expense. This means there is cash outflow—sales commissions and related expenses—at the time of the sale but no income statement effect, i.e. revenue or expense.

Another accounting treatment is to defer the revenue until the service is rendered but write-off the selling costs over the expected life of the contract (the time until it is estimated that the services will be rendered). Accounting for prepaid sales can be complicated, for tax accounting treatments are not the same in all jurisdictions and generally accepted accounting principles may introduce still another set of variables. Delving into the details of this subject is beyond the scope of this book and competent professional help should be sought when evaluating the tax or accounting aspects of trusts.

This isn't to underestimate the long-term financial statement effect of the accounting treatment of prepaid sales. The selling expense is "locked in" and doesn't increase. Expenses related to rendering services or buying merchandise are sure to go up with time. However, the amount of the sale increases and the funds to be received usually grow if either an insurance or trust vehicle is used to fund the prepaid arrangement.

## Bonding

Various states have adopted bonding as a means of trying to protect consumers. Under this method, the seller buys a performance bond that will pay for the services if the seller defaults. This is a somewhat flawed method of protection. Let me explain.

First, there are some underlying assumptions: (1) qualifying for a performance bond takes some level of assets, successful operating history, etc.; (2) bonds will be issued only for a fixed period, generally one year, and not on an open ended basis; and (3) if a seller's financial position deteriorates, the bonding company will not renew the bond.

If a state requires a bond as a condition for preneed selling, everything starts when a cemetery decides to sell preneed services. If the seller can qualify for the bond, it gets permission to sell. If not, then it can't sell preneed.

Once a company gets permission to sell, its financial position can go in one of three basic ways:

1. Stay the same or get better;
2. Be suddenly damaged by a major event (an uninsured loss, currency speculation, major lawsuit adverse judgment, etc.); or
3. Slowly deteriorate (could be from poor management, being undercapitalized, increased competition, or other reasons).

If the seller's financial position stays the same or gets better, then the seller is in a financial position to honor all contracts. Hence, a bond isn't needed to pay for services.

If the financial position deteriorates rapidly to a point where the seller is not in a financial position to deliver according to the contract, the bonding company will be called upon to make payment under the bond. This assumes that the precipitating event happens so fast the bonding company doesn't have a chance to cancel (or not renew) the bond. Two possible types of events that could cause a rapid decline in financial position would be uninsured losses from a catastrophe like a fire or losing a major uninsured lawsuit. Also, there is the implicit assumption that the bonding company cannot claim that material information was withheld from it that would make the application invalid. This is the only scenario where the bond will pay off.

The third alternative is that the financial position of the seller slowly deteriorates over a period of years. At some point, the seller's financial position will be so weak that the bonding company will not renew the bond. If the bond isn't renewed, there are three possible scenarios:

1. The seller does whatever is necessary to improve its financial position so that it can once again qualify for the bond;

2. The financial position remains weak so that the seller cannot qualify for a bond to cover additional sales; or

3. The seller goes out of business.

If the financial position improves so that the seller can qualify for a bond, no call is made on the new bond, as the seller is in a financial position to deliver services or merchandise as promised. If the financial position remains weak, the seller cannot qualify for a new bond, and the buyer remains at risk. If the seller goes out of business, the buyer has a general claim against the remaining assets—the likely range of what they might get will be from nothing to a few cents on the dollar. Under these two latter scenarios, no bond is in force, so no call can be made against a bond issuer.

In summary, bonding may appear good on the surface but actually offers little protection to the consumer.

The use of letters of credit to protect consumers has the same pitfalls as bonds, unless the letters are irrevocable. From the seller's point of view, irrevocable letters of credit can be a problem. They often must be backed by the entire proceeds of the sale, which is just about the same as a 100% of the retail trusting requirement.

## Consumer Guarantee Funds

None of the methods of securing performance are perfect. Each has its own set of strengths and weaknesses. The requirements of the various states are usually reflections of problems that have arisen in the individual states. If there was a problem with some firm not providing the goods and services contracted for, some enterprising legislator usually found a way to craft a new law on the subject. Some of the laws were written with input from industry, and some were not. Trusting and bonding requirements were sometimes deemed the best method of consumer protection. Recently, consumer guarantee funds have been gaining acceptance as a method of providing a pool of money to protect consumers from sellers who go out of business and cannot deliver the goods and services specified in preneed contracts.

A consumer guarantee fund is usually established by requiring all prearrangement sellers to contribute to a common fund. That fund may then be called upon to pay for the cost of buying services for consumers when the seller has not delivered as promised or is no longer in business.

Consumer guarantee funds often have a limit on the maximum required to put into the fund based upon some experience with defaults in a given state. There is usually some requirement that the seller be given the opportunity to deliver the goods and services called for in the prearrangement contract before a claim may be made against the guarantee fund.

From the seller's standpoint, guarantee funds may be a good thing if they ease restrictions on what can be done with proceeds from a prearranged sale. On the other hand, guarantee funds also can be viewed as a subsidy to inefficient competitors or as a way to mask poor administration of laws and regulations by regulatory agencies.

In addition to the differing views about the funds, it isn't easy to determine how much should be in such a fund. A frequently expressed concern is that if a legislature decides that there is "too much" money in the fund, that it might try to appropriate it for other purposes—making the assessment for the fund a tax on cemeteries to fund general government operations. Also administration of claims procedure for a guarantee fund may create an additional bureaucracy. It isn't surprising that consumer guarantee funds are quite controversial among cemeterians.

## Is there a right way?

The American Association of Retired People (AARP) has been concerned with the relationships between consumers, cemeteries, and mortuaries.[3] AARP has reached the conclusion that consumers are better off keeping control of their money rather than handing it over to others for prepaying cemetery or mortuary services or commodities.

There are many different products sold under a variety of regulatory requirements with diverse promises made by the sellers. However, many of the firms in the marketplace believe they offer the consumer something which will benefit both the seller and buyer.

Many state regulatory agencies have been concerned about preneed sales of services and merchandise. When large sums of money are set aside, temptation exists, and unscrupulous people have taken the money and run, leaving the consumer without anything. This has led to some very restrictive laws and regulations in certain states. The FTC has opined that extremely tough rules keep sellers out of the preneed marketplace, and that this cuts consumers' choices and limits competition. Most cemeterians understand the need to protect consumers by having rules that ensure delivery of goods and services. However, there is not general agreement about the best way to accomplish that.

It is possible for preneed purchases to be good for consumers as well as the organization selling the preneed arrangements. The various state regulatory plans provide some protection to consumers, but it is ultimately up to each consumer to do enough investigation of the fine print and the safeguards in place to determine if a preneed purchase of services makes sense for them.

## Selling

This is also a good place to make a short statement about selling. For years, many funeral directors considered cemeteries that focused on preneed selling to be high pressure, slick, take-advantage-of-consumers hucksters. While there may have been some who fit that description, this feeling stemmed more from the funeral directors' own lack of comfort with selling—due to lack of understanding of what good ethical selling is all about—more than pervasive problems with cemeteries' actions. This

*Figure 6–4 NFDA Prearrangement Standards.*

## Consumer Preneed Bill of Rights
### National Funeral Directors Association

Prior to purchasing any funeral goods or services or signing a preneed funeral contract, we urge you to ask us any and all questions you may have regarding your preneed purchases.

To ensure that you, as our client family, have a full understanding of the preneed funeral transaction, we guarantee the following rights and protections:

We will:

1. Provide you with detailed price lists of services and merchandise before you select services and merchandise.

2. Provide to you, at the conclusion of the funeral arrangement conference, a written statement listing all of the services and merchandise you have purchased and the price.

3. Give you a written preneed funeral contract explaining, in plain language, your rights and obligations.

4. Guarantee in the written preneed contract that if any of the merchandise or services you have selected are not available at the time of need, merchandise or services of equal or greater value will be substituted by us at no extra cost to you.

5. Explain in the written preneed contract the geographical boundaries of our service area and under what circumstances you can transfer the preneed contract to another funeral

home if you were to relocate or if the death were to occur outside of our service area.

6. State in the written preneed contract where and how much of the funds you pay to us will be deposited until the funeral is provided.

7. Explain in the written preneed contract who will be responsible for paying taxes on any income or interest generated by the preneed funds that are invested.

8. Inform you in the written contract whether and to what extent we are guaranteeing prices of the merchandise and services you are purchasing. If the prices are not guaranteed, we will explain to you in the written preneed contract who will be responsible for paying any additional amounts that may be due at the time of the funeral.

9. Explain in the written preneed contract who will receive any excess funds that may result if the income or interest generated by the invested preneed funds exceed future price increases in the funeral merchandise and services you have selected.

10. Explain in the written preneed contract whether and under what circumstances you may cancel your preeed contract and how much of the funds you paid to us will be refunded to you.

difference of viewpoints has contributed to tensions between the two industries.

As time has passed, many funeral directors have decided that preneed selling is all right and have begun preneed programs of their own. To their credit, NFDA adopted a "Consumer Preneed Bill of Rights" which outlines disclosures that should be made in prepaid transactions (Figure 6–4).

An owner of a small cemetery once told me he liked to keep his sales force small, so he could keep them out of trouble. Well, I admire his ethical standards in selling, because I agree with him. However, I believe better hiring decisions might allow him to sell more without having to spend so much time monitoring the sales staff.

Good selling isn't high pressure. Good selling is communication. It is helping consumers understand the benefit of a product or service, so they can make informed decisions. Businesses have known for a long time that consumers who make informed buying decisions are more content with their purchases and, thus, are more apt to come back again.

"Bait and switch" selling tactics are illegal. However, occasionally operators play that very close to the line. That isn't an effective long-term selling strategy. Nobody likes to be tricked, so selling that involves trickery or high pressure isn't a good long-term strategy. Because cemeteries need to be long term oriented—focused on building relationships that last generations—they must take the high road to sound, honest selling. Good selling is an honorable profession. It is ethical and serves consumers as well as business. The cemetery industry has long frowned on those who have been shortsighted with their approach to selling and the ICFA's Code of Ethics includes ethical standards for selling cemetery property.

## Summary

The principle of prearrangement has become widely accepted. While consumers like the idea of prepaid mortuary and cemetery services, consumer groups like AARP have been critical of prepaid arrangements. A major component of consumer satisfaction stems from price guarantees from sellers. On the other side, prepaid sales with price guarantees transfer all of the inflation risk to the seller—some sellers have not given adequate consideration to the downside potential of prepaid sales.

Subject to applicable state requirements, almost anything a cemetery or mortuary sells can be purchased on a prepaid basis. Prepaid sales are funded through a variety of methods and each method has its strengths and weaknesses. Not all funding methods are available in each state.

Sometimes prepaid sales have been perceived as being overly aggressive promotional programs. However, most sellers find that excessively assertive selling tactics lower customer satisfaction.

1. Adela Rogers St. Johns, *First Step Up Toward Heaven*, p.82-86.

2. Not all cemeteries have irrigation systems. In some areas they are considered unnecessary or are by custom are not used.

3. The AARP brochure "Prepaying Your Funeral," stock number D13188, is available from AARP Fulfillment, 601 E. Street, N.W., Washington, D.C. 20049.

Courtesy of Spring Grove Cemetery and Arboretum

*Figure 6–5 A private mausoleum in Spring Grove
Cemetery and Arboretum.*

Forest Lawn Memorial-Park Association

*Figure 6–6 Statue dedicated to World War I "doughboys" flanked by outdoor columbarium.*

# 7 Endowment Care Funds
## How BIG is big enough?

UNDOUBTEDLY, THE most important long-term issue for each cemetery is how big its endowment care funds will be in the future. Those responsible for each cemetery must be concerned about whether the income from endowment care funds will be adequate to care for the cemetery when it is substantially sold out. Concerned cemetery managers and boards of directors have long recognized the importance of building the size of endowment care funds to provide adequate income for the future care of the cemetery.

While present-day success depends upon currently generating sales and controlling expenses, the long-term success of a cemetery—what it looks like and how it is maintained when it is sold out—is directly related to the size of the endowment care fund. This is because the size of the endowment care fund is the principal determinant of how much income can be produced.

Some believe that a cemetery is unlike a typical business enterprise, because a cemetery cannot fail. That isn't true. Cemeteries can fail. Some cemetery scandals have been driven by financial failure. Maintenance costs were higher than the income from the endowment care fund and income from current operations, so shortcuts or illegal actions were taken to get through the short-term. That is failure.

It might be more accurate to simply say that cemeteries don't just go away when they fail. They're still cemeteries. A concern for both cemetery operators and society is that, in the future, many cemeteries may become eyesores, nuisances, or financial burdens to their communities. This problem may be caused by many factors.

Costs may increase faster than income available for cemetery care. The cemetery may be too small to ever have an endowment care fund that can pay all maintenance costs. A substantial portion of the interment spaces may have been sold before any endowment care amounts were collected. Poor planning may lead to higher costs of care. The endowment care fund may have been invested for current income rather than maintenance of purchasing power, ensuring disaster at a future time. Factors beyond the cemetery's control may create additional expenses. For example, flowers brought into the cemetery from the outside create refuse that is an outside-caused cost, and, of course, the higher the visitation rate, the greater the amount of trash brought into the cemetery. Whether the cemetery is required to haul the refuse to a licensed landfill or can dispose of it within the cemetery, a cost is incurred which has no direct relationship to revenue.

Some believe that those who express general concern about the size of endowment care funds are alarmists. Perhaps, but when one cemetery becomes run down or the subject of bad publicity, all other cemeteries tend to be colored with the problem. As an example of how bad things can be, read the following excerpt from a column in the Los Angeles Times:

> But what's this? Did those ugly stains come from rain leaking through the roof? And is that a breeze whistling through the missing panes in the stained glass? ... And outside the mausoleum, over on the pond, is scum really growing thick and green on the water next to where Marion Davies and Tyrone Power take the big sleep? Could that dead rodent trapped in the scum be a rat?...[The cemetery] is undergoing a kind of death itself. The place is flaking, peeling, disintegrating, falling to ruin, the victim of a sad fate that has left no money for repairs or upkeep.[1]

This description of Hollywood Memorial Park in Los Angeles is just about my worst nightmare-come-true for a cemetery and its endowment care fund. Hollywood Memorial Park is not the same place as Forest Lawn-Hollywood Hills and has no relationship to Forest Lawn! In a visit to Hollywood Memorial Park about six months before that article was written, I saw that the condition of the cemetery was probably worse than the description in the paper. The cemetery had defaulted on a $2.3 million loan. However, the lender didn't want to foreclose, because it didn't want to own the cemetery. So, the cemetery went into Chapter 11 bankruptcy in 1997. Next, the state regulators found problems with the endowment care fund. It seized the fund and prohibited the cemetery from selling any property until things were straightened out. Sometime, while all this was going on, the bankruptcy switched from Chapter 11 to Chapter 7. The cemetery was put up for auction under the jurisdiction of the bankruptcy court. Although a number of experienced cemetery operators looked at the bid package, none would bid. The successful bidder was the

*Figure 7–1 Hollywood Memorial Park, spring 1998.*

Callanan Mortuary which has been in the mortuary business since 1915 but has never run a cemetery. Callanan wouldn't close the deal, until they conducted a complete evaluation of the property. After their preliminary repair estimates topped $7 million, they aborted their purchase. After that, Tyler Cassity, a St. Louis funeral director, offered to buy the cemetery for $375,000. The buyer is taking on a huge challenge, and it isn't clear how enough funds will be found to bring the cemetery up to even a minimum level of maintenance. Cemeteries like this are embarrassing to all cemetery operators and are a prime example of why every cemetery must ensure the adequacy of its endowment care fund.

There are four basic questions which need to be asked about an endowment care fund to determine whether the fund will be large enough to provide the level of income required to sustain care of a sold out cemetery:

1. How much is in the fund now?
2. How much money currently is being put into the fund, and how long will those streams of additional contributions continue?
3. How is the fund invested, and what is the projected investment performance?
4. What are the total costs of care of the cemetery?

Obviously, there are a number of factors that must be taken into account when analyzing or planning for adequate endowment care funds. Objectives of the fund must be clearly spelled out, and testing must be performed to determine how well the plan will work.

Since cemeteries primarily are regulated at the state level, requirements and limitations differ greatly from state to state. Some states have very limiting rules about permissible investments—sometimes so limiting that the rules have an adverse effect, almost ensuring that the endowment care funds will not provide enough income to care for the cemetery. Because of the diversity of regulations, the comments in this chapter are general. Each cemetery needs to evaluate its action plans based upon the laws that apply to it. The common denominator for the objective of all cemeteries is that each endowment care fund ultimately should be able to bear the full burden of its cemetery's maintenance.

## Objectives

Agreeing on the purpose of the fund is the first step in determining the objectives of an endowment care fund. However, while it might seem easy to agree on the objectives, they are only obvious in a broad sense: to take care of the cemetery. Once the exercise gets more specific, disagreements may surface.

For example, should the fund income be adequate to care for both sold and unsold property? If the income should care for both, how much unsold property should reasonably be included? What about undeveloped property? What reserves should be established for infrequent events like roof replacement, road resurfacing, replacement of backbone utilities, and so on? How about facilities maintenance? The maintenance yard will still be needed when everything is sold, but what about the sales or administrative offices? Should the fund income be sufficient at the time everything is sold, or at some point before that, to allow some margin for error in predicting expenses or income?

As illustrated in the life cycle of a cemetery chart in Chapter 1, it is most likely that the cemetery won't just suddenly run out of things to sell. Sales of property will taper off as selection gets more limited, but sales of services and some commodities will continue long after that. For example, burials will be made in property purchased years or even generations earlier. Some of these families will purchase an outer burial container, and others may decide on some form of memorialization for a relative and purchase a memorial.

And then, there is the matter of overhead. How much of the insurance costs, management salaries, and utility bills should be covered by the endowment care fund's income?

At what point should the cemetery be primarily dependent upon endowment care fund income?

Forest Lawn Memorial-Park Association

*Figure 7–2 The income from endowment care funds needs to pay for far more than just mowing the grass, c. 1925.*

While some of these questions may seem as though they lead to "egghead" accounting games, they are very real and very important questions. It is possible to develop a scenario to justify almost any set of objectives and allocation decisions. The challenge is to make sure that the fund income will be able to take the full load of care at some time in the future. Because of the long time periods involved in forecasting the adequacy of income, it is easy to "prove" that everything is fine. The challenge to managers and boards is to use realistic assumptions that will lead to an achievable result.

Of course, there is also the matter of compliance with applicable laws and regulations of individual states. Some states are progressive about permitted investments, while other states have implemented restrictions that are most likely to be a long-term detriment to the regulated cemeteries. As long as an individual cemetery has some level of activity—sales of property at-need or preneed, sales of services, or sales of memorials-the cemetery's operations will be able to supplement the income from the endowment care fund. However, as a cemetery ages, sales will slow. If the fund doesn't produce enough income at that stage, sales will suffer, further compounding the problem.

The level of care will continue to decline as the purchasing power of the fund declines. At some point, the cemetery will be an eyesore, an attractive nuisance to vandals, and something everyone in the community will complain about.

An example of a well intentioned but disastrous restriction is a bill introduced in the California legislature in the 1996 session to require that endowment care funds only could be invested in government obligations. Since most cemeteries pay out all income and rely on capital gains for inflation protection, this would have guaranteed eventual financial disaster. If the fund paid out all of its income every year, the fund's purchasing power would decline every year, buying less and less maintenance, and thus, the cemetery's condition would erode steadily. Fortunately, the bill was defeated after protests by more enlightened members of the industry.

The subject of investment objectives must be part of the investment policy statement. Investing for current income is damaging in the long-term, because it tends to erode the real value of the endowment care fund's corpus over time. Consequently, the most important endowment care fund objective is maintenance of purchasing power.

Maintenance of purchasing power means the fund will be able to buy the same amount of services per space year after year. Most likely, this will mean the fund will give up current yield for capital appreciation. However, if the fund is going to take care of the cemetery forever, this is necessary.

Let me illustrate this principal with some arbitrary data. Suppose the current yield on a guaranteed investment contract (GIC) is 5% and the yield on stocks is 3%. On a short-term basis, the cemetery might prefer to have that extra 2% to take care of things. However, the 5% yield is fixed, so it produces the same amount of income per dollar over the life of the GIC. Even at a modest inflation rate of 2% over the life of a 10-year GIC, the purchasing power of the money received declines from $50 per thousand dollars invested to $41.02.[2] Remember this decline in purchasing power occurs over a short period in the life of a cemetery and uses an assumption of a small inflation rate.

Additionally, this illustrates that inflation is one of the great long-term concerns regarding endowment care funds. While it is important to make sure enough money is put in the fund, if the investment policy and performance don't keep pace with inflation, the cemetery ultimately will not be able to provide a uniform level of maintenance from year to year. Improvements in efficiency can help to offset inflation, but can't entirely offset increases in costs over the long-run. Failing to have a growing stream of income will produce a decline in purchasing power which will result in less care and maintenance each year.

## Investment Policy

Once the objectives have been identified, a formal written investment policy should be developed and adopted by the governing board. If investment advisors are hired, it should be shared with them as a formal set of directions. If the fund is invested in mutual funds, it should be used do determine whether or not a given fund has objectives and strategies that match those set in the formal policy statement.

At a minimum, an investment policy should clearly identify the fund's objectives, indicate what types of investments are acceptable, define asset allocation policy, identify the policy decisions that are to be retained by the fund trustees, and what decision making power is delegated to the investment manager.

The policy concerning acceptable investments can be in the form of a list either indicating what is permitted or what investments cannot be used. Obviously, any statutory or regulatory restrictions must be included in the parameters of an investment policy. The list should indicate any limitations placed on specific categories of investments.

In some jurisdictions, the laws allow realized capital gains to be taken out of the endowment care funds, while in others, only a portion of the gains may be taken out and only for improvements to the cemetery. Still, in other instances no restrictions are placed on what can be done with capital gains removed from the fund. A substantial removal of capital gains almost assures that the cemetery won't be able to stand on its own in the future, because capital gains are essential to maintaining the purchasing power of the fund. I suppose that some cemeteries will do this because it is legal and never think about whether or not it is right.

Loss of purchasing power is guaranteed without growth of principal. Capital gains and new contributions are the sources of growth of principal. Of course, new contributions can't go on forever, so even if they were large enough to maintain the fund's purchasing power, that form of principal growth will slow and stop entirely as the cemetery approaches the end of its selling life. Any law that allows removal of substantial portions of capital gains from an endowment care fund basically is asking cemeteries to fall into disrepair in the future.

Boards of directors should be very cautious about taking capital gains out of endowment care funds, even when a state's laws allow removal of the gains. I can't imagine taking capital gains out of an endowment care fund without some very conservative projections of future needs and a large cushion built in to protect the cemetery's future.

## Investment Advisors

As the financial world has become more sophisticated, it also has become more complex. There are now more than 7,000 securities listed on the major exchanges, more than 1,000 registered investment advisors, and over 10,000 mutual funds. Although the number of choices is bewildering, a decision must be made about who will actually invest the endowment care fund. Will it be the fund's trustees, the cemetery's board, a professional investment manager, a stockbroker, or someone's brother-in-law? Some guidance may be obtained from individual state laws and regulations, but in most cases, many options will remain and a choice must be made.

The fundamental point to remember is that the endowment care fund is a trust fund.

Whether or not the state has implemented some sort of investment standard like the prudent investor rule, the funds are necessary for the long-term good of the cemetery and its property owners.[3] Therefore, legally and morally, one must be long-term oriented and avoid wild risks and self-dealing. Most likely, this precludes choosing one of the directors' brother-in-laws to manage the fund. While one might argue in favor of using a fellow director's brother-in-law if he's truly a qualified investment manager, the first time he under-performs the market there is at least a theoretical risk that the board could be charged with violating their fiduciary responsibility. Since everybody eventually under-performs the market, why would cautious directors put themselves in that position?

How about the board making investment decisions themselves? This has similar problems. If the members of the board, or an investment committee that is delegated the responsibility, aren't qualified investment professionals, the board may not be living up to its fiduciary responsibilities. On the other hand, if the board merely picked an investment in one or more mutual funds and parked the money there, they actually did choose an investment manager. However, if they do a lot of switching between funds, at some point, they cross the line from using mutual funds as a way to choose investment managers to a point where they are really making investment decisions by switching between funds. Either of the extremes—putting everything in one fund and never changing or frequently switching funds—raises issues of how the fiduciary responsibility is being carried out. The challenge is to determine an appropriate place between these two extremes.

I know some cemeteries that use stockbrokers to manage the portfolio. This really bothers me, because a stockbroker is usually paid on a transaction basis, meaning they primarily are paid for trading securities. Consequently, this constitutes a built-in potential conflict of interest for the fund—a risk that the broker will be tempted to have a high turnover rate of securities, uncharitably called "churning" the portfolio. The problem is that it is hard to define what constitutes churning and what constitutes sound investment management. Stockbrokers are rewarded for being good salespersons—for generating transactions—rather than for being good strategists or analysts. While some may be good at "stock picking" and realize that is a way to get and keep business, it doesn't change the fact that a stockbroker typically is not a portfolio manager. If a stockbroker is going to be used this way, then the trustees should be sure to measure investment performance against appropriate benchmarks, net of commissions.

I have a bias toward using an investment manager—either by hiring the manager to manage the endowment care fund portfolio by itself or by hiring a manager who manages a pool of funds. The latter sort of manager could be hired by investing in a pooled institutional investment fund or a publicly traded mutual fund. Most investment managers (including mutual fund managers) are compensated on the asset value of the fund. Thus, they are rewarded and judged on how well they create increased value for a portfolio rather than for generating trading transactions.

Thus, the key is to select an outside investment manager who has a good track record as well as credentials that demonstrate good training and experience. Careful attention to the selection process will give those charged with overall responsibility for the endowment care fund some protection from individual liability (see the section on "safe harbors" in Chapter 9).

## Investments

Although the actual investment decisions will probably be delegated, it is still important that the endowment care fund's trustees understand the investment options available when they write a formal investment policy.

Asset allocation is one important aspect of choosing investments. All asset allocation decisions inherently are decisions about risk. Unfortunately, many of those involved in choosing investment managers and setting the overall investment policies don't understand investment risk very well. They often naively think of bonds as having no risk and stocks as being risky. This leads them to the conclusion that as fiduciaries they should avoid equities—a course of action that may

doom the endowment care funds by failing to preserve purchasing power or provide the income necessary to maintain
the cemetery in the future.

One of the best perspectives of investment risk is the result of work done by Dr. Harry Markowitz of the University of
Chicago. Dr. Markowitz was awarded a Nobel Prize in 1990 for
his ground-breaking work on investing and often is thought of
as the father of Modern Portfolio Theory. His award winning
work evaluated two dimensions of investing-rates of return
and risk. According to Markowitz, risk isn't just the chance of
losing money; it is the fluctuation or variability of returns. The
Markowitz Curve or the Efficient Frontier shown in Figure 7–3
shows risk on the horizontal axis and annual return on the
vertical axis. This shows that a risk-averse investor can reduce
the variability of a portfolio's returns by efficiently mixing stocks
and bonds to move back along the risk scale without giving
up return.

Some still believe a portfolio that is entirely in bonds is

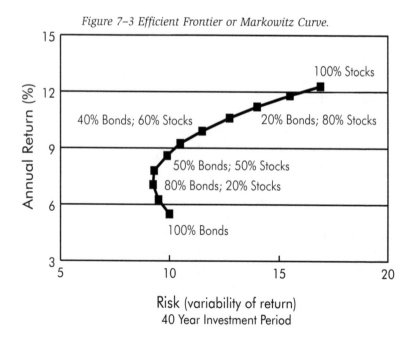

Figure 7–3 Efficient Frontier or Markowitz Curve.

very conservative and has little risk. However, Dr. Markowitz's studies showed that not only is there more risk in a portfolio with 100% bonds than a portfolio that is 80% bonds and 20% stocks, but the annual returns are also lower in the all bond portfolio. Given this historical relationship, it's hard to justify being entirely in bonds. Going up the curve shows that a portfolio of 40% bonds and 60% stocks has a much higher return without a large increase in volatility over the all bond portfolio.

There can be a big difference in results with a few changes in the facts. Most endowment care funds would not fit this model directly, because they pay out all the income from dividends and interest each year. However, the principles of Dr. Markowitz's work are worth noting, particularly in light of the fund's need to produce income which is at least level with an inflation adjusted basis.

Many factors affect the risks taken with individual investments, and these risks can have an impact on debt instruments—like bonds and mortgages—as well as equity investments. While there are broad risks that apply to governments as well as business, such as the condition of the world, national, or local economy, there are risks specific to each investment.

Most bonds have something behind them. It may be the "good faith and credit" of the issuer, or the bond may be secured by a stream of income—for instance, revenue anticipation bonds and mortgage backed securities. While it is uncommon for government agencies to default on bonds, the very fact that rating agencies exist to rate the quality of the debt instruments is testimony to the importance institutional investors place on evaluating risk.

Equity investments, like stocks, have risks that relate not only to the broad economic climate but also to specific industries and the decisions made by a particular set of managers and directors. Although some view fluctuations in the stock market with great concern, the underlying fact is that there are many companies that have a record of good or outstanding performance over a long period of time.

Real estate is perhaps the most common other type of equity investment. While real estate can be good for diversification of a portfolio, it is not a permitted investment in all states. Also, different skills are required to evaluate and manage real estate investments than publicly traded securities. Generally, only larger endowment care funds will use real estate as part of their investment portfolio.

It is the job of the investment manager to evaluate the relationship between risk and potential reward of each individual investment and to ensure that all investments are consistent with the objectives and policies of the endowment care fund.

## Diversification

Rather than try to discuss the many types of investments that might be held in an endowment care fund portfolio, let me just make a few comments about the importance of diversification.

A sound investment portfolio needs to be diversified. Diversification doesn't mean simply owning many types of investments nor does it mean more investments are better than a smaller number. Good diversification results from investments that have distinct, yet complementary characteristics. The idea behind diversification is that good diversification can help give more consistent performance and reduce volatility. A publication by PaineWebber likened diversification to musical instruments:

> For proper diversification, each type of investment should bring to the portfolio certain characteristics that, when blended, create a harmonious balance, much like musical instruments coming together in an orchestra. For example, a string quartet plays a beautiful tune. Yet add a set of woodwinds, bass and percussion to form an orchestra, and the music has more depth, strength, and resonance. If a clarinetist occasionally plays out of tune, all is not lost—the discord can be minimized by the melody carried by the rest.[4]

Good diversification is choosing instruments that make a beautiful "sound" when played together.

Diversification is more than just choosing different classes of investments; diversification is desirable even within a given asset class. For instance, the stock portion of a portfolio could include growth stocks or value stocks, or a decision might be made to hold a certain percentage of "mid-cap" stocks or to limit the amount of foreign equities in the portfolio. The goal of diversification is to increase a fund's performance by understanding and balancing the risk and reward attributes of various classes of investments.. The same type of understanding of subsets of asset classes is important for determining how to best use bonds and other types of investments for diversification.

Investment policies usually will address the issue of diversification by specifying either ranges or maximum amounts that can be held in a class of investments or individual investment.

## Testing Fund Adequacy

Setting objectives, quantifying diversification targets, and formalizing investment policy are important strategic determinations for an endowment care fund. Alone, however, these decisions give no information about whether an endowment care fund will be able to meet its ultimate objective of producing an adequate amount of income to care for a given cemetery. Thus, the whole package of strategic decisions must be tested, and these tests need to include estimates of how much will be contributed to the fund for the remaining life of the cemetery, a determination of current maintenance costs with appropriate overhead, and assumptions about future income and capital appreciation.

For smaller properties, this may be a good place to seek outside advice. An accountant may be able to help put together a financial model that can test the results of the assumptions. If the cost of this is prohibitive, talk to a local college—the financial modeling might make a good project for some of the students enrolled in a finance or accounting class.

Chapter 13, Testing Endowment Care Funds, contains the Metropolitan Cemetery Case which has examples of some of the items that might be taken into consideration in testing endowment care fund adequacy. It is not intended to be a comprehensive example, as each cemetery must make its own determination of what parameters are relevant to its individual circumstances.

On the surface, determining the cost of care seems easy. Most accounting systems are set up so the cemetery knows how much direct cost is related to things like mowing the grass, watering, maintaining roads, and so on. The difficult judgment calls are those related to overhead. How much supervision will be necessary in a sold out or nearly sold out condition? How much office staff? How many telephone lines? How much insurance will be needed?

I recently had a conversation with an executive responsible for a number of cemeteries. He said he wouldn't consider the cost of maintaining the chapels in his cemeteries when the cemetery was largely sold out, because they wouldn't be needed. Other cemetery executives consider chapels or other structures to be an integral part of the cemetery's atmosphere and would be shocked to find a peer who planned to raze them in the future. Judgment calls like this must be made when determining whether or not an endowment care fund will be large enough to care for a particular cemetery. This is the point where decisions are made about the cemetery's future and how the cemetery will meet its obligation to its property owners and community. Often the issue is whether the cemetery should be as well maintained in the future as it is today or if some lower standard of maintenance is acceptable.

This testing shouldn't be looked upon as a one-time event that can be done once and then just put on the shelf. If it isn't brought up-to-date periodically, managers and directors won't know whether or not the assumptions used are close to reality. When it is revised, the assumptions and objectives should be affirmed as still being appropriate. If they are no longer valid, they should be changed to reflect the new perspectives or changed circumstances. This periodic "reality check" is critical, because it forces reexamination of the assumptions if the results are unexpected. The testing, when done on an ongoing basis, provides a record of how good the assumptions are. A comparison of tests done several years apart will provide some clue as to whether or not changes need to be made in investment strategy, spending on maintenance, or amounts put into the endowment care fund.

Some cemetery managers I know have taken the position of "I'm putting $X$ percent of each sale into the trust fund. That's a lot more than the law requires, so I'm sure we'll be OK." That may show good intentions, but I don't believe it is as good as actually doing periodic testing. Whether the cemetery is for-profit or not-for-profit, handling the trust fund is a fiduciary matter. The long-term adequacy of the fund is a matter of fulfilling the public trust that is the obligation of all cemetery operators.

Testing is the interim report card on how well the cemetery is doing in fulfilling its ultimate responsibility to the families who have entrusted their loved ones to it and to the community. The ultimate test is the actual care given the cemetery as its revenue stream from sales dwindles to zero. Testing determines if the fund is on track and if improvement is being made. No matter what measures of success an individual cemetery decides are appropriate, an endowment care fund that will be large enough to provide adequate income for care of the cemetery far into the future is fundamental to the obligation of making the cemetery last forever.

## The Responsibility Is Today

It is sad that many endowment care funds are probably inadequately funded.[5] While we can look back and criticize preceding boards or managers for inadequate funds, current cemetery managers or board members who have not taken steps to correct insufficient funding are failing to fulfill their responsibilities for the future of the cemetery. Cemetery managers or boards may inherit problems from past generations, but that doesn't diminish their responsibility to take action to correct these problems. Even when a problem cannot be corrected fully, managers and board members have a responsibility to work toward improving the situation.

In the course of talking to cemetery managers about this book, I was told of a cemetery with approximately 140 developed acres that had an endowment care fund of about $2.5 million. While $2.5 million may seem like a large sum of money to some cemeteries, think about it like this: At a 5% rate, the fund will generate $125,000 a year in income. If the cemetery stopped selling property and services today, it would have less than $900 dollars per acre per year to take care of everything—mow the lawn, trim around memorials, treat weeds, fertilize, perhaps water, maintain roads, trim trees, repair and replace equipment, cover general overhead, and so on. That's about $74 a month per acre. Could an outside gardener be hired to provide all of his own equipment and supplies to take care of an acre of landscaping for $74 a month? What if he also is expected to keep the roads, fencing, roofs, and water systems in repair? Suppose he also was asked to maintain interment records for over a hundred thousand people? The "big" $2.5 million fund doesn't seem so big when compared to the task it is responsible for.

One of the things that isn't discussed much in an era of industry consolidation is whether the acquirers will be saviors of properties with inadequate care funds or profiteers with no regard for the future. The sale of a cemetery is an opportunity to make a difference in the future of the cemetery by providing a possible source of additional principal for the endowment care fund. Buyers and sellers have an opportunity to help correct inadequate endowment care funds by putting a portion of the consideration for the sale into the fund. If the endowment care fund isn't as large as it should be, sellers are faced with the moral dilemma of putting money in their own pockets or correcting the inadequate funding.

After purchasing a cemetery, the buyers encounter new challenges for the cemetery like debt service and quarterly earnings targets. Therefore, they must decide whether to yield to the pressure of the moment and adopt policies satisfying only the minimum legal contribution requirements or to make sure the endowment care funds are positioned to adequately provide for the cemetery in the future. Although people don't want to speak "on the record," more than one person within the acquisition firms has said they are concerned about the ultimate size of the endowment care funds. Many cemetery operators believe that the acquisition firms make only the legal minimum contribution to the funds. Even if this is true, they're probably not alone—independent cemeteries face the same temptation. Only time will tell whether or not the endowment care funds of any cemetery will be able to meet its intended purpose.

## Summary

The ability of an endowment care fund to care for a nearly sold out cemetery is one of the most important issues for cemetery managers and members of boards of directors. The key to satisfactory income levels is adequate principal. Adequate principal is a product of collecting enough money for the endowment care fund with each sale and investing the fund for growth of purchasing power. It is important that those responsible for endowment care funds have a clear understanding of the fund's objectives and a unambiguous statement of how those objectives will be met.

---

[1.] Robert A. Jones, "The Longest Goodbye," *Los Angeles Times*, June 29, 1997.

[2.] The real purchasing power (*PP*) is the reciprocal of 1 + inflation rate to the *x* power times the annual income where *x* is the number of years from the time the investment is purchased. For example, the *PP* of $50 of income in the 10th year where the rate of inflation is 2% would be $41.02:

$$PP = 50 \times \frac{1}{(1+0.02)^{10}} = 50 \times 0.8203 = 41.02$$

[3.] The Uniform Prudent Investor Act provides that: "A trustee shall manage trust assets as a prudent investor would considering the purposes, terms, ... and other circumstances of the trust.... The trustee shall exercise reasonable care, skill, and caution." Generally, this is a less stringent standard than the prudent man rule and gives trustees more guidance about what is permissible.

4. "Orchestrating a Diversified Portfolio," *Eagle*, PaineWebber, Third Quarter 1994, p. 1.

5. There is no hard data on this, but represents what I believe is an "off-the-record" consensus of cemeterians. As demonstrated in the Metropolitan Cemetery Case in Chapter 13, many subjective decisions must be made in making a financial calculation of endowment care fund adequacy.

Courtesy of Toledo Memorial Park

*Figure 7–4 An aerial view of Toledo Memorial Park.*

# 8 Master Plans
The key to the future

THE FINITE NATURE of cemeteries is one of the great challenges to those responsible for cemeteries. Once cemeteries begin selling, they start working toward going out of business—having nothing left to sell, although the cemetery will still exist. If producing revenue from current operations is the definition of being in business, all cemeteries eventually will go out of business. While it makes sense to do so in an organized way, most organizations go out of business in a painful way—they fail and cease to exist. Hopefully, most cemeteries will go out of business simply because they have nothing left to sell; however, a few will go out of business, because they have failed financially. No matter how a cemetery goes out of business, it will still be a cemetery; it will not cease to exist. For a cemetery, the key to going out of business in an orderly manner is planning (and, of course, making sure that the endowment care fund will produce adequate income to maintain the cemetery).

A cemetery's route to running out of space should be as efficient as possible, which means developing property in a logical and methodical way. It's an optimization process. The best vehicle for this is a "master plan"—a general development plan for the entire cemetery—which should include locations of roads, buildings, and interment property. A good master plan is a comprehensive picture of the cemetery's physical and fiscal future. It should encompass strategic engineering, operational, marketing, and financial planning. Although sometimes considered to only be a land-planning tool, a master plan is a foundation for many important decisions which cemetery directors and managers must make. A master plan is an important ingredient in planning cash flow as well

*Figure 8–1 Master planning needs input from all functions in the organization.*

as meeting the inventory needs of the sales force. It is also an essential ingredient to developing a financial model to test the adequacy of a cemetery's endowment care fund.

## Types of Cemetery Property

As part of the planning process, a cemetery must decide what types of inventory it wants to have available for sale. It may not be possible to have all types of interment property available at all times during the cemetery's entire selling life. During the planning process, the cemetery may find gaps in desired salable inventory, and the master planning process may enable it to determine ways to deal with those gaps. Some knowledge of the potential kinds of salable interment property is needed to understand the planning process. The following descriptions are generalities, so the details of usage may vary for individual cemeteries.

### Regular Ground Property

For most cemeteries, regular ground interment property is their basic product. Whether sold as single or multiple spaces, this property is often the "top of mind" image of cemeteries: areas of grass in which burials are made (Figure 8–2). Whether or not the cemetery allows monuments or restricts memorialization to flush memorials, it is still the basic commodity of cemeteries. Some cemeteries sell these regular ground spaces as "companion" spaces, meaning that two interments can be made in the space, one above the other. Different cemeteries have different ideas about how big these spaces should be. Some of these thoughts are driven by the history of the property, and some derive from practical considerations.

For example, in cemeteries that allow monuments, it is often desirable not to place the monument on the area where the interment is to be made due to the soil compaction needed to support a large, heavy memorial. The equipment used to back-fill an interment space cannot compact the soil enough to keep the monument from further compressing the soil that might result in the monument tilting or falling over. Placing the monument on undisturbed soil gives a higher degree of assurance that the monument will stay upright. Soil compaction beneath monuments is especially important to cemeteries in areas where the ground freezes.

*Figure 8–2 Regular ground interment areas in a memorial-park.*

Forest Lawn Memorial-Park Association

Forest Lawn Memorial-Park Association

*Figure 8–3 Modular companion lawn crypt construction.*

Over time, many alternatives to regular ground burial have been developed, including lawn crypts, mausoleum crypts, columbaria, and special memorials.

## Lawn Crypts

On the surface, lawn crypt areas are similar in appearance to regular ground burial areas, but there is a distinction. In a regular ground interment area, most cemeteries require an outer burial container to help avoid subsidence problems over time. However, in lawn crypt areas, concrete structures are placed below the ground, while the section is being developed. Therefore, no outer burial container is necessary (or permitted) at the time an interment is made. Lawn crypts may be single spaces for one interment or companion crypts for two interments.

Various construction methods are used for building lawn crypts. The earliest applications drew on the same poured-in-place concrete technology used in mausoleum construction.

Wooden forms were built, reinforcing bars were put in place, and the structure was filled with concrete. Although this resulted in very strong structures, they were expensive to construct.

To reduce costs, precast crypts were developed. First, the excavation is made for the crypts just as it would be for poured-in-place construction. Next, a bed of crushed rock is placed on the bottom of the excavation and leveled. Off site, concrete boxes are produced for the crypts. There are several variations in these, depending upon whether the development is to be for single crypts or double-depth companion crypts. Other variations result from a need for additional wall strength, accomplished by greater wall thickness, where the wall of the crypt unit is not placed directly against another unit. The units are as small as a single casket space and as large as four casket spaces. All are heavy, so a crane is needed to place the crypts on the crushed rock base. Figure 8–3 shows construction of a lawn crypt area with modular companion lawn crypts.

Some lawn crypts are constructed in a modular fashion. After the crushed rock is leveled, a concrete floor is poured. The crypt's walls are precast individually as flat pieces rather than the box-like units mentioned earlier. Although a crane is usually necessary to put the pieces in place, a much smaller crane can be used. The individual walls can be held together in a variety of ways—stainless steel pins and notches to interlock the pieces are common.

Sometimes lawn crypts are called garden crypts. In other instances, the term garden crypt is used for an underground crypt that is in a garden or other special area (Figure 8-4). The underground construction is the same; the principal difference is in what is done to embellish the above ground area.

## Mausoleum Crypts

The term "mausoleum" comes from a structure Mausolus, king of Caria in Asia Minor, built for his wife in about 1350 B.C. It was one of the Seven Wonders of the World. Although Mausolus' name is used to identify large structures for interment, at the time of his project, such structures had been around

Forest Lawn Memorial-Park Association

*Figure 8–4 A garden area with lawn crypts in Forest Lawn–Glendale.*

for centuries. Throughout most of history, these large structures were used for burial of kings and pharaohs, as well as for
the rich and powerful.

In the eighteenth and nineteenth centuries, entombment
was very popular in Europe. Many private mausoleums were
built in places like Père Lachaise in Paris and the Campo Santo
in Pisa, as well as in American cemeteries.

In the late 1870s, the concept of community mausoleums
was developed. A community mausoleum is a poured-in-place
concrete structure that is sold one crypt at a time to many
families in contrast to the earlier concept of a private, one-
family-only, private mausoleum. The appeal of a community
mausoleum is that it allows many more families to choose a
burial form previously associated with wealth and power.
For some, since mausoleum crypts are often above ground,
it also is comforting to think of burial in a dry area rather
than in the moist ground.

Community mausoleums often include embellishments,
such as stained glass windows, mosaics, statuary, or other art-

works. Often, the amount and quality of these embellishments indicates the price level of an area within the mausoleum. And although mausoleum areas usually are described in terms of corridors or sanctuaries (Figure 8–5), some mausoleums have chapels built as a part of the structure. This offers families a convenient place for a funeral or committal service and often is less expensive than building a freestanding church or chapel.

Generally, mausoleums are structures built of poured-in-place reinforced concrete, and while they are most often above ground, some have below-grade-level areas. The crypts are indoors and usually faced with marble or granite, and sometimes the walls are clad in rich stonework. Even though many states allow modular construction of mausoleums, most cemeteries have found that there is no cost saving in this type of construction, because it requires a significant amount of labor to tie the crypt modules together and properly seal each space.

Although community mausoleums have been popular in many areas, private mausoleums have retained their appeal to some families because of their exclusivity and perceived prestige (Figure 8-6).

Outside versions of community mausoleums are often referred to as garden mausoleums or wall crypts. While their construction is similar to that of indoor mausoleums, but there is no roof, and the em-

*Figure 8–5 Sanctuary of Heritage in Forest Lawn's Freedom Mausoleum.*

Forest Lawn Memorial-Park Association

Courtesy of Metairie Cemetery

*Figure 8–6 "Millionaires Row" in Metairie Cemetery, New Orleans, Louisiana, includes a wide variety of private mausoleum structures.*

bellishments must be appropriately durable for exposure to outdoor elements.

## Columbaria

A columbarium is composed of niches for the placement of urns containing cremated remains. It may be built as a free-standing structure or as part of a mausoleum and can be either an indoor or outdoor structure.

While columbaria are generally built of non-combustible material, it has become uncommon to build a columbarium with poured-in-place concrete. A common construction method is to build a poured-in-place concrete shell and use precast modular units for the actual niches (Figure 8–8) which vary in the number of urns that they can hold.

Niche fronts are made of many materials. Although marble and granite are probably the most common, many cemeteries use glass fronts in indoor locations. As cremation has grown in popularity, new approaches have been developed which include such things as mosaic and stained glass niche fronts.

## Engineering and Land Use

The master plan's most obvious component is land use. This portion of the plan focuses on what may be developed where. To accomplish this, marketing input is needed in addition to traditional land planning expertise.

It's up to the engineer to determine how much land can be used. For a hilly piece of property, this includes determining how cuts and fills can be used to make the maximum amount of usable acreage. Since grading costs money, this is a financial as well as physical optimization process. Among the many problems encountered is the problem of the time value of money. Good engineering optimization of acreage might require spending thousands of dollars today for property that probably wouldn't be sold for decades!

Many cemeteries face the problem that previous development decisions were made based upon an optimization heavily weighted by current costs. Thus, as plans are reexamined, it is

*Figure 8-7 Construction of outdoor mausoleum crypts (wall crypts) at Forest Lawn–Cypress*

Forest Lawn Memorial-Park Association

often true that the easiest development already has been completed, and future development will be more expensive than that experienced in the past. The previous decisions may not have been wrong, but the master planning process requires many trade-offs between the present and the future.

Not only will concessions be necessary, but one can safely assume that any plan created more than a couple of years ago will be subject to a lot of second guessing. This is all right if the plan is reviewed and updated on a periodic basis. No one has the vision to be absolutely 100% right

Courtesy of Jefferson Memorial Cemetery

*Figure 8–8 A columbarium at Jefferson Memorial Cemetery with a stained glass feature.*

about what will happen decades in the future. The important thing is to keep the plan current—putting it on the shelf to gather dust wastes the effort expended in generating the plan. It must continue to evolve as times change. Each review of the plan will test the validity of the plan's basic assumptions.

## Operations

Sometimes, the operations function is overlooked in the master plan process. After all, they aren't going to sell property are they? Of course, that depends on the organization's structure, but operations ultimately will have to cope with whatever is built. So, it is important that operations personnel participate in the deliberations about what will be developed and when. Here are a few examples of concerns operations people express in the course of developing master plans.

## Concentration of Services

If the master plan is too frugal with land development, there is a risk that many interments will be concentrated in a small area over a short period. This produces potential scheduling and proximity conflicts between committal services, making it difficult to serve the public well. Not only that, but it is very hard on the grass, because heavy equipment is moved repeatedly into a small area. Torn-up turf creates a poor appearance—it's not good for the image of the cemetery in general, is potentially harmful to sales, and adds unnecessarily to maintenance expenses. Plans that recognize the at need service needs result in improved operating efficiency as well as better service levels.

## Efficiency

The maintenance staff spends more time out on the property than any other group. Hence, it is important to think about travel time for staff and equipment. While it is common to put maintenance yards next to perimeters, this may not be the most efficient placement for the long haul. Ease of receiving deliveries from suppliers must be balanced against shorter travel routes for routine maintenance and interments. The master plan must allow areas for maintenance, so operations input is needed for determining the optimum location for these areas.

## Refuse Collection

Although some cemeteries are allowed to bury their waste, green and otherwise, many are prohibited from doing so. Those

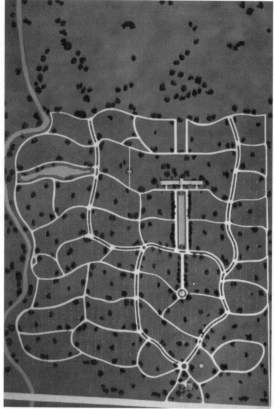

Courtesy of Toledo Memorial Park

*Figure 8-9 Toledo Memorial Park, Sylvania, Ohio,
has a model of the cemetery to help visualize
future plans.*

that can't need some place to store it until it is hauled off.
Strategically located collection points are essential for efficiency,
particularly since the intent is to cut the grass forever. The
trips within the cemetery will go on indefinitely from the places
the grass is cut or trees are trimmed to the collection points.

## Utilities

Most maintenance yards will need heavy electrical power, water, sewer, and, in some areas, gas. Mausoleums need power

for lighting and may have restrooms. Outdoor mausoleum crypts may need power for the device that raises the casket to crypt level in order to make an interment. The proximity of utilities is just one of the many important factors in determining the location of the maintenance yard and other facilities.

## Access

I can remember building a garden with the intent that we wouldn't use heavy equipment in it. However, we made the entrance so wide that maintenance workers soon figured out that a large, heavy backhoe could be driven into the area. It made work easier for them, but the area looked terrible because the constant maintenance equipment traffic tore up the grass. Although the problem could be solved with good management, the maintenance staff was always troubled that they couldn't use their labor saving equipment in an area where they knew it could fit! We had a somewhat similar problem with a stairway in a garden development. Even though it looked like it was wide enough on the plans, we soon found that carrying a casket up the staircase was quite cramped. As a result, we now have a different standard for stairway widths!

Some of these examples are short-term problems, and some are things that we'll have to live with as long as the cemetery exists. The principle is that it is important to include operating interests in the master planning process.

## Marketing

Marketing input is also critical for a good master plan. Generally, marketing is responsible for selling strategy, and a very important part of selling strategy is how the cemetery is developed. For many cemeteries, marketing is considered synonymous with sales. However, the term includes all forms of promotion, product planning, pricing, and competitive positioning as well. Seeking advice from the selling function is a very significant part of the marketing component of developing master plans, but selling is only part of the marketing picture.

Courtesy of Mount Olivet Cemetery

*Figure 8–10 Good master planning anticipates large features like Willow Lake in Mount Olivet Cemetery, Ft. Worth, Texas.*

Price points are the pricing strategy of the cemetery. Marketing must provide input about how fast it believes each price point will sell and how many price points there should be. An example of setting a price point strategy would be having property available in $100 or 10% increments. Sometimes a purely mathematical process won't determine the price points; instead, the points will be determined by a subjective evaluation of desirability of each area or section. It is common to price each row of mausoleum crypts differently, even though the crypts are all in the same area. Generally, the second and third rows are considered the most desirable, followed by the first and fourth rows. Crypts above the fourth row decline in value as they go higher.

Although the plan may be couched in terms of current price points, the relative pricing is what is important. Thus, if marketing says they need price points at $100, $200, $300, $400, and $500 based on current prices, for planning purposes, it won't make much difference if the actual prices are 50% higher in thirty years. Setting the number of price points is a strategic marketing decision and a change in that strategy can have an impact on the master plan. Moving from five price points to ten can ruin the plan! Eliminating price points might not have a great impact on the financial portion of the plan, development costs, and endowment care fund contributions; however, it can dramatically change the land use component of the plan and cause changes in the "mix" of property sold. The plan must address all property types that will be sold—above ground crypts, garden areas, and columbaria, as well as regular ground interment spaces.

Someone—most likely marketing in conjunction with operations—must provide input about setting aside land as being non-salable. This could be sites for churches, new entrances, maintenance facilities, reservoirs, or whatever.

Engineering, operations, and marketing must decide how much land to reserve for roads and on the maximum distance from roads to interment property. Generally, the distance from a road or walkway has an effect on pricing as does proximity to buildings or features. However, long distances from a road coupled with a steep slope may result in property that is virtually unsalable at any price. Conversely, building roads too close to the periphery of the cemetery may mean more roads are built than are really needed, resulting in a greater cost of development as well as tying up property unnecessarily in roadway easements.

## Financial

Leaving the financial function out of the master planning process has potential pitfalls for both the short-term and long-term.

Development is usually heavily dependent upon cash flow. Sales management generally has an excellent view of gross sales dollars, a fair view of net sales dollars, but little awareness of how much net cash actually comes in from the whole organization (except cash receipts where commissions are based on cash flow). Since cash flow forecasting is a crucial part of the budgeting process and the budgeting process is linked to development, financial oriented involvement is essential.

A master plan should be a financial-planning tool as much as a land-planning tool. It is the driving set of assumptions for projecting long-term financial performance and is the principal building block in determining the ultimate adequacy of an endowment care fund. Projections about the endowment care fund begin with projections about when sales will take place. The projected flow of funds into the endowment care fund is a by-product of the sales projections. When the estimate of additional funds is combined with projections of expenses and investment results, the framework is in place to test the adequacy of future endowment care fund income relative to projected expenses.

It just makes good sense to involve the financial function in developing the "big picture" a master plan represents.

## Putting It Together

In summary, a master plan needs to be put together in a multi-disciplinary manner. Architects and engineers need to be joined by the functions of operations, marketing, and finance. For properties where separate people do not represent those functions, it is still important that someone put on the hat of each discipline when developing the plan. The plan is far more valuable when it represents all aspects of the cemetery.

Finally, a master plan needs to be a dynamic product. Views of development possibilities, estimates of costs and sales rates, and consumer desires and needs change over time. The plan must be used as a guide and formally updated periodically, so that it is never far out of date. Having the discipline to update the plan may be the most challenging part of the process!

A well-done master plan is a wonderful tool for a variety of purposes. It provides a blueprint for engineering and architectural people to make sure there is some cohesiveness in the flow of the cemetery and that current development doesn't hinder future development needs. The operations staff benefits from efficiencies in future maintenance. A master plan helps marketing refine its strategy and provides the basis for a scorecard on the success of selling efforts relative to land use plans. A good master plan allows maximization of the finite resource of land and is necessary for planning an orderly development of the cemetery. The property sales information is essential to producing projections to test the adequacy of the endowment care fund. Chapter 13 is the Metropolitan Cemetery Case which shows how master plan information can be used in the projection of income and expense of an endowment care fund.

## New Cemeteries

Sometimes in the course of discussing a master plan, someone will suggest that the solution to the finite life of a cemetery is to start a new cemetery. That may be an excellent idea, but it is often very hard to implement.

With few exceptions, any cemetery started today will go through a local zoning process. The consensus is that it's a rather long process, which is one of the reasons that so few new cemeteries are started. The most often quoted figure is that less than three cemeteries are started anywhere in the United States in any given year. I don't know of any good source for that statistic and only am aware of three new cemetery projects in California in ten or more years. One was based on a land acquisition made almost eight years ago—the final regulatory approvals weren't obtained, and the project was abandoned. Another was in the governmental approval process for almost five years and recently had a ground-breaking ceremony. The third cemetery was very small—just several acres—and was completed on land adjacent to the church facility that owns it.

Part of the problem with obtaining zoning approval is that people don't want to live next to cemeteries. They are afraid that it will be depressing, that the people visiting or attending burials will put a traffic burden on local streets, and so on.

Once a cemetery opens, most of these fears go away. For the most part, cemeteries aren't noisy. Recently developed ones tend to follow the memorial-park model, so they aren't "depressing stoneyards" as Hubert Eaton called them some 80 years ago. Actually, they are rather nice open spaces and become appreciated as such—particularly in built-up urban areas.

## The Process

For any given cemetery, there is a start-up period. During this period, land will be acquired, zoning approvals will be secured, a master plan will be developed, and additional regulatory approvals will be obtained. This explanation is based upon a Southern California model, and the process will vary not only from state to state but from city to city and county to county.

The land acquisition process is similar in most areas, although different states have different practices regarding title protection—usually through a title insurance policy. The strategic concerns for cemetery land acquisition are similar to those of other real estate developments: Can the buyer tie the property up in escrow for as long as it takes to get all the approvals, and can the buyer back out if those approvals aren't obtained? Sellers don't like either of these ideas and will probably only agree to them if they're having trouble selling the property or if more money passes between the parties. Buyers typically want time for soils and geological studies, financing, and economic analysis as well as for zoning approvals.

Before closing escrow, a prudent buyer will make a financial feasibility study, regardless of whether the cemetery will be for-profit or not-for-profit. Prudent people go into new ventures with their best estimates of what will happen, even if an organization wants to run a cemetery at a break-even point as a service to members.

In Southern California, cemeteries tend to operate under conditional use permits rather than specific zoning. This means that a cemetery may be a permitted use in certain areas only if additional conditions are met. There are two reasons for this. First, there is little certainty that a cemetery will be developed on a given piece of land. No matter how much a city land planner wants a cemetery, economics ultimately will determine whether or not one is built. Second, conditional use permits give the city, or other zoning authority, more control over projects. This often is defended as protecting the public from unsightly projects, but experience suggests that it also has the effect of coercing developers into building or contributing to off-site improvements like road widening, traffic lights, curbs and gutters, schools, and so on.

At best, the zoning/conditional use permit process takes many months; at worst, time will be measured in years. Before anything is filed, environmental impact reports usually are required, and architectural and engineering plans must be completed. Then, after staff reviews, the whole package goes to the planning commission or similar body. They may have questions or public testimony may prod the commission into asking for more information, modifications to plans, or creating new restrictions on the development, thus making further delays.

At some point, either during the zoning process or immediately after its successful conclusion, applications will need to be filed for whatever state licenses are necessary for the new cemetery. In California, the state licensing process requires the applicant to deposit $50,000 in the new endowment care fund as one of the conditions to obtain a certificate of authority to operate a cemetery.

At the end of the zoning and licensing procedures, a new cemetery is "born." The proud "parents" can brag to their friends about how difficult the "labor" was and how healthy the newborn "child" is. Furthermore, the new cemetery needs as much attention as a newborn child does—it must be properly nurtured, so it will eventually become a self-sufficient adult. A friend of mine likes to describe the process of rearing a child as a battle for control that you want to gradually lose, as the child becomes self-sufficient. Similarly, the final measure of success in developing and running a cemetery is that it, too, will become self-sufficient—it will be well maintained long after it is sold out.

The process of beginning a new cemetery seems long and involved. In fact, the lengthy, complicated process is the reason so few cemeteries are started from scratch—indeed, why companies in the field have tended to grow by acquisition rather than starting new cemeteries.

## Summary

The master planning process is important for current operations as well as for fulfilling a cemetery's ultimate goal of being forever. In the short-term, a master plan helps ensure that the cemetery will have a proper mix of inventory to meet the needs of its customers and sales staff. This will contribute to the cemetery achieving its sales goals.

In the long-run, a good master plan helps attain efficient and orderly development of the cemetery. This is best accomplished with participation by key functional areas: marketing, operations, finance, and engineering. The master plan is also a key element in projecting the ultimate ability of an endowment care fund to produce enough income to care for a nearly sold out cemetery.

# 9 Governing Boards
Finding the right balance

CEMETERIES PRESENT unique challenges to management and governing boards.[1] Boards have a responsibility to set the direction for a corporation and make sure managers are in place who can follow the course charted by the board. It is important that each board discuss the role it should play for the institution it governs. As is often true with governance decisions, it is more likely that a mistake will be made by not making a conscious decision than by making one.

The legal responsibility of members of governing boards continues to evolve. Although most material written about board responsibility focuses on publicly traded corporations, much of the general material applies in principle to smaller corporations and non-profit organizations.[2] It also should be emphasized that directors of a wholly owned subsidiary have substantially the same responsibilities as directors of independent corporations.

Boards come in all shapes and sizes. Not only does each director bring a unique set of strengths and experiences, but the dynamics of each board depends upon the interaction of these unique personalities. Each team of directors and managers must find a point of equilibrium between board responsibility and management responsibility—a level which is comfortable for all and fits the size and complexity of the corporate structure as well as the sophistication of directors and managers.

An important part of creating an effective organization is carefully defining the roles of everyone involved. These roles often evolve over time and may include subtle divisions of authority. Despite the voluminous writings on boards and management, there is a great deal of variability in how organizations arrive at the split between board and management responsibility.

In general, there is usually agreement that the board sets policy, and management runs things on a day-to-day basis. The problem with this generality is that there is a huge gap between these two positions—if one is black and the other is white, there is a vast amount of gray in between. Each organization must determine where that dividing line is and communicate that conclusion to all involved. Problems and misunderstandings are more likely to occur because the line is not clearly drawn as opposed to where it is drawn.

The board of directors plays an important role in setting the stage for management, because it is responsible for hiring the CEO. However, because the CEO generally delegates some of his authority, delegation can occur only if it is clear what he or she has to delegate.

## Setting the Course

It is commonly believed that boards of large companies can plan first and then act according to that plan, but the boards of small companies are more oriented toward quick action. This view is a stereotype and, therefore, not universally applicable. However, it does serve to identify two distinct styles for boards. Each can be appropriate at certain times regardless of the size of the organization.

Small companies tend to have less depth of management and fewer internal resources than large companies. Accordingly, the boards of the smaller companies tend to behave differently. The quickness with which a smaller company and its board can react may be a strategic advantage as long as appropriate factors are considered. If they don't "look before they leap," they can be paving the way for disaster.

Planning can be a strategic advantage for big companies and their boards. A larger company can put more resources into the planning process, which allows for comprehensive thinking about the impact of decisions on all aspects of the business. However, in-depth planning can become a disadvantage when it becomes an obstacle to making decisions and acting on them.

Reaching a common understanding of an organization's purpose is essential to finding the balance between the roles of directors and management. This might be embodied in a mission statement or some other statement of principles. Often, the main benefit of a strategic planning process is this definition and understanding. Hubert Eaton's Builder's Creed gives Forest Lawn a vision of what it should be. We also have adopted a credo for employees to follow:

> At Forest Lawn, caring service is our reason for being. We pledge to provide the highest standards of ethical and personal service as well as the finest facilities to our guests and visitors. Our "Spirit of Service" anticipates the needs of those in sorrow and exceeds the expectations of all who enter our gates.

Some who write about boards of directors tend to see smaller firms as more entrepreneurial; this isn't always the case. A small firm can be downright stodgy and so comfortable with the status quo that change is impossible. This is common among boards of small organizations in a mature industry. However, whether a company is large or small, the directors have certain common responsibilities. No matter what the size of the organization, the boards should add value to the activities of the organization in the following ways:

- ✦ Ensuring legal and ethical conduct;
- ✦ Approving organizational strategy;
- ✦ Providing general oversight of the organization; and
- ✦ Succession planning including selecting, evaluating, compensating, and, when necessary, replacing the CEO and other senior executives.

## Legal and Ethical Conduct

A fundamental duty of a board of directors is to ensure the officers and other employees act legally and ethically. This duty doesn't change based on organization size or type of cemetery, although large companies tend to have more formal procedures than smaller organizations. In both cases, outside financial audits are usually one of the important elements of oversight to assure that the financial reporting is accurate and that good business practices are followed. Audits are discussed later in this chapter.

Many organizations have adopted statements spelling out standards of conduct for management, employees, and directors. A conduct policy doesn't have to be long or complicated. For example, the following is Forest Lawn's ethics policy:

> Forest Lawn Memorial-Parks and Mortuaries conduct business in accordance with the highest ethical standards of community leadership and citizenship. Respect and reverence for families who use our services and their loved ones is essential. Each employee is responsible for, and is expected to be positively committed to, a program of respect for those we take care of as well as full compliance with the laws, rules and regulations governing the organization. The desire to achieve company or personal objectives will not excuse lack of respect and reverence, wrongful activity, conflict of interest, or deviation from company policies. Violations will result in disciplinary action and may result in termination.

Although most organizations maintain they want to be ethical, the proof is in how they act rather than what they say. Cemeteries need to be concerned particularly about ethics, because they develop relationships that last for generations. Once the cemetery's integrity is bruised, it is difficult to heal it. Therefore, a cemetery's image is all-important. Setting high ethical standards and making sure the organization lives up to those standards is critical to maintaining that image.

More than twenty years ago, I came into frequent contact with a large number of people in the thrift industry—executives of credit unions and savings and loans. I was impressed when one of them said that when any customer thought their savings account interest calculation was wrong, the policy was to open the cash drawer and give the customer whatever they thought the shortage was. He didn't believe the calculations were wrong; he just believed in the importance of the good will of the customer.

Cemetery operators can learn from this lesson. A long-term view of relations with customers may often mean "giving in," even when the customer is wrong, rather than risking tainting the relationship for generations.

Furthermore, organizations should avoid adopting policies, unless they intend to live by them. A policy that isn't followed can and will be used against the cemetery.

Too often, business ethics is equated to legality. Many organizations believe that if something is legal it is acceptable to do. I don't agree with that. Ethics is about doing the right thing, not just about complying with the law. Laws governing the behavior of individuals and organizations are passed to provide guidance and set minimum standards of behavior. Through laws and regulations, society tells us that if we don't behave properly we will be fined, put in jail, or otherwise penalized. Ethical behavior is usually a higher standard than that required by the law. Because reputation is so important to cemeteries, they must uphold higher ethical standards than just legal standards. Boards of directors should set the example for ethical conduct and demand nothing less from management.

## Evaluating Strategy

Regardless of the size of the organization, outside directors have an important role in evaluating strategy. By virtue of their independence from the organization's day-to-day operations, directors have a broader perspective and may be able to be more objective than managers who are immersed in operating responsibilities. The quality of director participation is dependent upon several factors—principally each director's skills and the quality of background information provided each one.

In large organizations, directors often assess and ratify strategies proposed by management—either explicitly by reviewing the strategy or implicitly by approving plans and projects consistent with the strategy.

Frequently, directors of smaller organizations have a more proactive role in strategy development. This is particularly beneficial to the smaller organization, because its board of directors can provide supplemental knowledge and expertise to managers who are generally more "hands on."

Strategies cannot be perfected in a vacuum. In developing strategies, management will take into consideration factors such as local economic conditions, needs of ethnic communities, shifts in consumer buying patterns, and changes in competition. These factors can be set forth in a written document or be discussed in a more informal manner. The amount and formality of documentation needs to fit the personality of the organization. Some organizations find it helpful to be more formal and send information to directors before meetings. Other organizations may find that a cumbersome and unnecessary process.

Some organizations have embraced the concept of strategic planning as being essential to their survival. Others have dabbled with long-range plans, but have found that the plans had little value several months later. The benefits of planning often are derived as much from the process as from the result, because any discussion of the future and its possible impacts has value. Due to the nature of cemeteries, some long-range land planning must be done even if all other strategic planning is avoided. A master plan (described in Chapter 8) covers many aspects of a cemetery's future.

## Oversight

Board members of small and large organizations provide oversight by asking questions and providing general opinions on a variety of business issues, including defining the business, questioning short-term results versus long-term benefits, considering capital structure, and so on. The individual organization's specific needs usually govern what type of experience the organization looks for in potential directors.

Part of the board's oversight value comes from knowledge the individual directors have gained from general business or other experience. This can be from direct experience running their own businesses, serving on other boards, or obtaining specialized training. In some instances, outside directors can provide contacts that are useful to the organization.

Oversight shouldn't be confused with second-guessing. In properly fulfilling their oversight role, each member of the board will bring a different perspective to decisions and discussions. The board should help provide a broader perspective while still holding management responsible for results.

## Succession Planning

The late Fred Hartley, the rather crusty CEO of Unocal, often was quoted as saying that a board of directors only had two functions, "to set dividends and hire the CEO." While that limited view is not in keeping with the present view of the role of directors, ensuring proper staffing at the top of the organization is a very important function of the board.

Succession planning isn't merely ensuring that there is someone to follow in the CEO's footsteps upon retirement; it is having some understanding of the strengths and weaknesses of the senior management team and knowing whether or not there is a potential CEO backup within the organization.[3] If there isn't, it is the board's responsibility to determine how to cope with a foreseen or unforeseen vacancy in the position of CEO.

## Selecting and Replacing the CEO

I'm reminded of a story told by a management expert who spoke at a seminar for CEOs. He asked a number of CEOs what the most important part of their jobs was. The most memorable response he had was from a CEO of a large organization who said, "I decide who decides." In any organization that delegates responsibility, all decisions about who will be in what position are decisions about who will make decisions.

In the course of my involvement with the cemetery industry, I've seen boards choose CEOs for a variety of reasons, the most common being background. Each organization develops an expectation of what primary skills it expects its top managers to have.

Although any given manager may have risen through the ranks of a particular discipline—sales, finance, maintenance, law, or whatever—the nature of cemetery management is that managers must become generalists, once they are assigned broader responsibilities. This point is often a "moment of truth" for individual careers, because the greatest task of the generalist is to know when and how to involve experts.

Far too many organizations try to clone the existing CEO when trying to plan for succession. The problem with this approach is that it often ignores the fact that times and conditions have changed.

For example, for years, the directors of Spring Grove Cemetery and Arboretum believed that the organization had to have a "plant person" at the helm because of the arboretum role of the organization. However, after over a hundred years of existence, the directors decided they needed someone with broader business skills to ensure that Spring Grove would be financially sound when the cemetery property was all sold out. The directors realized that the needs of the organization had changed.

Directors cannot effectively plan for or replace a CEO or other senior manager, unless they understand the cemetery's unique strengths and weaknesses. They must possess an understanding of the human and other resources that make up the organization as well as the external changes and trends that may bear on the cemetery's future operation. This information can help the board develop a prioritized set of criteria for selecting a CEO.

Replacing a CEO is traumatic for organizations of all sizes, particularly when it is prior to the person's desire to leave. It is especially difficult when the CEO has been instrumental in bringing many of the directors onto the board—frequently the case regardless of the size of the cemetery. Many of these "retiring" CEOs have a tendency to think of the cemetery as "my cemetery" and have little desire to retire. Furthermore, while most cemeteries do not have mandatory retirement ages for executives, the advantage of mandatory retirement ages for CEOs is that it allows for a more definitive succession plan and may avoid the necessity of having a confrontation over diminished performance after many years of good performance.

## Evaluation and Compensation

Although it has long been dogma that performance and compensation should be linked, the theory often proves to be easier to say than to practice. Evaluation of personnel should be directly related to how they are compensated, but this carries an implicit assumption that the criteria for valuation are obvious.

Directors must have a clear understanding of the organization's goals if they are going to be able to evaluate management. If the board is doing its job, it has been a part of the strategic development, so that shouldn't be a problem. However, it isn't enough to just know what the goals are. Although management may be a part of the discussions and decisions about goals, many objectives do not directly translate into performance standards.

The idea of performance standards is good, but it may not be easy or even practical to put into practice for small organizations. Some boards have tried to specify what performance is by defining what levels of performance are acceptable, exceed expectations, and far exceeds expectations. Even though that looks great on paper, determining the performance standard for each level can be subjective, as some types of performance lend themselves to quantification better than others. For instance, a non-profit cemetery may expect the organization to break-even financially but not make more than a few percentage points on sales. This is an appropriate use of a numeric measure. On the other hand, many senior managers are held accountable for the organization's morale, but morale is difficult to quantify. While it can be done, it usually isn't worth the expenditure of effort and money to translate morale into numbers, unless one is dealing with a huge organization. Quantifying performance expectations is a laudable goal, but care must be taken to make sure that assigning numbers doesn't actually mask actual performance.

In large part, evaluation is all about communication. An excessive desire to quantify all aspects of performance may actually make it difficult to assess performance, because some responsibilities of senior management can best be evaluated subjectively.

As large publicly traded firms in many industries have discovered, the concept of matching performance and compensation is easier to articulate than to put into practice. Any quick study of executive compensation of publicly traded companies shows that there is a huge disparity of the amounts paid CEOs. The differences cannot be accounted for solely by industry, size of revenues, number of employees, or profitability. Despite many studies and articles about the lack of correlation between pay and performance, no uniformly satisfactory approach has been found. It is up to the directors to determine what is right for the corporation they govern.

To smaller companies, particularly non-profits, compensation may seem like a black art. There is an element of truth to this, but it doesn't diminish the board's responsibility to fairly compensate senior management. The work force is far more fluid than it was several decades ago. This makes the board's job of ensuring the right people are hired and retained in key executive positions even more difficult. Paying fairly for performance is an important component of keeping good people.

## Transitions

The board has an important role to play in the transition from one CEO to another. In the best of cases, this should be a smooth transfer of power; one regime leaves office, and the other takes the ball and runs with it. At this time, new plans and strategies should be reviewed with the board. When the organization is ready for a change, the board should evaluate recommendations for changes without allegiance to the prior CEO. The board's responsibility is to the organization and stockholders if it is a for-profit cemetery, not to the former CEO.

Several years ago Harvard Business School professor Jeffrey Sonnenfeld wrote a book about what happens when CEOs of major corporations retire.[4] He identified four different styles that CEOs adopted upon retirement:

| | |
|---|---|
| *Ambassadors* | leave gracefully. They never try to sabotage their successors but provide continuity and counsel after their retirement. |
| *Governors* | also exit willingly and then maintain little contact with their companies. Typically, they involve themselves in community affairs and other worthy endeavors. |
| *Monarchs* | cling to their crowns until the end. |
| *Generals* | depart reluctantly, only to plot their return. They want to rescue the company from their successor's real or imagined inadequacy. |

Although Sonnenfeld wrote about people who led Fortune 500 companies, the principles seem to be applicable to all organizations, because the book is more about human behavior than large organizations.

My ideal of an "ambassador" is Ben Dwoskin who was general manager of Mount Sinai Memorial-Park in Los Angeles. Ben had been with Mount Sinai since it opened in the early 1950s, so when he decided to retire, it was a big change for him and the organization. Despite Ben's attachment to Mount Sinai, he decided the best thing he could do for it was to allow his successor, Arnold Saltzman, to manage without interference or a lot of advice. Arnold has told me how great

Ben has been when he's been called with questions, but that Ben has never tried to meddle with the organization—a demonstration of a real ambassador.

Examples of typical "governors" can be found outside the cemetery field. A friend of mine, Bill Lochmoeller, retired from a senior management position with a national retailer. When he retired, he immersed himself in community activities, serving on the local boards of the Boy Scouts, Goodwill Industries, Volunteers of America, and others. He has had a great time, has felt useful, has made a valuable contribution to the community, and hasn't had much at all to do with his former employer. Another friend was CEO of a Fortune 500 company. When he retired, the board kept him on as chairman for one year but moved his office out of their headquarters to a facility some 40 miles away from the main corporate offices. Like Bill, he still serves on many community boards as well as boards of publicly traded companies. He's behaved like a governor, partly by choice and partly by the structure imposed on him.

Forest Lawn's builder, Hubert Eaton, was a "monarch." He ran the organization from 1917 until his death in 1966. Although very few people are left who were working at Forest Lawn during his reign, the lore about him gives a clear picture of a man who remained in control until the end. One drawback, though, was that he wasn't always around because of health reasons and did exhibit some of the normal signs of aging. Nonetheless, although there certainly are disadvantages to monarchs, there is a basic honesty in their approach—there is no question who is in control. The biggest downside, however, is that the organization feels stifled—people feel as though they can't, or shouldn't, make decisions. The result is that the organization needs a recovery period after the loss of the monarch—the loss of a monarch often leaves a leadership vacuum, because managers aren't used to making decisions. Either the loss is followed by a transition period where a new monarch steps in or managers begin to make decisions without someone looking over their shoulders.

The "general" is the most damaging style. Generals keep in touch with people who used to work for them. Not only do they keep in touch, they give a lot of advice. In fact, a lot of their advice sounds like orders—they behave just like they did when they were "at the helm." This has the effect of undermining their successors and confusing the organization—the organization isn't sure who is in charge.

Shortly after joining one of the Forest Lawn boards, Bob Skothiem, president of the Huntington Library and a former college president, sent me a book about corporate governance by William G. Bowen called *Inside the Boardroom*. Bowen is a former president of Princeton and has served as an outside director of for-profit organizations such as American Express and Merck, as well as not-for-profit boards like the Sloan Foundation and the Smithsonian Institution. Here are Bowen's thoughts about the pros and cons of continuing involvement from a former CEO:

> It is evident that retaining the services of the former CEO on the board has advantages. Key relationships with investors, customers, and donors can be maintained. Historical knowledge—"institutional memory"—is available to the board. The benefits of continuity are maximized....Nonetheless, the arguments against continuing service on the board are stronger.
>
> A wise commentator (Arjay Miller) observed that a perverse pattern may develop because, in his words: "The CEOs who would be okay as continuing members of the board do not usually want to stay, whereas the CEOs who want to stay on the board after their retirement are the very ones who should leave...."[5]

This book is well worth reading for it explores the role of directors in a way that is relevant to both publicly held corporations and private companies. It also explores the role of directors of both for-profit and not-for-profit enterprises, pointing out the similarities of the directors' roles as well as the differences.

Thomas J. Shapiro, a psychologist who works with boards of directors on succession planning, echoed a similar sentiment:

> Even a well-handled succession can fail when the former CEO stays in place after the succession....The former leader can feel ignored and cut out. When the rumor mill starts grinding out stories about how the new CEO is shaking things up, the former CEO can be less than objective....And soon, without a lot of overt fuss, the seed is planted and the successor is discredited and undermined...it is best [for] the former CEO to leave after a very brief transition.[6]

There is a related myth that many boards and retiring CEOs buy into—the myth of partial retirement or "half-time." This sounds good—you keep the old CEO around so the organization can benefit from his expertise; the old CEO isn't thrust into the emotional turmoil of suddenly being a general without an army; and he can take it easy without fully retiring. The problem with this is that no matter how good (or bad) the retiring CEO is it is hard for the organization to give up that allegiance. The new CEO is the boss—everybody should know that—but there is a lingering feeling about the old boss that doesn't go away.

Keith Renken, a former managing partner with Deloitte & Touche, one of the "Big Six" accounting firms, who was responsible for the Southern California practice, has said that almost no one could semi-retire effectively. He saw recurring patterns of tension resulting when CEOs tried semi-retirement, either working part-time or remaining on the board as a director for more than a year. Energy soon was wasted on the struggle for control between the old CEO and the new CEO. He noted that everyone lost in those cases. The old CEO was frustrated—sometimes even angry—because he no longer had the power or respect. The new CEO was frustrated, because attention and energy was put into dealing with conflicts with the predecessor rather than being used for the benefit of the organization. The employees were confused, not sure that a transfer of authority had actually taken place, and scared to cross either the old or the new CEO. The boards sometimes ended up refereeing between the points of view, not realizing they were being drawn into a conflict they shouldn't have let happen in the first place. Some boards actually tried to continue the awkward situation under the misguided belief that they either owed it to the old CEO or that the old CEO wouldn't be around for long. The organization they were responsible for was the ultimate loser.

A few years ago, the long-time CEO of the Braille Institute of America decided to retire. Russ Kirbey had carefully groomed his successor, Les Stocker. Russ gave his understudy plenty of opportunity to interact with board members and made sure he had transmitted to Les a sense of organization history, culture, and values. With all of that done, when it came time to retire, Russ moved out of the area—removing the possibility of inadvertently interfering or seeming to undermine Les.

An organization can only have one chief. The board is responsible for choosing that chief and for doing whatever is necessary to make sure everyone understands there is only one chief, including insisting on the full retirement of the old CEO. If the old CEO is going to be on the board, the term should be limited to not more than one year.

## How active?

The level of board activity in businesses varies. Some boards function as management committees that become the functional CEOs of the organizations, while others work hard at limiting themselves to a policy and oversight role.

It has been my observation that small cemeteries are often much closer to the first than the latter. While the heavy involvement of the board can be a great aid to a small cemetery, it also can ensure the ineffectiveness of the CEO. It is the responsibility of the board to ensure that a proper balance is found between helping the CEO and controlling the CEO. Although a strong case can be made for intense board involvement in the small organization, caution must be exercised so the board doesn't lose its perspective. Directors don't want to put themselves where they can't see the forest for the trees. If a board becomes too involved in decisions and details, it is unfair to hold the CEO responsible for results. When boards become management committees, it is difficult to provide the broad oversight that only those above the fray of day-to-day decision making can do.

## Meeting Frequency

There is no established "norm" for how often boards should meet. A 1993 study by the Conference Board reported that the average small company board met five times per year, while the average large company board met seven times per year.[7] Another study by Wyatt Data Services suggested that the meeting pattern was "u" shaped—the smallest companies had seven meetings per year, the largest had ten, and there was a dip in board meeting frequency for mid-sized companies. This second study reported that the board meeting frequency for all non-profits was seven times per year. Each board ultimately must decide how often it should meet, taking into consideration how much is going on and how involved it wants or needs to be.

## Committees

How many board committees are established depends on how the board interacts with management and the division of responsibilities between the two. The number of committees and scope of activity helps define where the line is drawn between the board's policies and operating decisions which management is expected to make. The size and complexity of the enterprise appear to have a bearing on the need for committees.

In some cases, the regular meetings are so full of material that committees are necessary to bring policy matters to a summary position the board can deal with. In other cases, the board is more comfortable with acting as a committee of the whole. Another variable is the size of the board. Larger boards tend to use committees to get more effective discussion of important issues than can be accomplished in a larger group.

Most boards have at least an executive committee. Other common committees include audit and compensation committees.

It is also quite common for special committees to be formed as needs arise. For example, a board may form an ad hoc committee to deal with specific planning issues.

Just as it is important to define what functions are to be performed by management and what will be done by the board, it is important for the board to clearly define the roles of its committees and what authority is delegated to each.

## Board Size and Composition

Boards vary in size and composition as much as the organizations they govern. However, many formal studies of group effectiveness suggest things to consider when developing a board organization structure.

Small groups often don't bring the depth and diversity to discussions that help a board provide high level perspective. At the other extreme, large boards can be so big they are not efficient or productive.

I've served on the boards of several eleemosynary organizations that had approximately one hundred board members. They often had trouble getting a quorum—many directors didn't attend regularly, because there was no substantial discussion of issues at the board meetings. The meetings generally were filled with reports and presentations, but issues and policies were seldom discussed; therefore, many directors felt that they couldn't contribute anything at the meetings. The real work of the board was carried on in committees. Those board members who were active on committees generally felt a high level of involvement and sense of contribution. Those directors who weren't on active committees didn't have the same sense of responsibility or active, engaged interest.

Ultimately, each organization must determine what board size is appropriate. This will depend on the size of the organization and such factors as the background and abilities of management and diversity of constituencies being served. The goal is to have a board that provides a variety of perspectives while not being so large that it becomes ineffective.

The composition of board membership is as important as the size of the board. Board members should be chosen for what they can contribute in the way of experience, contacts, and knowledge. One clear trend has been a reduction in the number of inside directors serving on all boards—large, small, for-profit, and not-for-profit. Usually, the CEO is a member of the board and often the only employee member.

As an example of board members being chosen for multiple reasons, I'm familiar with a medium-sized cemetery that is owned by a fraternal group. The parent organization purchased the cemetery to offer a service to its members, but later it realized that the cemetery had substantial positive long-term cash flow which it might use somewhere else. Thus, in this case, the cemetery's board members were chosen for their contribution to the cemetery's governance as well as for their standing and influence with the parent organization. As with most cemeteries, though, cash flow is erratic—cash builds up and then large amounts are used in development. Despite the purposes for their selection and regardless of their relationship with the parent company, the members of the cemetery's board have an obligation to the cemetery to fulfill its long-term responsibilities and prevent it from just serving as a short-term source of funds for the parent organization.

## Relations with Management

A great deal of the literature on corporate governance is written about the relationship between boards and management. Many members of cemetery boards of directors don't identify with the problems faced by directors of large publicly traded organizations; however, how the board relates to management is an issue organizations of all sizes should address.

Fundamentally, the problem is defining roles of each group—board and management—and having each group understand its role and how that role affects the other group.

It is here that a board determines its personality. Each organization must determine how much involvement the board will have in day-to-day issues and how much will be left to management. The problem for smaller organizations is the big temptation for the board to become more like a management committee than a policy-setting, governing board. Many boards don't realize that, if they become a de facto management committee, they should hold themselves as accountable as they do the people in management positions, for they have allowed themselves to become part of management. While this may be an appropriate decision for some cemeteries, it should be done only with a clear understanding that the decision changes the dynamics of responsibility and accountability between the board and management.

The cemetery's board and management are a team and should work toward common goals, but it isn't unusual for their individual objectives to differ. When there is a possibility of this occurring, it is important to identify potential differences, disclose those differences, and discuss them so everyone is keenly aware of what is going on.

## Safe Harbor

Directors have a clear responsibility for the corporation's overall operation and cannot transfer the liability for some kinds of actions or inaction to others. On the other hand, if they get too involved in management rather than policy, they can lose some of the protection they have under law. This is known as the "safe harbor" concept. As long as the directors don't cruise outside of the harbor, they have some measure of safety.

Under the safe harbor concept directors have a great deal of flexibility—and some limits to their liability—if they keep within a set of legal guidelines. Every board of directors should have their own outside attorney explain how this applies to their particular board.

Directors have the duty to make reasonable inquiries about management's information and recommendations. In fact, this is a fundamental responsibility—but only to a point. As long as the inquiries don't go beyond that, the directors remain within the safe harbor. They can cruise around setting policies and business strategies without any problem. This is because they are held to be able to rely on management to give them accurate information. Similarly, they may rely on outside experts like certified public accountants and attorneys.

Once the directors begin to second-guess management or outside experts by getting involved in too much detail, they risk cruising outside the safe harbor. And, if they leave the safety of the harbor, they may be exposed to whatever legal storms may come up.

Although this sounds rather simple, it isn't always clear how to apply the principle. It is an important concept to keep in mind, so the board and management must be sensitive to its application and seek advice on their respective responsibilities at appropriate times.

Paying attention to the safe harbor concept has a side benefit in that it helps provide some framework for delineating responsibility between the board of directors and management.

## Audits

Audit statements are often misunderstood. Having an audited financial statement isn't a guarantee of the absolute accuracy of the financial statement—an unqualified opinion on an audit statement doesn't mean the books are right to the penny. The auditor only provides an opinion that the financial statements prepared by management (or under the direction of management) "fairly represent" the organization's financial condition.

However, the accounting profession does have standards for what they deem to be "material" inaccuracies with financial statements. For example, if a cemetery had a net profit of $100,000 and if an expense item of, say, $1,000 was missed, the financial statement would still probably be a fair representation—the omission wasn't material. At some point, though, the errors, individually or collectively, may not allow the auditor to say that the statements are a fair representation of the financial position of the company. This results in a qualified opinion of the auditor that explains the potential problems with the statements or, in the extreme case, no opinion at all. Types of exceptions that might be encountered are records which are so incomplete the accountant cannot verify them, disagreements of how to account for transactions, or a company so financially weak that it might not be able to stay in business (a "going concern" exception).

Some naively believe that if they have an audit the auditor is certifying that there hasn't been any embezzlement or other "bad stuff" going on. This is not true. The outside CPAs are supposed to examine "internal controls" to evaluate how easy it would be for someone to either steal from the company or "cook the books." Internal controls are the procedures the cemetery has for financial transactions. They're called controls, because they should be designed to minimize the chance for improper actions or incorrect booking of transactions. For example, a common internal control is to have someone other than the bookkeeper sign checks under the theory that whoever signs the checks should not account for them—don't let the fox count the chickens in the hen house. Internal controls can't entirely prevent problems, but they can reduce temptation or require complicity of two or more people. The assumption is that if the auditors feel the internal controls aren't strong enough they will examine things more closely or make recommendations for changes in procedures. The catch to the auditor's review of controls is that to accomplish the audit they only have to follow the trail far enough to get below the materiality threshold before they stop further investigation.

Readers shouldn't be left with the impression that an audit with a certified opinion by a CPA isn't valuable. Many people won't serve on the board or as an officer of any organization that doesn't have an independent audit. In fact, most would be quite concerned about staying in a situation where the audit opinion was qualified, unless there is ample evidence that corrective action is being taken.

When done by the book, audits are almost a fungible product. The product is the auditors' opinion, and that does have value. However, given the cost of an audit and the competitive nature of the field, an organization should expect more than just the audit. During the course of an audit, the accountants should gain a different perspective from that of the board or management.

A common by-product of an audit is a "management letter" which will reflect the CPA's observations about how internal controls or other procedures may be improved. A good auditor will provide ideas beyond internal controls as well as make observations about other aspects of the business. While not all of these observations or recommendations may be things that the cemetery wants to consider, it should be a valuable source of objectivity which is already being paid for. A good CPA firm should provide a valuable outside perspective of the business.

It should be noted that just having an outside accountant prepare the financial statements isn't auditing the books. In fact, outside accountants who work on the books and prepare financial statements cannot render an independent opinion on the financial statements because of their involvement in the preparation of the statements. From the board of directors or bank's standpoint, the certified public accountant's unqualified opinion on the audit, which requires independence, is crucial to the credibility of the financial reporting.

It is important to understand the meaning of an audit. Yet, even though it's not perfect, the independent opinion is important, and it is better than having nothing. Additionally, there always should be an expectation of value added beyond the pure audit function.

The CPAs have had their share of litigation and, not surprisingly, have tried to restrict their own liability. Audit firms usually will have the organization sign documents such as letters of engagement and representation that attempt to absolve the CPAs from all responsibility. While they can perform a valuable service, accounting firms will go to great lengths to avoid responsibility and liability for any shortcomings in what they do.

Nonetheless, an audit should be done, but it doesn't mean that the board or officers are off the hook. They still must accept the final responsibility for what the organization does (or doesn't do).

## Selling a Cemetery

Whether to sell, or merge, a cemetery is one issue that may come before a board, and with respect to this, each cemetery is unique and has its own set of issues for its board to consider. As directors ponder this subject, they undoubtedly will need outside experts to give them accounting, legal, and tax advice in order to evaluate and consummate a transaction.

In the case of for-profit cemeteries, sales are often motivated by tax or succession considerations. Inheritance taxes are confiscatory, so the desire to avoid them to any extent possible is understandable. For those owners who have built a business, either by managing it or investing in it, there comes a time when they may want liquidity. Sometimes a family has run a business for a generation or more, and no one in the next generation has any interest in managing the operation. Unfortunately, there are also times when bad management makes a sale or merger the best way out. This may come about due to generally poor performance, a woefully inadequate endowment care fund, or even some sort of malfeasance.

Sometimes, a not-for-profit cemetery cannot be sold per se, but it can decide that the affairs of the cemetery could be better managed by another, perhaps larger, organization.[8] This can lead to a management contract with a for-profit company. As some not-for-profit cemeteries realize they've missed the mark on endowment care fund additions for years, a management contract might lead to a cash infusion to the endowment care fund. This cash infusion might be in the best interests of the property owners, as it would help ensure the level of maintenance in the future.

In any of these scenarios, the board has some heavy responsibilities. This kind of situation brings the directors' responsibilities really to the fore, with the exception of a sole proprietorship or a situation where all the owners are members of the board. Not-for-profit directors need to be aware of their fiduciary duty. Directors of for-profit cemeteries are accountable to stockholders, but directors of not-for-profit cemeteries have a fiduciary duty that is at a higher level of responsibility than their for-profit counterparts. Lucrative management or consulting contracts stemming from a transaction can give the appearance of a conflict of interest. Presumably, the directors of the not-for-profit organization serve for the benefit of the property owners and society, not for personal economic gain. Any hint of personal gain to the detriment of the organization may cause personal liability, something most directors don't want.

An example of a particularly sensitive situation would be when a not-for-profit cemetery board discovers that the only way to deal with severe inadequacies in the endowment care fund is to have someone else take over the operation of the cemetery and, in return, put cash into the fund. I see this as creating a great dilemma for the directors. On the one hand, a not-for-profit cemetery turning over the keys to a for-profit entity troubles me. There are legal ways to do this in many jurisdictions, but it probably will result in a fundamental change in operating goals. On the other hand, I realize cemeteries that don't have large enough endowment care funds will not be community assets forever, and that also troubles me.

Despite the obstacles and sensitive issues involved, some not-for-profit cemetery boards reluctantly have concluded that turning over the cemetery's management to a for-profit organization is the only way to preserve the cemetery's integrity into the future. They have reached a point where they believe that a drastic action is necessary to put enough cash into the endowment care fund to bring it up to the level it needs to be. When that conclusion is reached, it is important that the new management have a contractual obligation to continually augment the endowment care fund as property is sold to ensure its adequacy in the future. Although prices may be raised when operations are sold to a for-profit entity, this still may be better than having the cemetery become an eyesore or, in the extreme case, abandoned.

In 1996, the not-for-profit cemetery operation and for-profit mortuary of Rose Hills Memorial Park in California was sold for approximately $285 million dollars.[9] The buyer was a joint venture composed of the Loewen Group, Inc. and Blackstone, a venture capital group. The not-for-profit association sold its cemetery assets and converted itself to a 501(c)(4) tax-exempt foundation. It previously had sold its for-profit mortuary subsidiary to members of management who concurrently sold their interest in the mortuary to the same joint venture. The money from the sale of the cemetery's assets went into a huge new charitable foundation that will do wonderful things for the community. However, nothing from the transaction went into the endowment care fund. According to John Argue, chairman of the non-profit association, both the sellers and the trustees of the not-for-profit corporation thought that the fund was big enough, so nothing was put into the endowment care fund from the sale. Under California law, the sale of the majority of the assets of a mutual benefit corporation have to be approved by the California Attorney General. Since the Attorney General approved the transaction, the presumption was that it was fair to society and the property owners.

Discussions with various people involved in the Rose Hills transaction pointed out some of the dilemmas faced by directors of a non-profit cemetery, as they contemplate major changes in a cemetery. The basic, and probably most obvious, question is whether the property owners will be better off if the cemetery is sold. In the case of Rose Hills, the cemetery directors also had to weigh the interests of the community benefit derived from the large foundation against the interests of the property owners.

The question of putting money into the endowment care fund isn't always so easy. At first, it might appear that this obviously benefits the property owners. After all, a large endowment care fund is good. However, the acquiring company will receive the income from any money put into the fund, so it might be argued that the money put into the endowment care fund is for the acquirer's benefit. Once the additional money is put into the endowment care fund, if the level of maintenance doesn't improve, then the additional contribution has done nothing for the property owners. In that case, it actually might be deemed to be a reduction in the purchase price. On the other hand, for a cemetery that has an inadequate fund, if the level of care of the cemetery improves, the property owners have received a benefit. Even in this latter case, the acquirer also receives a benefit from the funds, because a better-maintained cemetery is a more desirable place to consumers. These are tough decisions for directors to make and ones that surely need qualified outside advice.

Cemetery acquisitions will continue to happen, and there will be a variety of motivations for these transactions. Directors must remember that they have responsibilities that are dictated by the organization's structure. They must put their responsibilities to the organization ahead of any gain they might realize personally, whether in the form of actual money realized or a more intangible type of value such as an increase in community stature.

Some not-for-profit cemeteries are exploring cooperative arrangements with other nearby not-for-profit cemeteries as an alternative to selling their cemetery. For example, some have entered into equipment and overhead sharing arrangements that attempt to cut expenses while maintaining independence. This is a viable alternative only when the problems are small. In cases where income from endowment care funds is severely short of what is needed, new operating efficiencies may not be enough to correct the shortfall.

At one time, the common thought was that an acquirer should only acquire assets. This was seen as the best way to avoid unknown liabilities. Some still take that view. However, another point of view has emerged that favors buying corporations through mergers or pooling of interests. This latter perspective has to do with reported earnings. When assets are acquired, the buyer must use the acquisition price as the basis for depreciation and cost of sales. However, when a cemetery is acquired by merger, the buyer uses the existing tax and accounting basis of the firm being purchased. The difference between the book value of the company being acquired and the price paid the selling shareholders is goodwill. As the goodwill is written off over a forty-year period, the acquirer generally has higher earnings to report under the merger method than the asset purchase method.

The companies acquiring cemeteries are experts at acquisitions. They've been through many acquisitions and have developed a legal and financial expertise that a seller is unlikely to have. Sellers, and potential sellers, should remember this and make sure they get high quality, skilled, and experienced lawyers and accountants to represent their interests. A cemetery may have an attorney or accountant who has done a good job in day-to-day matters, but that doesn't mean that person is the best resource to use in a transaction of this type. Other types of advisors that might be valuable resources in structuring a transaction include consultants, brokers, and appraisers. Advisors should be chosen for their individual experience in similar situations.

## Small Cemeteries and Boards of Directors

I've noticed that small cemeteries, like other small businesses, occasionally think they should avoid the trappings of being a corporation. They believe that tools like budgets and planning are overhead expenses they cannot afford. Sometimes this thinking extends to resisting having a board of directors that actually functions as a governing body.

One study reported that less than half the boards of small companies with annual sales of more than $1 million met more than twice a year.[10] This is often shortsighted thinking, as a small cemetery may have even more to gain from a board of directors than does a larger cemetery. This relates to the very smallness of the organization. A larger organization has more people in management, supervisory, and specialized positions that can add perspective and specialized knowledge to execution, evaluation, and planning. A board of directors composed primarily of outside directors can provide this for the small cemetery. Of course, the outside directors aren't cemetery experts, but they can bring experience and detachment from the fray that has a tremendous value to the small cemetery.

## Summary

Being a director is a big responsibility whether the organization is for-profit or not-for-profit. Each cemetery's board must develop its own unique style and relationship with management. The nature of endowment care funds as trust funds means that the directors are required to exercise fiduciary levels of oversight and management. In all other aspects of cemetery management, the governing board has the responsibility not only to maintain the cemetery's short-term economic viability but also to adopt strategies that fulfill the cemetery's long-term obligations. The board is obligated to ensure that they are governing the cemetery in a way that will make it last forever.

[1] Members of governing boards may be called directors or trustees, but their role is essentially the same. For ease, the term "director" is used to apply to both.

[2] Governance of corporations continues to evolve. In addition to books on the subject, a good source for information about boards and their responsibilities is the National Association of Corporate Directors, 1707 L. Street, NW, Suite 560, Washington, D.C. 20036. Phone (202) 775-0509. In addition to a monthly publication regarding board and director issues, it offers seminars on various topics, including the relationship between the CEO and the board, the role of the board in closely held corporations, and building an effective board.

[3] The term "succession planning" has taken a specific meaning to the acquisition companies in the cemetery field. To them it means whether or not the cemetery will be sold when the CEO or owner is ready to retire or move on to other things.

[4] Jeffrey Sonnenfeld, *The Hero's Farewell*.

[5] William G. Bowen, *Inside the Boardroom*, p.63-64.

[6] Thomas J. Saporito, "Pitfalls in the CEO Selection Process" p. 7.

[7] *Director's Monthly*, National Association of Corporate Directors, March 1996, p.6

8. Some states have a provision for a not-for-profit corporation converting to a for-profit corporation.

9. Financial Statements, *Loewen Group, Inc. 1997 Annual Report*, Footnote 4(b). In addition to describing the relationship between Loewen and Blackstone and the operating results of Rose Hills, the statement was made that "The excess of the purchase price over the fair value of net assets of approximately $130 [million] was established as goodwill in RH Holdings *[the company owned by Loewen and Blackstone]* and is being amortized over 40 years."

10. Sara Cliffe, "Family Business: Facing up to Succession," *Harvard Business Review*, May-June 1998, p. 17.

Forest Lawn Memorial-Park Association

*Figure 9–1 Garden of Honor, Forest Lawn–Glendale.*

A History of Mourning

*Figure 9–2 A Greek Tomb: the Monument of Themistocles, Athens.*

# 10 Management
### Responsibility for the past, present, and future

MOUNTAINS OF MATERIAL have been written about the theory and practice of management, dealing with all facets of management and its relationships with a variety of constituencies— boards of directors, employees, customers, and society at large. Often, these works address the topics of focus and communication in one way or another.

Focus means knowing where the organization is going. The often-quoted Chinese proverb fits well: If you don't know where you are going, any road will get you there. The corollary to that is if you don't know where you are, you have little chance of getting where you want to go. If they are to endure, organizations must have some idea of why they exist.

Poor communication is probably the most common failure of people and organizations. Since management is defined as getting work done through others, it makes sense that communicating what needs to be done is essential to the process.

## The Cemetery Manager

The demands on a cemetery manager are similar to the demands on the cemetery itself:

+ Do well in the short-term;
+ Always be aware of the long-term needs of the cemetery; and

✦   Make sure that, long after you're gone, nobody can look back and say, "If it weren't for the shortsightedness of [former manager], the cemetery would be in good shape today."

It's been said that running a cemetery is something like running a city. A cemetery manager oversees many of the same types of activities that a city performs—zoning/land use (master planning), road maintenance, utility operation (backbone utilities like water), budget balancing (sales to cover expenses), long-term financial concerns (the endowment care fund), community relations, enforcement of rules and regulations, and so on. This requires the cemetery manager to be something of a generalist in order to be effective.

## Operations

Although it is easy to accept the generalization that the board of directors sets policy and management is responsible for operations, often this seemingly neat and clean policy statement doesn't well define the separation of powers or responsibilities. It is difficult to establish a clean line of demarcation between management and board responsibilities, because various responsibilities are not always just black and white; many fall on more than one person in the organization. Thus, this overlapping is inevitable in any hierarchical organization. Indeed, the problem of defining responsibility not only occurs between boards and management but also among the different levels of management.

In most organizations, management participates with the board in developing policy. Even though the board has the ultimate authority, few boards fail to seek the opinions of management on major issues, especially when management will be required to implement the decisions.

For cemeteries with more than one level of management, the line between policy and operating implementation may begin to blur. For example, consider an organization with a mission statement and the task of fertilizing the grass. The mission statement says the cemetery grounds should be beautiful and the lawns well maintained at all times. The mission statement, even if recommended to the board by management, is a policy statement that is a board level responsibility. It sets a direction for the organization but doesn't tell how the objective will be achieved. It is management's responsibility to determine how to implement that policy and, thus, when it is necessary to fertilize the grass—an implementation of the policy contained in the mission statement.

For a cemetery with more than one level of management, a determination still must be made regarding which level of management is responsible for implementation. Should the grounds superintendent be responsible for deciding when to fertilize, or should he only be responsible for fertilizing well once the CEO tells him to do it? Both the CEO and the superintendent are accountable for the condition of the grass. Through the board-set policy, the CEO is directed to accomplish something, but he can delegate part or all of that responsibility to someone else. That delegation makes someone else, the superintendent, accountable to the CEO for accomplishing the objective but doesn't change the basic accountability of the CEO to the board. So, responsibilities often overlap as a result of an organization's structure rather than poor definition of authority and accountability.

The above example clearly illustrates the implementation of a policy set in a mission statement, but consider something like setting prices—is that policy or implementation? If pricing is seen as a strategic way of growing the business, then it may be policy. On the other hand, if it is merely a way of achieving the annual budget or another long-term financial plan, it may just be implementation. At some point, management is making interpretations of board policy, and those interpretations become policies themselves. Consequently, in the normal course of business, management will make policies in areas where the board may not want to (and, most of the time, shouldn't want to) become too involved in details—credit, administrative procedures, evaluation of staff other than senior management, and so on. The important point for both management and the board to recognize is that the line separating where boards are involved and where management has freedom and responsibility to act isn't the same for every cemetery. Each organization must choose its own comfort point regarding what the board should reserve to itself and what management's duties are.

Although methods of operation in cemeteries do not change rapidly, changes do occur. Advances in equipment design, materials available, and many other things offer opportunities for cemetery managers to find ways to do things better and more efficiently.

## Budgeting

Budgeting is usually viewed as a control and planning mechanism. It is a control, because most organizations use it as a limit on spending and a minimum revenue target. Most organizations with budgets have experienced a supervisor or manager who believes that if the money in the budget is not spent completely that there will be less money in the budget next year—a penalty for being efficient. While those who act this way simply are proving they don't have the capability to handle larger responsibilities, all organizations need to be sensitive to this mentality and seek ways to avoid its result. Budgets are a planning tool, because they result in a resource allocation that charts the financial course for the budget period.

Budgets also should be viewed as communication tools. While developing a budget, many assumptions are made about how the organization will function. Anything affecting income, expense, or cash flow is part of the budget. There are endless discussions and articles about whether budgeting should be bottom up, zero based, or some other variant. Yet, no matter what methodology is chosen, involvement and explanation throughout the organization is essential for developing commitment to and good execution of the plan.

Budgets cannot be developed in vacuums. Input needs to be sought from supervisors who will actually oversee the spending of labor and material dollars. Sales management must be

Forest Lawn Memorial-Park Association

*Figure 10–1 Over time, improvements in equipment can provide more efficient methods of operation (Cemetery development, c. 1930).*

involved in the projections of sales revenue and selling expenses. However, it is important to differentiate between the concept of sales goals and a revenue budget. The revenue budget is usually the basis for spending, so it must have a relatively high achievement probability. Conversely, spending must be a variable amount based upon actual sales production. This is an important concept to a cemetery, since a large portion of the operating expenses are fixed costs—office salaries, mowing, and so on. For sales organizations paid on a commission basis, it is common for a budget to be a variable amount based upon actual sales production.

As with other forms of planning, a great deal can be gained merely from discussing the assumptions and strategies contained in the budget. Each level of review and participation has something unique to contribute, so widespread involvement is essential. Finally, senior management must convey the proposed budget to the board to secure agreement on strategic decisions contained in the budget.

## Financial Performance

Generally, financial statements for cemeteries are in a format much like the financial statements of other organizations. Like other associations, cemeteries must cope with seemingly endless changes in accounting standards as well as the names of the statements themselves. For instance the balance sheet became a "statement of financial position" and the income statement became an "activities statement" with recent accounting pronouncements. Management needs to be aware of the impact these changes have on the substance of the information presented. While the accounting community contends that the changes are aimed at making statements more understandable and meaningful, users don't always agree.

For many purposes, a cemetery's financial statements are useful for measuring its financial performance and condition. However, managers and board members should be aware of the shortcomings of generally accepted accounting standards applied to cemeteries, particularly to older cemeteries. This caution is aimed primarily at audited statements. However, the caution is also valid to the extent that the preparation of regular internal financial statements conforms to generally accepted accounting principles.

One of the most common problems with judging financial performance of cemeteries results from using historical costs. Current accounting methods calculate the cost of sales expense from the historical cost of cemetery property and related improvements. Thus, if the cemetery hasn't changed hands for decades, the land costs are quite low. A friend of mine who runs a 150-year-old cemetery told me that they had long ago written off all land cost, so they had no land component in their cost of sales. That makes a lot of sense, because the 150-year-old cost would be so low that it would approach nothing.

Theoretically, using replacement cost rather than historical cost might make sense. Because gains from inflation in land value would be identified as inflation gains and not treated as profits, this would be an improvement over the historical method of accounting, as it would more accurately measure the true financial performance of a cemetery. However, using replacement cost would usher in an entirely new set of complications—disclosures, new schedules, higher fees to the accountants, and so on. I doubt the increased "accuracy" would be worth the effort and expense. Additionally, replacement cost accounting implies that cemetery property could be replaced easily; however, given the finite size of an existing cemetery and the difficulty of starting a new one, the implication of easy replacement may be false.

Financially, a cemetery is somewhat analogous to a mine, oil well, or other natural resource. A mine has only so much ore in it; similarly, a cemetery has only so much property. A mine is depleted as the mineral bearing ore is removed; likewise, a cemetery is depleted as interment spaces are sold. Both are depleting assets with a finite life. Cemeteries face the problem of when to recognize income and expenses. Should everything be booked at the time of sale? What if commissions are only payable as cash is received? How about the sale of predeveloped interment property? What is the income tax accounting treatment of these things (as opposed to generally accepted accounting)? Obviously, many questions need to be addressed.

Some cemeteries don't worry about financial accounting, for they are primarily concerned with taxes. To them, all this discussion of the theoretical accounting is a waste of effort. At the other end of the spectrum, the publicly traded companies must comply with the dictums of the accountants and the tax law while being careful to convey an accurate performance picture to investors.

The point is that accounting is not nearly as clear cut as some might believe. Reading some of the disclosures and notes to audit statements of any of the public companies in almost any industry can eliminate any doubts about this. While the complications and expectations may vary considerably from one cemetery to another, this is a strong argument in favor of having a good CPA.

## Record Keeping

Cemeteries have some common record keeping responsibilities that are always present regardless of the additional other roles they may adopt—arboretum, park, art museum, open space, and so on. These record keeping responsibilities involve ownership of interment property and records of where each decedent is interred—information that is critical in determining who may be buried where.

A cemetery is much like a county recorder's office. While it must maintain accurate records of who is interred in which space, a cemetery also must maintain a timely and accurate record of ownership of all land in the cemetery, including a description of the property and the names of all the owners. Since property is often held in more than one name, the records must reflect how title is held—joint tenants, tenants-in-common, community property, trustee, and so on. Property ownership records must be accessible by a description of the property as well as by the owners' names.

Because property can be transferred, ownership is important. For example, unused property often is left to relatives by bequests in wills. In its role as registrar, the cemetery must be able to ascertain whether the interment right can actually be transferred. Furthermore, property is transferred when an owner sells the property to someone else or conveys it to another family member. The record keeping responsibilities are broader than just ownership records because cemeteries also must keep records of who is interred in which space. Consequently, all of these records are important. Their accuracy is an integral part of the mission of the cemetery, and their mere existence is part of what gives value to a cemetery.

It is important that a cemetery's records be protected to ensure their availability. Several levels of physical security are possible to protect records. Original records are usually kept in fire-resistant storage of some sort. This can be a vault or a high quality fire-resistant cabinet. Often back-up copies of records also are kept. Cemeteries that do not have their records computerized often make microfilm copies of the records and store that microfilm off the premises. For those cemeteries with computerized records, copies of computer files can be easily kept in storage away from the cemetery offices. Generally it is best for the back-up records to be stored at a separate physical location as a disaster that damages the original records might also damage the back-up records if they are stored at the same location.

## Rules and Regulations

In most states, individual cemeteries have the authority to set the rules and regulations to govern the cemetery. Even when there isn't a statutory provision for this, most cemeteries adopt rules and regulations to clearly articulate policies and uniformly deal with property owners. Rules and regulations usually include items related to the care, control, management, and other restrictions on the use of the cemetery.

Restrictions on use typically include limitations on size and type of memorials, prohibitions of burial of anything other than human remains, restrictions on what structures may be built, and other reservations of rights to the cemetery operator.

It is also common for the rules and regulations to allow the cemetery to make the final determination of the appropriateness of memorialization. This usually is intended to give the cemetery the right to refuse to have memorials placed that are offensive due to profanity, racial slurs, or other words and images that are in poor taste. Although this restriction is subjective in its application, many cemeteries believe this right of censorship is important to maintaining the dignity of the cemetery.

It should be noted here, as reinforcement of what was said in Chapter 5 about restrictive practices that led to antitrust lawsuits, that one of the ways cemeteries got into trouble was to have rules and regulations that weren't applied uniformly and that had the effect of making it difficult or impossible for outside monument dealers to sell merchandise for placement in the cemetery.

Although purchasers may have a right of interment, cemeteries control their appearance by controlling the type and location of all structures in the cemetery. Thus, rules and regulations often limit the erection of structures to those which have been specifically approved by the cemetery. Generally, the definition of structures and construction is very broad and includes anything that might have a degree of permanence. Prohibitions against placement of upright monuments in specific sections and limiting private mausoleums to specific sites are examples of these types of restrictions. Often, the rules and regulations also will give the cemetery the right to remove anything placed or constructed without prior approval of the cemetery.

Another common provision in a cemetery's rules and regulations is a restriction on plantings and landscaping. Plantings and landscaping usually are construed as broad terms and include small fences and coping or edgings on interment spaces.

These restrictions are particularly important for memorial-park cemeteries, as they base their image on sweeping vistas of lawn. If property owners began planting shrubs on individual spaces, the openness would disappear, thus eliminating the panoramas that attracted many of the purchasers in the first place.

However, each cemetery has its own ideas about what restrictions are important for its image. These grow out of the vision of what the cemetery is to be as well as from community practices. Hence, some cemeteries may allow artificial flowers, while other cemeteries may ban them entirely.

Sometimes, rules and regulations define appropriate or permissible conduct of visitors in the cemetery. This can be as simple as setting the hours the cemetery is open to the public or as broad as imposing limitations on "improper assemblages" in the cemetery.

The rules and regulations also are the logical place for the cemetery to set restrictions concerning where remains may be buried and what cemetery authority approval is required before an interment can be made. This might be in the form of a statement regarding the procedure for receiving interment authorization.

Although it was common at one time for rules and regulations to allow the cemetery to prohibit interment based on some moral judgment, most cemeteries would now run to lawyers before refusing to make an interment because of moral turpitude.

As a final note, care must be taken to avoid using the rules and regulations for anti-competitive purposes. Most of the litigation regarding cemeteries and monument dealers mentioned in Chapter 5 also involved questions about law violations in rules and regulations. The cemetery trade associations have avoided drafting model rules and regulations for fear of inadvertently creating antitrust problems for their members.

## Checking and More Checking

While the significance of record keeping may be obvious, it is important to stress why it is so critical. Each piece of property is unique, and families choose a given space or spaces for personal reasons. They are very unhappy if they're eventually told that someone else already owned the property or it was sold to someone else after they bought it.

Even greater than the problems that can be caused by selling property a second time is the problem caused by making an interment in a wrong space. Making the interment in the wrong space within property the family owns is almost as bad as making it in a space owned by someone else. Even mistakenly making an interment in an unsold space is a major problem.

There can be many reasons for an error to be made—a document that hasn't been recorded, a transposed lot number, or a misspelled name. The preventive measure is to check and double check.

Even more error prone is the act of identifying the physical interment space on the grounds. This error is easier to make, because in most cemeteries, not every single interment space is marked. Often only the corners of lots are marked, and each lot may have numerous interment spaces. Because of the cemetery's layout, lots often are not uniform in the number of interment spaces. Additionally, older cemeteries often have some early numbering systems that lend themselves to causing errors rather than preventing them. Some cemeteries have addressed this by insisting that every family visit the cemetery and physically select the interment space before a burial. Other cemeteries have avoided or abandoned this practice as an inconvenience to families.

Sometimes the numbering scheme adopted early in a cemetery's life is error prone but cannot be changed without causing greater problems. As an example of problematical numbering schemes, Forest Lawn acquired an older cemetery several decades ago that had a multi-story mausoleum. As is typical for mausoleums, each crypt had been given a distinct number. The problem was that the difference between one floor and another was a leading zero as a significant digit—a crypt numbered 1234 was on the main (second) floor and a crypt numbered 01234 was on the ground (first) floor. Most of us have been trained in school that leading zeros aren't significant in mathematics—a number like 01234 is the same as 1234—so we have a tendency to ignore leading zeros, and computers have only reinforced that view.

From a practical standpoint, we were stuck with the numbering system. Thousands of deeds had been issued with the leading zero number scheme, and the interment records used it as well. We changed the numbering method for areas where no sales had been made, but we have had to increase our vigilance when checking the older areas.

This problem isn't uncommon for older cemeteries. Fortunately, those designing cemeteries have learned from the mistakes of others, so numbering methods have improved over the years.

The preventive measure for identifying interment spaces is usually a "blind" check. Employee "A" goes out on the grounds with a list of interments to be made, finds the appropriate space, and marks it. Employee "B" is told to go out on the grounds and find all marked spaces. Upon finding the spaces, "B" duly records the property description: section, lot, and space. When "B" returns the list to the office, a third employee, "C," then compares the list that "A" was given with the list "B" prepared. Any discrepancy between the lists must be resolved.

Additional checks can be added as appropriate for a given cemetery.[1] The checks can be viewed as a costly burden, and some depend upon a large enough staff to have a separation of duties. However, the cost becomes insignificant when compared to the potential cost of a single mistake. Unfortunately, errors are usually judged only in hindsight.

## Professional Support

Without question, knowing when to call in experts is an art rather than a science, and the range of possible experts is bewildering! The most obvious sources of expert help are members of the board of directors, accountants, attorneys, and specialized consulting firms. Nonetheless, there are a multitude of other sources of advice, including government agencies (some of them really do want to help), colleges and universities, trade associations, civic groups, and so on.

However, before calling in the experts, it's a good idea to know what management/staff is capable of doing itself. When management has expertise, it's often a mistake to call in outside specialists. On subjective matters, an "expert" may not be what is needed, just someone with some distance from the issue who can provide some perspective. Even when experts are needed for their specialized knowledge, management and the board should never lose sight of the fact that they have responsibility for the enterprise, not the outsiders. They must temper whatever advice they receive with its practical application to the organization. The board and management still will be in place and responsible for the cemetery long after the experts are gone.

## Lawyers

Attorneys are one of the most commonly used outside resources. The vast number of lawyers and the related litigious nature of our society make attorneys an indispensable resource. The key, however, is to find ones that are right for the organization. Just as with any other profession, some are well suited for some purposes but not for others. General practitioners are fine, but they are most valuable when they understand their own limitations and send the client to specialists as needed. In California, at least, the increased competition among law firms often leads attorneys to claim they can handle any legal matter. Just as most of us have become accustomed to seeking specialized medical advice, we should recognize the parallel situation with lawyers. A general corporate attorney shouldn't be asked to develop a complex tax strategy.

The most common complaint about attorneys is the cost, but attorneys' fee structures seem to be changing. Some attorneys who once only worked on an hourly basis will now consider working on a fixed fee basis for a project. Although most attorneys will work against a budget, unexpected situations or problems often arise, necessitating a revision to the budget—which is rarely revised down—another important reason to make sure you tell your attorney everything related to a matter when you start.

Therefore, building relationships is important. Over time, an attorney comes to understand both your organization and the industry. This knowledge helps an attorney give the best advice possible, making the process more efficient since background information doesn't need to be provided repeatedly.

I'm surprised to still run across business people who don't give their attorneys the entire set of facts to start with, hoping to keep the bill down, but that is often a very shortsighted approach. When relevant information is withheld from any advisor, not just attorneys, the advice received won't take into consideration all of the facts. And, when information changes, conclusions often change. So, while holding back on information may work some of the time, it also can be the business equivalent of playing Russian roulette.

Although attorneys are thought of most often concerning litigation and contracts, don't lose sight of their value in interpretation of regulations and statutes. An attorney with a strong general business practice should be able to offer business perspective as well as legal advice. A skillful legal practitioner realizes that it is far better to be proactive and take preventive measures than to need a good defense after the fact.

## Accountants

I suspect accountants often fret about being misunderstood. They've probably contributed to this themselves by being apologetic about their detail-oriented, number-crunching approach to life. While accountants can drive those of us who are not detail-oriented a little crazy, this is due to a difference in personalities rather than any lack in their importance. Thus, outside accountants should be viewed from a proper perspective— as accounting professionals who are not part of the cemetery's work force. They may be certified public accountants ("CPAs") or public accountants, which are not the same thing, but each group considers themselves accounting professionals. Since it is more likely that CPAs will be used, let me focus on them.

Some smaller cemeteries use a bookkeeper to do the day-to-day posting to accounts, pay the bills, prepare payroll, and so on. The cemetery uses the services of an outside accounting firm or CPA to prepare the actual financial statements. It is accurate to refer to this outside firm as the cemetery's accountant, because the firm is doing the accounting work as distinct from the lower level bookkeeping work. This can be very efficient for the cemetery that isn't large enough to justify having a full accountant on its payroll. Over time, the outside accountant will develop knowledge and perspective about the cemetery and should be able to provide valuable insights relating to financial and operational matters to management. In this instance, the outside accountant is acting as the chief financial officer or controller.

Outside accountants can become a valuable source of perspective regarding the organization. The accountants involved should acquire a sense of what is important in the business and what is trivial. They also should be able to give helpful suggestions and observations from the perspective of professionals who have experience in many industries and businesses as well as being far enough away from the trees to see the forest.

In Chapter 9, Governing Boards, I discussed the role of outside auditors as distinct from outside accountants. Outside auditors can benefit the cemetery with their focus on the quality of accounting systems and controls in the course of their audit. Although management may sometimes squirm from their comments, there is little doubt that the observations generally will be helpful in the end. Management needs to think of these comments as constructive criticism—a valuable resource for improvement—rather than an attempt to point fingers and embarrass someone.

## Consultants

Smaller organizations often see the use of consultants as an extravagance; however, when used properly, consultants should add substantially more value than their cost. Smaller organizations usually don't have on-staff expertise in all disciplines. Not only would it be too expensive, but it also would be impractical. Failing to have enough work in a specialty area would leave the experts bored, and they'd leave to seek true challenges. While good consultants can be expensive, they can be an invaluable resource. However, when used, they must be carefully managed.

Often, consultants are criticized for only telling management what it wants to hear. The reason for this isn't always that the consultants are pandering to management. Frequently, management knows what to do, but lacks the confidence to do it. In fact, sometimes management lacks the courage to take an unpopular action and needs the consultant or someone else to blame. While this latter use of consultants is common, it is wrong.

The key to using consultants is to use them wisely and manage what they do. Each consulting project needs to have a clearly defined scope and budget.

However, there are a few areas where consultants shouldn't be used. The first has already been suggested: Don't use consultants for tasks that should be done by management. If management can't do its job, then it should be trained to do the job or be replaced. Second, using consultants as scapegoats for tough decisions is damaging to the organization and just advertises management's weakness. Third, consultants shouldn't be used as referees for internal squabbles. Conflict resolution is a part of management's responsibility. This holds true whether the dispute is between peer level managers or different levels of management.

Which leaves the question: When should consultants be used?

Consultants are appropriate when some skill, expertise, or experience is needed that the organization doesn't possess. For example, an organization might need specialized assistance if it is moving into a new type of operation or has a need for computer/technology planning. Engineering consultants may be necessary to help plan major utility layouts, while computer experts might be needed to help evaluate the technological side of a local area computer network. After deciding to open a mortuary, one cemetery operator not only hired an architect with experience in designing funeral homes, but also hired a consultant who was a merchandising expert to help with the planning. The consultants not only provided valuable service, but in the process of their engagement, management gained a lot of knowledge.

Consultants also can be appropriate for short-term "overload" projects—tasks that could be done internally, but need to be done before internal resources can complete them. This can be an expensive alternative to reordering priorities.

Cemeteries contemplating a sale or acquisition may find consultants helpful in appraising the cemetery and negotiating the transaction. A variety of consultants can be of value in these types of transactions. People experienced in valuations and deal structuring are necessary whether they carry the title of appraiser, valuation consultant, financial analyst, or investment banker.

In summary, consultants can be a valuable resource that can be quite cost effective when used properly. When used unwisely or not managed well, they can be expensive and even wasteful.

## Service

Most cemeteries are concerned with the quality of service they give families. The term "service" is used often but is seldom defined. Delivering high quality service means exceeding customer expectations. That's an easy generalization but a much more difficult concept to put into practice. Each organization must create its own definition of what makes high quality service. The quality of service provided is clearly the responsibility of management. Although board members may have ideas about what is important, providing service is an operating responsibility.

A cemetery may intend to provide care for an interment space forever, however it only has one chance at getting the burial made right. This is the same challenge that mortuaries face in rendering funeral services. A mistake in a burial or funeral service mars the memory of the event forever. Thus, high quality service, defined as getting it right the first time because it is the only chance, is an integral part of the funeral and burial process.

High quality service will remain an elusive goal, unless it is defined and ways are found to measure it. One of the axioms of the quality control movement is that there cannot be improvement if you cannot measure what is happening. Only by measuring the components of quality service can an organization know if it is improving, is stuck at the current level, or is experiencing a decline in service.

Part of the problem with identifying ways to measure service is that everyone seems to have a different idea about what makes good service. The CEO has one idea, a first-line supervisor another, a front line employee may have still another view; and, of course, to make matters even more difficult, each consumer has a different view on service. Many organizations will define service with a list of standards they believe customers will value. While this is a start, it is even better to prioritize the list. Sometimes, good service isn't just doing the special things; it primarily is avoiding doing the things that really irritate. The work of Frederick Herzberg in defining satisfiers and dissatisfiers for employees also suggests a way of looking at customer satisfaction.

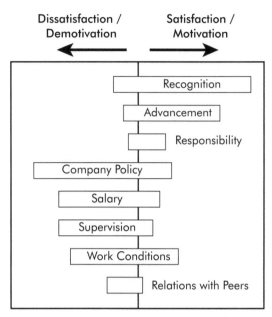

Figure 10–2 An example of Herzberg's motivators and demotivators.

### Herzberg's Theory

Psychologist Frederick Herzberg studied what motivates and demotivates workers and developed what he called the "motivational-hygiene theory."[2] His theory is that some things can motivate workers but have little potential for dissatisfaction (motivation factors). Conversely, other things can produce dissatisfaction, but the removal or correction of them cannot provide much satisfaction or motivation (hygiene factors).

According to Herzberg, things like company policies, salary, and working conditions have more potential to be dissatisfiers than satisfiers. When a worker was paid less than they thought they were worth, they were dissatisfied or demotivated. However, he found that raising the pay rate to one they thought was fair didn't produce much satisfaction or motivation. Other factors such as recognition, advancement, and responsibility operate in the opposite way—they have more potential for satisfaction/motivation than for dissatisfaction. Under Herzberg's model not receiving recognition doesn't produce much dissatisfaction, but receiving it does produce a lot of satisfaction and motivation.

Herzberg found that the degree of satisfaction and dissatisfaction from individual factors didn't apply equally to all types of employees. For example, groups of professional and managerial employees tended to receive more satisfaction from the work itself than did factory workers.

In conclusion, there are factors that primarily dissatisfy and factors that primarily satisfy. The absence of a dissatisfier doesn't produce satisfaction, and the absence of a satisfier doesn't produce dissatisfaction. The absence of either factor tends to produce nothing. This theory also can be used to think about how a cemetery's actions effect a consumer's perception of service.

## The Service Model

Using Herzberg's principles, a cemetery can develop a model for understanding high quality service and customer satisfaction. His theory can help develop a framework for determining what must be done to meet customers' expectations and what should be done to exceed them.

The core of Herzberg's theory is the axiom that customers expect certain things. As long as customers receive what they expect, they are not dissatisfied. (Note that here, as in Herzberg's model, not being dissatisfied is not the same as being satisfied; it is only the lack of dissatisfaction.) Providing what customers anticipate only meets their expectations, so there is no satisfaction. Conversely, there are things customers do not expect, but the absence of them doesn't produce dissatisfaction. Yet, when a customer receives an unexpected service, it can create great satisfaction.

Suppose a person goes into a nice restaurant for dinner. The waiter takes the order and goes away. When he brings the meal, it is just what was ordered. Odds are that the fact the order was right won't get much more than a passing thought. However, if the meal that is put on the table isn't what was ordered, the customer is unhappy or dissatisfied.

Consider the other side of this. The meal is ordered and is just as expected, but the restaurant adds some touch the customer isn't expecting. This could be an unusually attractive presentation of the food, a chilled fork for the salad, some sorbet between courses, a complimentary drink at the end of the meal, or a single long-stemmed rose to a lady. The customer now has been nudged into the satisfaction zone, as expectations have been exceeded.

Thus, the key to high quality service is identifying the customer's basic expectations—recognizing the potential dissatisfiers. These are the points of service that shouldn't be missed. Once the dissatisfiers are avoided, then an understanding of what will produce satisfaction can produce a very happy customer.

Here's the challenge for an individual cemetery: How does this apply to that specific cemetery? To a specific depart-

*Figure 10–3 Herzberg's principles applied to a restaurant experience.*

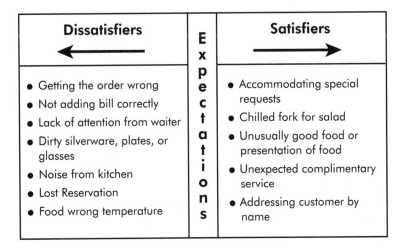

| Dissatisfiers | E x p e c t a t i o n s | Satisfiers |
|---|---|---|
| • Getting the order wrong<br>• Not adding bill correctly<br>• Lack of attention from waiter<br>• Dirty silverware, plates, or glasses<br>• Noise from kitchen<br>• Lost Reservation<br>• Food wrong temperature | | • Accommodating special requests<br>• Chilled fork for salad<br>• Unusually good food or presentation of food<br>• Unexpected complimentary service<br>• Addressing customer by name |

ment within the cemetery? To an individual who works for the cemetery?

No matter how dramatic a satisfier may be, I suspect that it is quite hard to overcome the negative effects of a dissatisfier. So, if this model is valid, organizations need to first focus on avoiding the things that will cause dissatisfaction and then turn their attention to the satisfiers.

Herzberg also discovered that different types of workers were motivated by different things and in different degrees. Similarly, the satisfiers and dissatisfiers for the customers of a given cemetery will vary based upon many factors. It's easy to realize that getting the wrong interment space is a big dissatisfier, but how high can the grass grow before it becomes a negative factor? What about mistakes in addition on contracts, employees who aren't empathetic, not being on-time/keeping people waiting, or employees giving wrong directions to an interment space? I imagine all of those are dissatisfiers.

Satisfiers, of course, would be things like an employee taking the time to help a visitor find an interment space rather than just giving directions to it (an example from the Ritz-Carlton hotels) or a cemetery which had particularly high levels of maintenance.

Each cemetery must determine what affects its customers and visitors. While it takes effort to identify satisfiers and dissatisfiers, the undertaking can help improve service and provide a way to differentiate a particular cemetery from its competition.

## Summary

The job of the cemetery manager includes a large slice of stewardship. The cemetery manager must carry out policies adopted by the board of directors and be ever mindful of the commitment cemeteries make to present and future generations. These managers are charged with the same type of responsibilities as all business managers—perform well financially by generating sales and controlling expenses, comply with legal and regulatory requirements, make sure the organization is a upright community citizen, and be a good employer. At the same time, cemetery managers act with the understanding that many things done today will have an impact on what the cemetery is like tomorrow. Each cemetery manager is a steward of the cemetery's future.

---

[1] There's almost no end to how complicated these checks can be. Forest Lawn has settled on a seven-step process for identifying and verifying interment locations.

[2] Frederick Herzberg, *Work and the Nature of Man.*

© Crown Hill Cemetery and Funeral Home

*Figure 10–4 Community mausoleum in Crown Hill Cemetery, Indianapolis, Indiana.*

Courtesy of Woodlawn Memorial Park

*Figure 10-5 A visitor to Woodlawn Memorial Park has a moment of contemplation before the reproduction of Michelangelo's* La Pieta.

# 11 Trade Associations
Support from the industry

THE DECISION of whether or not to join one or more trade associations is often made based on perceived cost—the cost of dues, cost of traveling, and time away from the cemetery. While cost is important, the softer side of the analysis is determining the benefits derived from membership and participation. Does the cemetery gain more in value from the participation than it spends?

I know several prominent cemeterians who make a point of writing reports after every meeting they attend. These written records help them organize the ideas they have gained and share new thoughts with those who didn't go. It's also good documentation about the business purpose of the trip. While I'm not that organized or disciplined, I certainly can appreciate the value to those who do put in the effort.

There are cemetery trade associations at the state, regional, and national/international level. Each type of association has something different to offer, and the cost of participation in each must be weighed against the value of knowledge received.

## (Inter)National

For many years, there were two dominant national trade associations for cemeteries, the American Cemetery Association (ACA) and the National Association of Cemeteries (NAC).

With roots dating back to 1887, the ACA generally was comprised of people involved in traditional and not-for-profit cemeteries. Most members were quite interested in day-to-day operational issues. Consequently, the association was viewed from the outside as being composed of superintendents and others who were more interested in maintenance than in sales. The association did a good job on maintenance and operational issues, but over time, it lost membership as an increasing number of cemeteries became concerned with sales and expanding revenue.

The NAC was primarily a sales-oriented group. Although it tried to include maintenance and operational topics in its programs, its strength was in sales—selling techniques, sales management, and sales training. Its membership tended to include sales-oriented managers and owners of for-profit cemeteries as well as a few managers of more progressive non-profit cemeteries.

As the ACA membership declined and the NAC's membership increased, a heightened awareness developed that a large portion of ACA's membership also belonged to NAC. Over time, as managers looked at their expenses, they decided to drop their ACA membership and retain the NAC membership. Eventually, and inevitably, the two associations merged in 1980. The "new" association took on the American Cemetery Association name, as it was the older organization and a way of honoring the industry's heritage.

As ACA's membership gradually expanded beyond the United States, there was talk of changing the name. However, the association's leadership was reluctant to change a name that had been used for nearly one hundred years.

As time went on, it became apparent that the ACA had programs that were of interest to a broader audience than just cemetery operators. A number of ACA cemeteries had gone into the mortuary business, and independent mortuary operators were interested in what ACA's members knew about preneed selling. So, in 1988, the ACA began admitting non-cemetery members to a non-voting class of membership. Even though very few joined, it marked the beginning of a period of introspection for the organization that ultimately led to changing its name to the International Cemetery and Funeral Association (ICFA). Under the new ICFA banner, it began to admit anyone who sold retail products related to cemeteries, burials, or funeral services as full voting members. At the same time, the large publicly traded firms agreed to have all of their funeral homes become members of the ICFA. Almost overnight, the ICFA membership more than doubled, going from about 1,900 immediately prior to the change to just over 5,000 members in March 1998.

The ICFA holds major conferences each year, and its spring convention includes a large primarily cemetery-related trade show. It also holds a number of seminars on various topics throughout the year.

One of the ICFA's important activities is to monitor and proactively deal with legislation and regulation at a federal level. It has successfully represented the industry in regulatory and legislative matters and has filed amici curiae (friend of the court) briefs in important civil cases.

In 1997, the ICFA's executive vice president, Steve Morgan, resigned after twenty-five years with the organization to accept a position with a member firm, SCI. Members had a mixed reaction to Morgan and with so many changes occurring in the cemetery industry, a change in management will undoubtedly be good for ICFA. Linda Christenson, an experienced association executive and attorney, replaced Morgan as the ICFA's executive vice president.

It isn't clear yet how successful the ICFA is going to be in meeting the more diverse needs of this larger membership. Members who are not part of the large firms worry about the amount of influence the large firms wield. At the 1997 fall convention, approximately 25% of the pre-registrants were from publicly traded firms. When the ICFA met in Atlanta in the spring of the following year, about 31% of the pre-registrants were from publicly traded firms. At least three presidents in a row will be from the largest publicly traded firms. Some members have questioned the heavy emphasis many ICFA leaders have placed on "promoting the selection and funding of funeral, cemetery and memorial products and services in advance of need" (from ICFA's Mission Statement).[1] A number of independent operators believe that industry-specific program content has declined, while large acquisition firms compete with each other in sponsoring nationally recognized speakers. I think the sentiment is that the association has lost some sense of balance and is too heavily influenced by one segment of the membership. This is a common problem for most trade associations, but that doesn't lessen the importance of the issue to the future of the ICFA.

For the moment, ICFA is *the* national trade association for cemeteries in the United States. However, I suspect that the climate remains ripe for a new association that understands the needs of the independent operators who do not view themselves as acquisition candidates.

## Specialized

Other specialized national organizations include the Monument Builders of North America (MBNA) and the Cremation Association of North America (CANA).

CANA's focus is on cremation related topics, including operations and sales. This group is mindful that cremation is only a step towards disposition and isn't necessarily a low cost disposal option. CANA has an active membership that is interested in this specialized focus of the organization.

For years, there was strife between the MBNA members and cemeteries. This led to some of the litigation that was mentioned in Chapter 4. The fundamental issue was competition—cemeteries and monument dealers were going after the same customers. Some of the cemeteries were greedy and adopted exclusive installation and sales rules. These rules restricted consumers to memorials purchased from the cemetery and specified that the cemetery was the only one who could perform the installation of the memorials.

It was hard to justify the exclusive sales rules, and two federal appeals courts found that those rules were prohibited, "tying arrangements" under the anti-trust statutes. Cemeteries had a more appealing rationale for the installation rules: they had to maintain the cemetery forever and were, therefore, more concerned with long-term quality issues than an outside installer would be. However, the exclusive installation rules were so tainted by the exclusive sales rules that they also were banned by the appeals court decisions.

For years, the Prearrangement Association represented the most aggressive sellers of preneed services. It is now defunct, and ICFA has made a strategic decision to position itself as the prearrangement association. Although some ICFA members have expressed concern that the focus on prearrangement is too limited, it is unlikely that the IFCA will change its position. Instead, it more likely will attempt to form sub-groups to meet the needs of various constituencies.

Although this is primarily a book about cemeteries, the National Funeral Directors Association (NFDA) was mentioned in an earlier chapter and, thus, deserves to be mentioned as a major funeral trade association. The NFDA is primarily a funeral directors group. Although the ICFA admits funeral directors to full voting membership, NFDA does not admit cemeteries. The ICFA and NFDA seem to continue to appeal to different market segments.

## State and Regional

I've combined the discussion of state and regional trade associations, because there is considerable overlapping between the two. I'll use the term "state association" to refer to both state and regional associations. A number of states do not have active trade associations for their state alone, so cemeteries participate in a multi-state association. Other states have large active state associations—the Interment Association of California and Texas Cemetery Association are good examples of strong state trade associations.

For most cemeteries, the state trade association is a critical part of their existence, because most cemetery-related legislation is passed at the state level. Accordingly, state associations usually have a heavy emphasis on legislative efforts that make participation in the state association crucial.

Some managers of cemeteries that are exempt from regulation under their state's laws question if they should be spending the money to belong to a state association. Ultimately, most of them decide this is a good idea.

First, monitoring legislation is often a defensive activity. Even when current laws don't apply to a given situation, anything is possible when a legislature is in session. For example, religious cemeteries in California are exempt from the California Cemetery Act. However, several years ago, when a legislator was introducing a bill on minimum burial depth, he carefully worded it to include "all cemeteries in the state" because of a problem with a cemetery that was exempt from state regulation. Although there was a lot of discussion about whether or not this was the beginning of a trend, it was clearly an encroachment on the exemption. As a side note, the religious cemeteries didn't oppose the provision, and it passed.

Second, all by itself, exchange of information with other members is usually well worth the price of membership. The opportunity for exposure to points of view of other managers faced with similar types of problems is invaluable. Most people who have made the effort to participate in state associations have found it to be well worth the time and expense.

## Summary

Cemetery managers have many trade associations to choose from. Although there are potential benefits from many of them, it is important to join those that best meet the needs of the individual cemetery and manager. Generally, the highest priority will be on the state association membership because of the importance of state regulation. National organizations can give a broad perspective of what is happening in the industry or within a segment of the industry. Ultimately, the decision of what trade association(s) to join is a question of time, money, and perceived benefits of membership.

# 12 Regulation
The role of government

CEMETERIES ARE subject to many of the same laws and regulations that affect all businesses. A few laws exempt small business and some cemeteries fall under these exemptions. For the most part, though, cemeteries must comply with the same employment and safety laws that apply generally.

Because of the diversity of operations of a cemetery, cemetery managers need to be aware of the breadth of their legal responsibilities. It is beyond the intent of this book to discuss these at length, but it is worth mentioning that cemeteries need to be sensitive to laws regarding safety, primarily the Occupational Health and Safety Act (OSHA), and hazardous materials handling. The safety related laws are important because cemeteries use heavy equipment and a wide variety of machinery. The use of paints, solvents, fertilizers, and pesticides can usher in various sets of laws and regulations relative to use, training, and disposal of hazardous substances. Operating a mortuary further expands the regulatory demands with sanitation requirements and regulations related to blood born pathogens as well as various state and federal mortuary rules.

## State Regulation

The majority of cemetery regulation is done at the state level. As can be seen from a perusal of Appendix B, the extent and type of regulations varies by state. Although each state has its own particular political personality and philosophy of regulation, generally, the trend seems to be toward more regulation. Elected officials may talk about lessening regulation; however, their appointees and the civil service employees who administer the rules—not to mention surviving in their positions through each election—still have a vested interest in more rather than less regulation.

Cemeteries should not be able to operate without any regulation. Most consumers come to a cemetery because of a death in the family, so they come with the burdens of stress and grief. They are vulnerable. Also, the implied promise of taking care of the cemetery forever through the endowment care fund creates a valid public concern about those promises and the integrity of the funds.

Not only is there a valid societal interest, but the ethical players want a level playing field—equal administration of laws and regulations to everyone performing the same business functions. When problems have occurred with cemeteries, they often have been with operators who had a track record of violating consumer confidence and, at best, operating right on the edge of the law. Most of the dedicated cemeterians I know realize that protecting the public in reasonable ways also means protecting themselves, for when any scandal hits a cemetery, all other cemeteries are damaged to some extent.

Having said why regulation is necessary, I also am obligated to present the negative side of regulation—efforts that do nothing to protect consumers and only increase costs of what consumers buy. Let me give examples from what has happened in California.

For many decades, California had an independent cemetery board with the members appointed by the governor. When Jerry Brown was governor, the board was changed from a membership of only industry members to a five-person board with only two industry members—three of the members were required to be from the "public" and couldn't have any relationship with a cemetery. Almost twenty years after that, several members of the California legislature and some appointed officials began talking about an "industry dominated board."

This never made much sense, since less than half of the members of the board were from the industry and more than half were, by law, appointed by the governor or legislature. The heat grew for several years, until the board finally lost its budget. Its responsibilities were swallowed up by the Department of Consumer Affairs, a 14,000 plus employee agency that also regulates more than three dozen other unrelated industries.

Although the Department has meant well, it underestimated the time required to understand the cemetery and funeral industries. For example, in 1997, it published a booklet titled "Consumer Guide to Funeral and Cemetery Purchases." At the end of the booklet, sources for more information were listed. Listed in the section "Consumer/Government Organizations" was a federation of memorial societies. What the Department had failed to understand was that the memorial societies are competitors to cemeteries and funeral homes. Listing one group of competitors as consumer organizations and another as industry organizations reflected the Department's lack of understanding of the industries it was regulating.

Also, the Department had a difficult time training its field investigators, since the staff was covering cemeteries and mortuaries in addition to many other industries. Inspectors would arrive at Forest Lawn wanting lists of celebrity interment locations and lists of our rolling stock—everything from cars and trucks to backhoes. They wanted a list of the cemetery salespersons licenses, because they couldn't produce one from their own records. They asked for information they had no right to request under the statutes. In a question and answer program at a meeting of the Interment Association of California, I asked Peter Brightbill, Chief of the Cemetery and Funeral Section, why the investigators were asking about things that weren't covered in laws or regulations. His response was that they were just trying to "build up their files," and each cemetery could appropriately decline to give information that wasn't required by law. Surprisingly, they didn't seem to care about the endowment care funds.

The point of recounting this isn't to criticize the Department or other states' regulatory bodies. The point is that those charged with enforcement need to understand the industries they are regulating if the rules are to result in meaningful consumer protection.

Unfortunately, the concept that regulation costs are a business expense that is passed on to consumers often is forgotten. The regulatory process must weigh all costs of regulation—those incurred by the government and those incurred by the regulated firms—against the benefits derived from that regulation.

## The FTC Funeral Trade Rule

Although the Federal Trade Commission's Funeral Trade Rule only covers sellers of funeral goods and services, cemeteries should be familiar with its provisions.

Historically, the federal government's efforts to regulate mortuaries is filled with controversy. The FTC began investigating the funeral industry in 1972. In 1975, the FTC staff proposed a rule to regulate the selling methods of mortuaries; however, it wasn't until March 1979 that the FTC actually approved the regulation. As with any other FTC rule, Congress had a period of time in which it could veto the rule before it went into effect. And, veto it, the House did. In a compromise in the Senate, new procedures were required for promulgation of the rule, necessitating a second proposed rule.

In January 1981, the FTC staff issued a new version of the rule after receiving approval from two funeral industry trade groups. However, consumer groups and senior citizen groups protested, because the rule required consumers to specify the items they didn't want. The consumer groups favored an itemized pricing approach to regulation as had been done in earlier versions of the rule. The FTC commissioners decided they wouldn't agree with the compromise worked out by the staff and put the requirement for itemized pricing back into the rule.

The NFDA was unhappy with the version approved by the FTC and began legally challenging the rule. When the legal battle hit the U.S. Court of Appeals, the AARP joined the fray with a friend-of-the-court brief in 1983. Although the rule was to take effect on January 1, 1984, it was delayed, because the court hadn't rendered its decision. Finally, in January 1984, the 4th Circuit Court disposed of the last of the NFDA's challenges. Although the NFDA had vowed to fight the rule all the way to the U.S. Supreme Court, it capitulated and said that its 14,000 members were prepared to comply with the "federal intervention." David Bonhardt, executive director of the NFDA, said that the NFDA "does not think it (the FTC regulation) is necessary. We still think state and local laws are adequate."[1]

FTC spokesperson Amanda Pederson said that the regulations did not reflect an FTC judgment that funeral costs were excessive, but rather an acknowledgment that funeral shopping was traumatic and that pricing information had not been uniformly available. She indicated that the FTC was uncertain about the effect of the rule on funeral prices. However, Dale L. Rollings, executive director of the Order of the Golden Rule, a mortuary organization, predicted that prices would rise as a result of the rule.[2]

It should be noted that not all mortuaries agreed with the NFDA's position and challenge to the rule. Indeed, some were embarrassed by the NFDA's seemingly anti-consumer position. Firms in California, Texas, New York, New Jersey, and Florida already had some form of price itemization. A number of firms in other areas indicated that they had long had a practice of quoting prices when asked. A number of mortuaries simply were opposed to the methods mandated for price disclosures and not the principle itself.

On April 30, 1984, the FTC Funeral Trade Rule went into effect. The entire current version of the rule is included in Appendix A, but some of the most important provisions are:

+ Prices must be quoted over the telephone.
+ Itemized price lists must be provided.
+ Consumers must be given the option to decline some services.
+ Prohibits saying that embalming is required by law when that is not the case and requires disclosure that it can only required in certain cases.

+ A casket cannot be required for cremation.
+ Claims cannot be made that items are being delivered "at cost" if there was any mark-up.
+ Requirements of state or local law cannot be misrepresented.

Most mortuaries have learned to live with the FTC Funeral Trade Rule; however, follow-up studies by the FTC have shown that many firms have not complied fully with the rule's provisions. This led to the FTC agreeing to a regulatory partnership with the NFDA to establish a Funeral Rule Offenders Program (FROP). The FTC would have the option of sending violators into the FROP program rather than taking them to court. Violators going into the FROP would be required to make voluntary payments to the treasury and agree to comprehensive staff training and testing for five years.

The FTC promoted the FROP as a means to obtain more compliance using industry resources rather than government resources. The NFDA pitched the idea on the theory that it would save the government litigation costs and lower fines and legal costs to mortuaries. Eileen Harrington of the FTC's Bureau of Consumer Protection stressed that "Nothing about [the FROP] immunizes [funeral] homes from enforcement."[3]

## Summary

The seemingly endless amount of regulation on any business represents a substantial cost. While cost is a reason to lobby against adoption or for repeal of regulations, it is not a valid reason to fail to comply with laws and regulations (unless there is a specific reasonable expense test in the law). Those responsible for cemeteries need to understand the principles of the regulations and laws that apply and know when to seek advice about the applicability of the various statutes and rules. Membership in trade associations is one good source of information for cemetery operators about applicability of regulations and for status reports of proposed new government requirements.

1. Winifred I. Cook, "Funeral Homes Welcome New Regulations: FTC Requires Cost Disclosure," *Miami Herald*, May 5, 1984.

2. Joyce Gemperlin, "FTC Backs Consumer in Funeral-Data Hassle," *Boston Globe*, May 1, 1984.

3. Cindy Skrycki, "The Regulators: Price Viewing—Funeral Group, FTC Undertake a Partnership on Rules," *Washington Post*, January 19, 1996.

Courtesy of Swan Point Cemetery

*Figure 12–1 Crematory building in Swan Point Cemetery.*

Forest Lawn Memorial-Park Association

*Figure 12–2 Church of Our Fathers, Forest Lawn–Cypress.*

# 13 Testing Endowment Care Funds
A case study

THE MATERIAL in this book addresses many philosophical issues—some of the issues related to the central thesis that a
cemetery should be forever might seem theoretical. To help
put some practical perspective on these points, a simple case
study was developed for a fictional cemetery, the Metropolitan
Cemetery. The purpose of the case study is to demonstrate
how one cemetery might examine the issues relative to its desire to be a positive community asset when it is sold out.

This case study is fictional and intended to stimulate discussion about endowment care funds for all types and sizes of
cemeteries rather than present pat solutions. A similarity to
any person or organization is coincidental. The policies and
business strategies contained herein are neither an endorse-
ment nor a representation of any "normal" practice. The mythi-
cal Metropolitan Cemetery operates under California law; laws
differ in other states.

## Metropolitan Cemetery

Located in a suburb of Fresno, California, Metropolitan Cemetery was dedicated in 1929 with a total size of just over a
hundred acres (Figure 13–1). For its first twenty years, it was
just a nondescript local cemetery. However, in 1959, Gordon
Reeves, who had more than 10 years' experience in the cemetery field, was hired as president. As a student of cemetery

history, Reeves was fascinated by Hubert Eaton's story of opening a funeral home on dedicated cemetery grounds in 1933. Foreseeing the inevitability of other cemeteries operating funeral homes, Reeves convinced Metropolitan's board of directors to open a funeral home in 1965, but zoning approvals and construction delays kept the mortuary from opening until 1969.

After returning from Vietnam, Clyde Smith went to work as a salesman for Metropolitan. He sold preneed cemetery property door-to-door for ten years before being promoted into sales management. Once in sales management, Clyde created an innovative program to recruit new salespeople, and Metropolitan experienced an unprecedented growth in revenue. After demonstrating his skill for eleven years, Clyde's boss, Gordon Reeves, decided to broaden Clyde's responsibility and, thus, put him in charge of all cemetery operations.

Clyde soon realized that simply worrying about day-to-day cemetery operations would not permit him to be an effective manager. Much of what he needed to do today was heavily influenced by decisions that had been made years earlier. Thus, he decided he needed to develop a comprehensive long-term plan for Metropolitan. Clyde gave a great deal of thought to this. Most of the businesses he knew created plans for five years, but that didn't seem like a long enough time-horizon to him. Given the finite nature of the cemetery's boundaries, Clyde concluded that the only time frame that made sense was the entire life of the cemetery. This would enable him to adequately plan for roads, utilities, grading, building sites, and inventory mix. Being a realist, Clyde also realized that a life-of-the-cemetery plan would have to be updated periodically, because the underlying assumptions probably wouldn't remain static.

Upon further contemplation, Clyde decided to call his plan a "master plan" instead of using the usual terms of "strategic plan" or "long-range plan." Clyde wanted his master plan to accomplish something similar to what city planners achieve with zoning plans—he wanted to make long-term decisions about land use that would allow orderly development of the

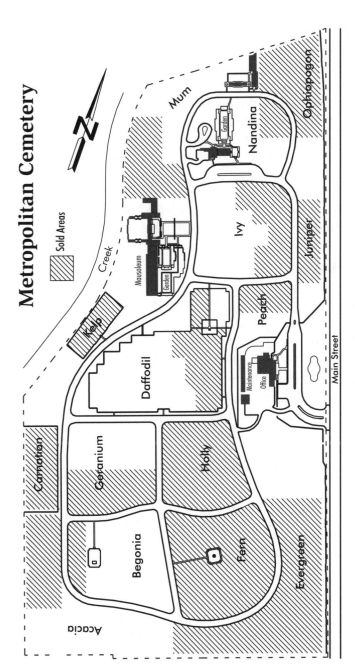

*Figure 13-1 Metropolitan Cemetery.*

entire property. The master plan's principal building block would be assumptions about land use absorption rates, which would have to be driven by projections of unit sales at various price levels. Having just completed an executive MBA program, Clyde quickly realized that this master plan also was an essential element in marketing strategy. He understood that the master plan could give him information necessary to monitor Metropolitan's endowment care fund—whether or not enough money was being put into the fund to care for the cemetery when it becomes almost sold out.

So, Clyde set out to develop a master plan for Metropolitan cemetery and to follow it with a forecast of future endowment care fund income and expenses.

## The Master Plan

Clyde began the master plan by making a list of the items he would need. These included:

1.  An accurate map of the cemetery showing all existing roads, walkways, buildings, utility easements, and unusable portions of the property.
2.  Acreage information:
    - ✧ Gross dedicated acres.
    - ✧ Acreage devoted to existing roads & utility easements.
    - ✧ Size of building sites and support areas—parking, utilities, walls, fences, and so on.
    - ✧ Property unusable for any reason—too steep, swamp land, endangered species habitat, soil conditions, or other reasons.
    - ✧ Amount of property already sold (including property that had been paid for in full as well as property sold on terms and not yet fully paid for).
3.  Projections of unit sales (in interment spaces) by price level.

Clyde found that some of this information was easy to gather and some wasn't. The cemetery didn't have good records regarding the number of spaces sold, but Metropolitan did file an annual report with the state regulatory agency that indicated the number of square feet of ground and number of mausoleum crypts sold each year. This report was designed to allow the state to determine whether or not the cemetery was collecting at least the minimum amounts required by statute for deposit into the endowment care fund required by statute for each kind of property.

However, the problem with the square footage data was that it included spaces of all sizes—small spaces used for cremated remains of infants, as well as large spaces for oversized caskets. Since Clyde had to seek a common denominator between the sales projections and the historical sold data, he decided that he'd just assume every space had 26 square feet. He figured that given the decades long horizon of the plan the errors this would introduce wouldn't be material to the big picture decisions he had to make.

Early in the process, Clyde realized that determining the usable amount of undeveloped land was something of a "chicken and egg" problem. The decisions he made in one area about slopes and road locations often would have an effect on other areas because of cuts or fills in the grading. He knew he wouldn't make it through this process without at least some input from his outside civil engineer who could help him make sure he could balance the use of dirt through the end of the cemetery's practical life. Part of the balancing calculation would need to be based on the additional dirt that was generated from each interment—the volume displaced by the burial vault.

To begin the process, Clyde developed a table to show the current usage of Metropolitan Cemetery's acreage (Table 13–1). Even though a title report indicated that the land owned by the cemetery was somewhat higher, Clyde discovered that the amount of dedicated land within the cemetery actually was just over 105 acres. Metropolitan Cemetery's engineer, Bill

|  | Acres | % of dedicated |
|---|---|---|
| Gross Acreage | 107.138 | |
| Dedicated Acres | 105.374 | 100.0% |
| Building and Infrastructure Site Acres | | |
| Administration/sales buildings | 1.592 | 1.5% |
| Entrances and frontal areas | 2.185 | 2.1% |
| Chapel sites | 0.621 | 0.6% |
| Mausoleum sites | 0.889 | 0.8% |
| Roads in developed areas | 3.384 | 3.2% |
| Maintenance Yard | 2.132 | 2.0% |
| Utilities & wells | 1.457 | 1.4% |
| Total Buildings | 12.260 | 11.6% |
| Net Usable | 93.114 | 88.4% |
| Developed Areas | | |
| Sold and deeded | 1,451,937 sf | |
| Sold, not paid-in-full | 82,095 sf | |
| Total Square Feet Sold | 1,534,032 sf | |
| Sold Acres | 35.217 | 33.4% |
| In inventory | | |
| Reserved property | 2.782 | 2.6% |
| Inventory (developed) | 5.369 | 5.1% |
| Inventory (predeveloped) | 2.494 | 2.4% |
| Total Inventory | 10.665 | 10.1% |
| Total Sold and Developed | 45.882 | 43.5% |
| Remaining Acres | 47.232 | 44.8% |

*Table 13-1 Metropolitan Cemetery acreage usage.*

Thomas, explained that the difference in acreage was due to the ownership of the land being to the center of the adjacent city roads and the dedication only going to the edge of the city sidewalks. The gross acreage included a portion of city streets, sidewalks, and city maintained planting areas. According to Bill, the dedicated acreage was actually what had been approved by the city for cemetery use. Hence, Clyde started with the amount of dedicated land.

Next, Clyde had Bill determine how much land couldn't be developed because of its use—property devoted to the maintenance yard, roads, administration and sales facilities, and so on. Everyone was surprised to discover that almost 12% or 12 plus acres of land was tied up in some non-salable use.

Because Metropolitan recently had invested in converting its records to a computer system, Clyde was able to obtain a report that indicated the status of interment property inventory—property developed and available for sale, property reserved for some specific use, and property that was available for sale prior to development.

When Clyde added the property in building and infrastructure to the property in inventory, he couldn't balance to the total dedicated acreage. He found that part of the discrepancy was property in the process of being sold—tied up in accounts receivable. This was property that had been sold but hadn't been deeded to the buyers, because they still owed money on their account. Although the interment right wouldn't be conveyed to the purchasers until their account was paid in full, for planning purposes, the property was sold.

Clyde found that he still couldn't balance the total area of sold, in process of sale, and inventoried property to the dedicated acreage. He went back to Bill Thomas, explained his problem, and showed Bill his area breakdown (Table 13–1). Bill pulled out a lot map of the Begonia section and pointed out that there was property in all sections that couldn't be used.

To demonstrate this, Bill used his pencil to fill in the spaces between lots, on corners, and at the edge of the road (Figure 13–2). These areas were too small to be used for burials but were planted in grass or landscaping and needed to be cared for. Bill reminded Clyde that although Metropolitan had used some interment spaces that were shorter than Metropolitan's standard eight feet, it was impossible to use every square inch for interments.

Clyde thought they needed a label for this type of property. They kicked around several terms to describe this—Bill wanted to call it "wastage," and Clyde wanted to call it "fractional excess" which sounded less harsh to him. After some

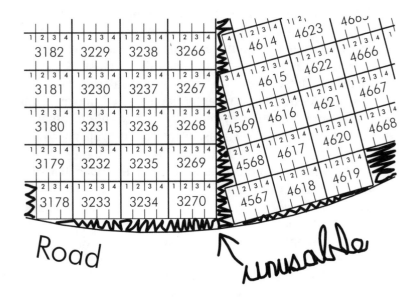

*Figure 13–2 Bill's explanation of unusable area.*

discussion, they decided to call it "unusable." Bill showed Clyde that including the unusable property resulted in a corrected amount of net remaining acreage that tied-in to Bill's maps (Table 13–2). Table 13–3 shows the final calculation of acreage available for development, including roads, mausoleum sites, and the estimated amount of unusable property in the undeveloped areas.

Now that Clyde knew how much property Metropolitan had that could be developed, he was ready to start thinking seriously about his master plan.

Largely because of the training he'd received from Gordon Reeves, Clyde believed that Metropolitan needed to offer its customers a variety of cemetery property—different locations, features, and prices. Consequently, he determined that they should have approximately twelve different types of interment property for ground burial, including lawn crypts, mausoleum crypts, and niches. Certain areas of the cemetery lent itself well to high priced property because of location or topography, while other parts were much less desirable. Clyde met with some of his sales team and debated the relative value of different areas of the cemetery. They didn't try to put prices on the areas; they just put the areas in order according to value.

They discovered some interesting things from this exercise. First, the portion of the cemetery easiest (read that as least expensive) to develop was the portion that had been developed first. The remaining property had some big challenges—a lot of dirt to move, some possible riparian habitat, and an area with a ground water problem. Not only that, but the designations they put on value for their first attempt didn't balance at all. They'd run out of property inventory at some intermediate price levels long before they ran out of lower priced or higher priced property. They wanted to have the higher priced inventory last to the end of the sales life of the cemetery but thought they could accept running out of the lowest price levels before the intermediate price levels. So, it was back to the drawing board.

After a series of meetings and many calculations, they found a comfortable way to achieve an inventory mix for the remaining sales life of the cemetery. They determined that if they set aside enough area for above ground inventory—mausoleum crypts and niches in columbaria—they would be able to have those types of property inventory all the way to the actual end of the sales life of the cemetery. Figure 13-4 shows the fi-

Table 13–2 Bill's adjustment to Clyde's figures to give the actual amount of remaining acreage.

|  | | Acres |
|---|---|---|
| Dedicated acres | | 105.374 |
| Used for buildings and infrastructure | | 12.260 |
| Usable for development of interment property | | 93.114 |
| Sold Property | 35.217 | |
| Property in inventory | 10.665 | |
| Unusable | 3.517 | |
|  | | 49.399 |
| Net available for development | | 43.715 |

| | | Acres | % of dedicated |
|---|---|---|---|
| Remaining Acres | | 43.715 | 2.5% |
|    Roads in undeveloped areas | 2.930 | | 2.8% |
|    Future mausoleum sites | 4.167 | | 4.0% |
|    Unusable area | 2.807 | | 2.7% |
| | | 9.904 | 9.5% |
| Net Usable Undeveloped | | 33.812 | 32.1% |

*Table 13–3 Metropolitan's net remaining area.*

nal distribution of the estimated life of each price level. While developing this data they determined that they didn't need to assign actual prices. Rather, they just needed to determine how many price points they had.

Clyde was pleased with this result. Also, because he'd included many people in the process of developing this, he felt it had the benefit of diverse points of view and represented the differing needs of the organization—maintenance, sales, and financial.

Clyde had his master plan, but he realized that it would be necessary to update it periodically, as things undoubtedly would not play out exactly as forecast. However, with the master plan in place, Clyde knew he could then test to make sure that there would be adequate funds to take care of Metropolitan Cemetery at the time it was nearly sold out. Thus, he moved on to the endowment care fund income and expense study.

## Assumptions

Clyde met with several of his financially astute board members before getting too far into projecting endowment care fund income and expense into the future. He realized that some subjective decisions needed to be made about the projection assumptions.

The first issue they discussed was when the endowment

care fund income should take care of all maintenance costs. As they talked about this, everyone was convinced that it wasn't when the cemetery was entirely sold out. While they expected the sales rate would continue to decline as selection dwindled, there still would be property left on which they could build niches and crypts for a long time after everything else was sold. So, the cemetery could be sold out from a practical stand-point, although some spaces would remain unsold.[1] As a result, the cemetery might have decades of nominal income from sales, but still not be entirely sold out. Also, waiting until the very end of the sales life of the cemetery wouldn't give any

Table 13-4 Acreage, interment spaces, sales rate, and estimated inventory life by price level.

| Price Point | Area Available (Acres) | Spaces Possible to Develop | Annual Sales Rate | Life in Years |
|---|---|---|---|---|
| A | 2.323 | 3,718 | 143 | 26 |
| B | 3.305 | 5,289 | 123 | 43 |
| C | 6.573 | 10,518 | 235 | 45 |
| D | 4.347 | 6,956 | 148 | 47 |
| E | 3.712 | 5,940 | 135 | 44 |
| F | 3.982 | 6,372 | 118 | 54 |
| G | 3.782 | 6,052 | 89 | 68 |
| H | 1.954 | 3,127 | 59 | 53 |
| I | 1.530 | 2,448 | 36 | 68 |
| J | 1.292 | 2,068 | 22 | 94 |
| K | 0.515 | 824 | 8 | 103 |
| L | 0.375 | 600 | 4 | 108 |
| M | 0.120 | 192 | 2 | 96 |
| Mausoleum Crypts | | 4,500 | 40 | 113 |
| | 33.812 | | | |

opportunity to take corrective action if their projections weren't accurate. Therefore, they determined it would be prudent to build a cushion into their ultimate goal. They decided, rather arbitrarily, that they wanted to have the endowment care fund income entirely maintain the cemetery by the time the cemetery was 80% sold, reasoning that this would give them enough time to take corrective action if the fund income wasn't adequate by that time.

The discussion about when the fund's income should entirely take care of the cemetery led to a discussion about how long the projection period should be. Although it would be possible to project the fund income and expense for the entire expected life of the cemetery, they realized that errors would compound over a long projection period. Consequently, they agreed to use a 50-year projection period with the understanding that the estimates at the end of the 50 years were very soft.

For purposes of this study, they resolved to keep adding to the endowment care fund's reserve accounts as they had in the past. Half of the realized capital gains would go into the reserve for extraordinary repairs and replacement, and 15% of the fund's net income would go into a reserve for investment losses. The effect of additions to the reserve for investment losses would be similar to the effect of contributions to principal. The amounts added to the reserve for repair and maintenance would have the effect of additional contributions only if they were not taken out of the fund, even though the law specifically provided that reserve amounts could be spent for certain purposes. Consequently, they did not make any use of the reserve for repair and maintenance in their projections; and thus, the fund generated an income stream that was somewhat larger than if they took out the funds as allowed by law.

Given the uncertainty of what might happen in the economy over a 50-year period, they decided not to forecast any price increases. As a result, the projection would be in terms of real or constant dollars, allowing them to avoid forecasting inflation.

The hardest decision was what to do with growth of the fund from investments and the assumption of income rate.

Clyde discussed this with Metropolitan's investment advisors. They discussed what had happened in the stock market in past and recent years and what was likely to happen in the future. Everyone seemed comfortable with the portfolio being heavily invested in good quality common stocks, and there was agreement that the equity investments were necessary for maintenance of purchasing power. Finally, it was decided to take the recommendation of their investment advisor: assume a 0.5% real growth from investments and a 4% income stream.

## What are the Real Expenses?

Perhaps, the hardest part of gathering the necessary data for this study was determining the expenses for caring for the property. Some of the people who had been around Metropolitan for a long time believed the endowment care fund was to take care of only the sold property, while others believed it should take care of the entire cemetery. After a great deal of discussion, and even a little heated debate, all agreed that the maintenance of the entire cemetery should be the basis for the study. Even if they were wrong and the endowment care fund should only take care of the sold property, Clyde determined that this method would err on the conservative side. Considering the maintenance expenses for the whole cemetery might overstate expenses, but that would be far better than under-estimating them. Clyde recruited Metropolitan's outside accountant to help allocate the expenses between maintenance and operations.

Metropolitan's accounting system had been set up with management accountability in mind rather than cost accounting, so quite a bit of analysis was needed to determine how much of the general expenses should be properly allocated to take care of the property.

It wasn't difficult to identify the accounts that covered direct property upkeep expenses, such as mowing the lawns, trimming around memorials, fertilizing, and irrigation. The challenge arose when they began to consider how much of the overhead items should be included as care expense. Clyde was

| Prices, Expenses, and Contributions | |
|---|---|
| Real annual price increase rate | 0.0% |
| Real annual increase in expense | 0.0% |
| Endowment care fund contribution rate | 10.0% |
| **Investment Assumptions** | |
| Real capital gains growth rate | 0.5% |
| Income available for distribution | 5.0% |

*Table 13–5 Assumptions for Clyde's first projection.*

concerned about how to handle general management, insurance, vehicle depreciation, accounting, and other overhead items and functions. He realized that many of these expenses would continue once Metropolitan was sold out, but also realized they were probably higher now, given the current levels of activity, than they would be in a sold out condition. Consequently, Clyde and his accountant developed a series of allocation formulas to consider the variables.

For example, the electrical power was supplied through a number of meters. The entire bill for the meter that was for the irrigation pumps clearly reflected a care related utility expense, but the meter that fed the administration offices and maintenance yard served current selling, operations, and administrative functions. The question was how much power would be necessary for administration when Metropolitan was virtually sold out. Clyde decided to split the electrical expense on the ratio of direct care expenses to total expenses. He applied similar allocation formulas to a variety of expenses to determine how much was really related to care of the cemetery.

Once Clyde had a total dollar cost for care-related expenses, he divided it by the number of developed spaces in order to project the cost of care on a constant dollar basis, as more and more property was sold. This led him to another problem, though; he had to account for the cost of caring for mausoleum crypts and niches. He was fairly sure that the cost of caring for these would be less than for property outside that had grass that grew all year. As a result, he decided to use a formula that gave each mausoleum crypt one quarter of the maintenance cost of a ground space and a niche one twelfth of the cost of a ground space. Table 13–5 shows the first set of assumptions that Clyde used in his first projection.

## The Results

As Clyde put together his projection, he was confident it would show that Metropolitan would have more than ample earnings from its endowment care fund when the cemetery was 80% sold. Part of this confidence came from Metropolitan's past practice of exceeding the minimum endowment care fund contribution rates set by the state and the balance came from the past investment performance of the fund. Metropolitan's directors long ago had recognized the need to invest for capital appreciation and had maintained good growth in the fund, while other cemeteries had invested primarily for current income. The Metropolitan Cemetery Endowment Care Fund was considered large by many in the industry.

Clyde plotted the results and produced the graph in Figure 13–3. Needless to say, he was surprised with the results.

First, the projection showed that Metropolitan would be 80% sold in the year 2024. At the end of the 60-year study in 2050, it would be 94% sold. Second, the current annual shortfall of endowment care fund income relative to care expenses was about $340,000. Third, and the bad news, was that by 2050 there was still a shortfall—just over $150,000 a year!

Not only was Clyde surprised, he also was very troubled. He knew he could solve the problem on paper by changing the sales mix to get higher prices and, therefore, higher contributions to the endowment care fund, or he simply could increase the real growth earnings assumption. A real earnings growth of approximately 1.5% would make things just break even in 2050, but more than 5% real growth would be necessary to break even by the time the cemetery was 80% sold. He knew that the 0.5% real growth rate was conservative but also understood that 5% real growth was impossible to attain and that other measures would be necessary to achieve the goal.

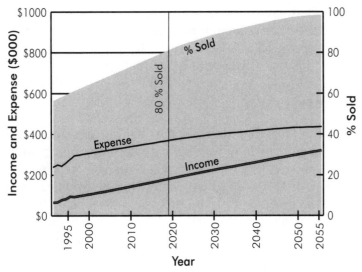

*Figure 13–3 Results of first projection.*

Additionally, because the 0.5% real growth rate had been developed by the fund's investment advisors, Clyde was reluctant to override their professional judgment.

## Possible Approaches

Other than using an unattainable real growth rate assumption, Clyde only saw three possible ways to deal with the shortfall:

1. Decrease maintenance costs
2. Increase average prices faster than inflation (real growth of prices)
3. Increase the amount of the endowment care fund contribution per space

He wasn't thrilled with any of the choices. He could see potential problems with all of them but realized that something must be done.

If he spent less on maintenance, the cemetery wouldn't look good and sales might suffer. He could surely look for ways to be more efficient but wasn't sure how much he could cut out and still maintain the desired appearance.

Increasing prices faster than inflation would be a challenge. Metropolitan had competitors who might not follow suit, which also could have a negative impact on sales and, perhaps, cause a loss of market share. He realized that market share was very hard to change, so he was quite reluctant to do anything that might have an adverse impact on Metropolitan's market position.

His third option, to increase the amount of the endowment care fund contribution, would increase what consumers would have to pay. He didn't know if consumers would view it as a price increase or if they would see it only as a larger payment for care of their interment property.[2]

## Clyde's Recommendation

As Clyde experimented with his financial model, he found that nominal increases in real prices had almost no impact on the occurrence of the break-even point. Similarly, decreasing the maintenance cost on undeveloped property had no significant impact. Thus, Clyde decided to present a recommendation to Metropolitan's board of directors that used a little of each of the three options listed above. First, he'd try to cut 15% from his maintenance budget and commit to having the cost per

Table 13–6 Assumptions for Clyde's final projection.

| Prices, Expenses, and Contributions | |
|---|---|
| Real annual price increase rate | 0.0% |
| Real annual increase in expense          0.0% | |
| Endowment care fund contribution rate | 20.0% |
| Reduction in maintenance cost/space | -15.0% |
| **Investment Assumptions** | |
| Real capital gains growth rate | 0.5% |
| Income available for distribution | 5.0% |

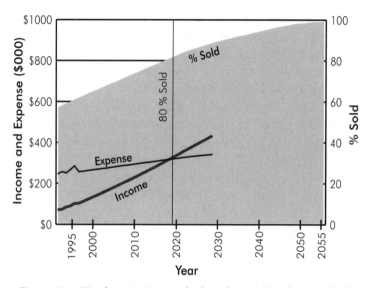

*Figure 13–4 Final projection results based on policy changes Clyde recommended to the board of directors.*

space rise no faster than the inflation rate. Second, he'd recommend that the amount of the endowment care contribution be raised from 10% to 20% of the purchase price. Table 13–6 shows the final assumptions.

These changes wouldn't be easy to accomplish, but Clyde realized Metropolitan should have made this careful study years earlier when such difficult changes wouldn't have been necessary. Even with these changes, the projected break-even point for endowment care fund income and care expenses was eight years after the 80% sold target date, as shown in the graph in Figure 13–4. Clyde explained to his directors that the proposed action didn't fully solve the problem. He recommended that the study be updated annually, so the board and management could see whether or not progress was being made in building up the income and principal of the fund. Corrective measures then could be taken in a timely manner, depending upon whether the results were better or worse than the projections.

Clyde also cautioned the board members about the cumulative impact of compounding in projections. He warned them that small changes in significant items could have a large effect on the results at the end of 50 years. This principle would hold true for estimation errors in any direction. He told them that it was important to look at the trends any changes would cause while remembering that the projections would result in figures that actually would be very soft at the end of the 50-year period.

Metropolitan's board directors also were surprised at the results of Clyde's analysis. They thanked Clyde for his work and told him they agreed that the adequacy of the size of the endowment care fund needed to be tested routinely. Everyone left the meeting feeling good about taking measures to protect the cemetery's future, but each also had a renewed commitment to make sure they would do everything they could to ensure that Metropolitan Cemetery would be forever.

---

[1.] The situation reminded Clyde of the problem that had been posed to a class when he was in school: If you go half way across the road, and then half the remaining distance, and then half the remaining distance, etc., when will you get across the road?

[2.] California requires that the endowment care fund contribution be listed separately from the property price.

Forest Lawn Memorial-Park Association

*Figure 13–5 An actor portraying Abraham Lincoln as part of Forest Lawn's Living History Programs discusses Lincoln's life with school children.*

# 14 Meeting The Challenge
The job is never done

THE PERMANENCE of cemeteries produces many challenges. Sometimes, the simultaneous demands from the past, present, and future create conflicts. These needs often compete for the attention of management and allocation of whatever resources are available.

The demands from the past stem from the history or heritage a cemetery represents. Cemeteries are the sacred repositories of the mortal remains of loved ones, relatives never met, and the memories of generations gone before.

For cemeteries to remain places that honor the memories of the past, they must be well run and well maintained in the present. Because cemeteries deal with consumers at the time of loss, when grief is new and raw, the expectations for cemeteries' business practices are higher than for those of other kinds of enterprises. Communities view the way cemeteries currently are maintained as a reflection of how much honor is given the past. Hence, families measure the respect given their loved ones by the way cemeteries are maintained and operated.

Cemeteries cannot escape concern for the future. Because cemeteries tend to stay cemeteries forever, it is good business practice, and the fulfillment of a moral obligation, for a cemetery to concern itself with how it will fare in the future. Managers and directors must concern themselves with the cemetery's active economic life as well as what will happen when the cemetery is virtually sold out. There are two major elements to this—planning for the future and building an adequate endowment care fund.

Planning for the future and building the endowment care fund are related activities as demonstrated in the Metropolitan Cemetery Case in Chapter 13. Cemetery master planning is essential. It is easy to continue developing based on intuition and ease, but it is far better to develop based on sound planning, taking into account all the needs of the cemetery. In order to be financially successful during its active selling life, a cemetery must have well thought out strategies. It also must have a vision of the distant future as well as a strategy to achieve that vision if it is to remain a valuable asset to the community long after the last burial is made.

## Community Asset

Cemeteries are community assets because of their links to the history and culture of a community, their long-term nature, and the position of trust they hold with society. Each of these factors underscores the importance of the cemetery's image which is key to its financial success as well as to its long-term stature. Consequently, maintaining a positive image is an important responsibility for each cemetery manager.

To some extent, this challenge is a public relations issue. Keeping a cemetery in the public's awareness is a way to foster the image of the cemetery as an asset to the community. There are many ways individual cemeteries do this: public programs, general advertising, support of community organizations, property owner newsletters, free use of facilities to community groups, concerts, and so on. The list is as broad as management's imagination.

Involvement in the community can be effective; however, it only helps support an image that is based upon a sound foundation. Since cemeteries deal with a sensitive subject— burial of loved ones—they will maintain a positive image only

Courtesy of Allegheny Cemetery

*Figure 14-1 Memorial Day parade at Allegheny Cemetery, Pittsburgh, Pennsylvania.*

as long as their operations are based on high principles. A cemetery is expected to act ethically and should go the "extra mile" to treat everyone fairly. As a community institution, regardless of the legal status of ownership, a cemetery is held to higher standards when dealing with consumers. Recognition of this fact, before problems occur, is essential to maintaining its image.

The public is as disgusted with unethical conduct by cemeteries as it is with dishonest clergy or politicians. The cemetery manager's challenge is to maintain an extraordinary level of integrity for the cemetery, as it is far easier to keep a reputation than it is to rebuild a lost or tarnished one. Here, the challenge is not only to have the individual manager act with integrity but to have everyone in the organization embrace the spirit of high ethics.

## Finite Life

It is crucial for a cemetery to have a long-term vision and commitment. Although a cemetery does have a finite life—there is only so much dedicated ground that can be sold—it has a very long life. Not only is the cemetery going to be around for quite a long time, it is almost impossible to do anything with land where burials have been made. Even when it is possible to use the unsold land for other purposes, the process of removing the cemetery dedication can be cumbersome.

Recognizing the fact that a cemetery's sales life is finite is crucial to the premise that a cemetery should be forever. Only with a great deal of care, planning, and discipline can a cemetery maintain itself in the distant future with the income from its endowment care fund.

The challenge of finite life is multi-faceted. Cemeteries must meet the day-to-day challenge of running a successful business—meeting payroll, covering other expenses, and doing what is necessary to fulfill the individual cemetery's definition of success. In the long-term cemeteries are challenged with running a business that has a finite sales life—making sure that land use is optimized and having a variety of products to sell to meet consumers' desires as well as the cemetery's economic interests. Thus, long-range financial planning for the endowment care fund is essential for ensuring care of the cemetery after the end of its sales life. The dichotomy of a finite sales life and the intent of lasting forever are the unique challenges presented by a cemetery, resulting in obligations to the owners of the cemetery, the cemetery as a place, lot owners, families of those interred, and to the community.

The limited sales life of a cemetery creates a set of challenges that must be addressed in the present even though the results won't be known until some time in the distant future. The challenge to directors and managers is be good stewards of the cemetery—to achieve immediate goals and to have the vision and courage to protect the future.

## Failure

This book is titled *A Cemetery Should Be Forever*, because it is possible that some cemeteries may not last forever. There can be many reasons for this, some foreseeable, some not. When a cemetery does cease to exist, it surely has failed. However, like many things in life, failure may only be relative. Some cemeteries have ceased to be cemeteries in the sense that they have been forgotten or abandoned. No more burials are made, and no one cares for the area. However, the ground is still a cemetery, because it has burials. As I was in the final stages of writing this book, an article appeared in the *Los Angeles Times*, telling the story of a developer who found six interments, including "disintegrating coffins," near Tehachapi, California. Old timers in the area speculated that early settlers had made the burials in a family cemetery. This was a forgotten cemetery, perhaps not unlike burial grounds of native Americans.

Other cemeteries have ceased to be cemeteries for other reasons, one of which is business failure. Some of these cemeteries existed more recently and even were subject to state regulations. Nevertheless, they failed, because they didn't work economically—they couldn't produce an adequate sales volume to pay the current expenses, and they didn't have adequate endowment care funds to take care of what had been sold.

What happens to these cemeteries varies greatly. One such cemetery located in Whittier, California, was transformed into what the state calls a "pioneer cemetery"—the memorials were all removed and it became a park. In another, Home of Peace in Los Angeles, the state seized what little there was of the endowment care fund, and no one is sure what to do with it. (Fans of the "Quincy" television program may recognize this as the inspiration for the episode about the cemetery where caskets were washing out of the hillside.)

One of these failed cemeteries became a public park. The individual memorials that marked the lives of those interred there were gone, but at least it wasn't entirely neglected and abandoned. The other cemetery is an unresolved dilemma. Although the state seized it, the state doesn't have the money to maintain it, and the local government doesn't want to take on the liability, either. It's in limbo.

Although these two examples are located in Southern California, the issues are not unique—failure can happen anywhere. Cemeteries with similar problems date back to colonial times when no one thought of endowment care funds and the cemetery's future care. Cemeteries of all types have failed—for-profit, not-for-profit, and those owned by religious orders. No cemetery of any type or age has a monopoly on the potential for failure. Fortunately, cemetery failure has been an infrequent occurrence.

Perhaps, it can be argued that the notion of "once a cemetery, always a cemetery" is a product of the twentieth century. I don't accept that, because I believe humans always have tried to treat burial places with dignity. Despite our focus on technology, I believe that society has a growing appreciation of the past, and that respect for cemeteries is part of that appreciation. And, it is our respect for cemeteries that makes us so uncertain about what to do when they fail. We want to respect these final resting-places, yet we also recognize that part of capitalism in the United States is the freedom to fail. We just haven't found a good way to reconcile these two positions.

## A Cemetery Should Be Forever

After years of exposure to cemeteries and those who operate them, I continue to find them interesting on many levels and for many reasons. I have a great respect for those who run cemeteries. As a group they are people who understand the unique aspects of cemeteries and the special obligations of cemeteries. It is hard to spend time with these people and not be left with the impression that this group wants to do the right thing. They are caring conscientious people.

While cemeteries appear to be simple businesses on the surface, increased understanding of cemeteries makes one aware of their complexity. They have the same financial pressures in the short-term as most businesses, but they also have some unique long-term challenges.

Due to their finite nature, cemeteries present a planning challenge. The objective is to plan well and to have inventory remain balanced for as long as possible—hopefully, until the end of the cemetery's sales life.

A cemetery's endowment care fund is its financial commitment to its future care. Over time, these funds must grow to meet the maintenance needs of the sold out cemetery. It is essential to collect enough money as sales are made and to invest the funds wisely, so the purchasing power will grow and keep pace with increases in maintenance expenses.

In spite of all of the interesting and challenging aspects of cemeteries, I have a growing appreciation of their importance as institutions. The family of each person buried in a cemetery has an emotional tie to that cemetery. This is true no matter how many generations go by. As the ICFA says, cemeteries are the "guardians of our heritage."

In *The Comemoral*, Hubert Eaton's first chapter—"Who Wants To Be Forgotten?"—describes the "why" of cemeteries as the "memorial impulse." This desire to remember or be remembered has evidenced itself in history as well as in art and architecture. In fact, the world is replete with structures and artworks conceived for this purpose. Consider the Egyptian pyramids, the Taj Mahal, universities, libraries, and public buildings dedicated to individuals, not to mention the countless thousands of individual interment spaces in cemeteries. The answer to Eaton's question "Who wants to be forgotten?" is: no one.

Cemeteries provide their communities with continuity. They furnish us with a link to the past while providing a frame of reference for understanding the mystery of life. Unfortunately, when a cemetery falls into disrepair or is abandoned, memories are damaged—some only bruised, others lost forever. This fading or disappearance of cherished memories is a tragedy.

In a world of change and turmoil, cemeteries give us a place to pause and reflect and a place where we feel connected not only with our pasts but also with the pasts of others. Even though some were famous and some just ordinary, they all, like us, lived on this earth at some point and time.

However, cemeteries are not just a place to reflect on the past. They remind us to keep the present in perspective. As we seek meaning in our lives, cemeteries are an appropriate place for contemplation. They can reinforce religious beliefs, stimulate a sense of the spiritual, or be a place to discover new visions of the meaning of life.

To be all of these things, a cemetery should be forever.

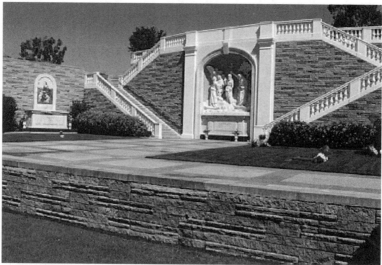

Forest Lawn Memorial-Park Association

*Figure 14–2 Forecourt to Triumphant Faith Terraces, Forest Lawn–Glendale.*

# Funeral Trade Rule
Federal Trade Commission

Code of Federal Regulations
*Title 16—Commercial Practices*
*Chapter 1—Federal Trade Commission*
*Subchapter D—Trade Regulation Rules*
*Part 453—Funeral Industry Practices*

## 453.1. Definitions.

(a) **Alternative container.** An "alternative container" is an unfinished wood box or other non-metal receptacle or enclosure, without ornamentation or a fixed interior lining, which is designed for the encasement of human remains and which is made of fiberboard, pressed-wood, composition materials (with or without an outside covering) or like materials.

(b) **Cash advance item.** A "cash advance item" is any item of service or merchandise described to a purchaser as a "cash advance," "accommodation," "cash disbursement," or similar term. A cash advance item is also any item obtained from a third party and paid for by the funeral provider on the purchaser's behalf. Cash advance items may include, but are not limited to: cemetery or crematory services; pallbearers; public transportation; clergy honoraria; flowers; musicians or singers; nurses; obituary notices; gratuities and death certificates.

(c) **Casket.** A "casket" is a rigid container which is designed for the encasement of human remains and which is usually constructed of wood, metal, fiberglass, plastic, or like material, and ornamented and lined with fabric.

(d) **Commission.** "Commission" refers to the Federal Trade Commission.

(e) **Cremation.** "Cremation" is a heating process which incinerates human remains.

(f) **Crematory.** A "crematory" is any person, partnership or corporation that performs cremation and sells funeral goods.

(g) **Direct cremation.** A "direct cremation" is a disposition of human remains by cremation, without formal viewing, visitation, or ceremony with the body present.

(h) **Funeral goods.** "Funeral goods" are the goods which are sold or offered for sale directly to the public for use in connection with funeral services.

(I) **Funeral provider.** A "funeral provider" is any person, partnership or corporation that sells or offers to sell funeral goods and funeral services to the public.

(j) **Funeral services.** "Funeral services" are any services which may be used to :

(1) Care for and prepare deceased human bodies for burial, cremation or other final disposition; and

(2) Arrange, supervise or conduct the funeral ceremony or the final disposition of deceased human bodies.

(k) **Immediate burial.** An "immediate burial" is a disposition of human remains by burial, without formal viewing, visitation, or ceremony with the body present, except for a graveside service.

(l) **Memorial service.** A "memorial service" is a ceremony commemorating the deceased without the body present.

(m) **Funeral ceremony.** A "funeral ceremony" is a service commemorating the deceased with the body present.

(n) **Outer burial container.** An "outer burial container" is any container which is designed for placement in the grave around the casket including, but not limited to, containers commonly known as burial vaults, grave boxes, and grave liners.

(o) **Person.** A "person" is any individual, partnership, corporation, association, government or governmental subdivision or agency, or other entity.

(p) **Services of funeral director and staff.** The "services of funeral director and staff" are the basic services, not to be included in prices of other categories in §453.2 (b) (4), that are furnished by a funeral provider in arranging any funeral, such as conducting the arrangements conference, planning the funeral, obtaining necessary permits, and placing obituary notices.

**453.2 Price disclosures.**

(a) Unfair or deceptive acts or practices. In selling or offering to sell funeral goods or funeral services to the public, it is an unfair or deceptive act or practice for a funeral provider to fail to furnish accurate price information disclosing the cost to the purchaser for each of the specific funeral goods and funeral services used in connection with the disposition of deceased human bodies, including at least the price of embalming, transportation of remains, use of facilities, caskets, outer burial containers, immediate burials, or direct cremations, to persons inquiring about the purchase of funerals. Any funeral provider who complies with the preventive requirements in paragraph (b) of this section is not engaged in the unfair or deceptive acts or practices defined here.

(b) Preventive requirements. To prevent these unfair or deceptive acts or practices, as well as the unfair or deceptive acts or practices defined in §453.4(b)(1), funeral providers must:

(1) Telephone price disclosure. Tell persons who ask by telephone about the funeral provider's offerings or prices any accurate information from the price lists described in paragraphs (b)(2) through (4) of this section and any other readily available information that reasonably answers the question.

(2) Casket price list.

(i) Give a printed or typewritten price list to people who inquire in person about the offerings or prices of caskets or alternative containers. The funeral provider must offer the list upon beginning discussion of, but in any event before showing caskets. The list must contain at least the retail prices of all caskets and alternative containers offered which do not require special ordering, enough information to identify each, and the effective date for the price list. In lieu of a written list, other formats, such as notebooks, brochures, or charts may be used if they contain the same information as would the printed or typewritten list, and display it in a clear and conspicuous manner. Provided, however, that funeral providers do not have to make a casket price list available if the funeral providers place on the general price list, specified in paragraph (b)(4) of this section, the information required by this paragraph.

(ii) Place on the list, however produced, the name of the funeral provider's place of business and a location describing the list as a "casket price list."

(3) Outer burial container price list.

(i) Give a printed or typewritten price list to persons who inquire in person about outer burial container offerings or prices. The funeral provider must offer the list upon beginning discussion of, but in any event before showing the containers. The list must contain at least the retail prices of all outer burial containers offered which do not require special ordering, enough information to identify each container, and the effective date for the prices listed. In lieu of a written list, the funeral provider may use other formats, such as notebooks, brochures, or charts, if they contain the same information as the printed or typewritten list, and display it in a clear and conspicuous manner. Provided, however, that funeral providers do not have to make an outer burial container price list available if the funeral providers place on the general price list, specified in paragraph (b)(4) of this section, the information required by this paragraph.

(ii) Place on the list, however produced, the name of the funeral provider's place of business and a caption describing the list as an "outer burial container price list."

(4) General price list.

(i) (A) Give a printed or typewritten price list for retention to persons who inquire in person about the funeral goods, funeral services or prices of funeral goods or services offered by the funeral provider. The funeral provider must give the list upon beginning discussion of any of the following:

(1) The prices of funeral goods or funeral services;

(2) The overall type of funeral service or disposition; or

(3) Specify funeral goods or funeral services offered by the funeral provider.

(B) The requirement in paragraph (b)(4)( i)(A) of this section applies whether the discussion takes place in the funeral home or elsewhere. Provided, however, that when the deceased is removed for transportation to the funeral home, an in-person request at that time for authorization to embalm, required by §453.5(a)(2), does not, by itself, trigger the requirement to offer the general price list if the provider in seeking prior embalming approval discloses that embalming is not required by law except in certain special cases, if any. Any other discussion during that time about prices or the selection of funeral goods or services triggers the requirement under paragraph (b)(4)(i)(A) of this section to give consumers a general price list.

(C) The list required in paragraph (b)(4)(i)(A) of this section must contain at least the following information:

(1) The name, address, and telephone number of the funeral provider's place of business;

(2) A caption describing the list as a "general price list"; and

(3) The effective date for the price list;

(ii) Include on the price list, in any order, the retail prices (expressed either as the flat fee, or as the price per hour, mile or other unit of computation) and the other information specified below for at least each of the following items, if offered for sale:

(A) Forwarding of remains to another funeral home, together with a list of the services provided for any quoted price;

(B) Receiving remains from another funeral home, together with a list of the services provided for any quoted price;

(C) The price range for the direct cremations offered by the funeral provider, together with:

(1) A separate price for a direct cremation where the purchaser provides the container;

(2) Separate prices for each direct cremation offered including an alternative container; and

(3) A description of the services and container (where applicable), included in each price;

(D) The price range for the immediate burials offered by the funeral provider, together with:

(1) A separate price for an immediate burial where the purchaser provides the casket:

(2) Separate prices for each immediate burial offered including a casket or alternative container; and

(3) A description of the services and container (where applicable) included in that price;

(E) Transfer of remains to funeral home;

(F) Embalming;

(G)  Other preparation of the body;

(H) Use of facilities and staff for viewing;

(I)  Use of facilities and staff for funeral ceremony;

(J)  Use of facilities and staff for memorial service;

(K) Use of equipment and staff for graveside service;

(L) Hearse; and

(M) Limousine.

(iii) Include on the price list, in any order, the following information:

(A) Either of the following:

(1) The price range for the caskets offered by the funeral provider, together with the statement: "A complete price list

will be provided at the funeral home"; or

(2) The prices of individual caskets, disclosed in the manner specified by the paragraph (b)(2)(i) of this section; and

(B) Either of the following:

(1) The price range for the outer burial containers offered by the funeral provider, together with the statement: " A complete price list will be proved at the funeral home" or

(2) The prices of individual outer burial containers, disclosed in the manner specified by paragraph (b)(3)(i) of this section; and

(C) Either of the following:

(1) The price for the basic services of funeral director and staff, together with a list of the principal basic services provided for any quoted price and, if the charge cannot be declined by the purchaser, the statement: "This fee for our basic services will be added to the total cost of the funeral arrangements you select. (This fee is already included in our charges for direct cremations, immediate burials, and forwarding or receiving remains.)" If the charge cannot be declined by the purchaser, the quoted price shall include all charges for the recovery of unallocated funeral provider overhead, and funeral providers may include in the required disclosure the phrase "and overhead" after the word "services"; or

(2) The following statement: "Please note that a fee of (specify dollar amount) for the use of our basic services is included in the price of our caskets. This same fee shall be added to the total cost of your funeral arrangements if you provide the casket. Our services include (specify)." The fee shall include all charges for the recovery of unallocated funeral provider overhead, and funeral providers may include in the required disclosure the phrase "and overhead" after the word "services." The statement must be placed on the general price list together with the casket price range, required by paragraph (b)(4)(iii)(A)(1) of this section, or together with the prices of individual caskets, required by (b)(4)(iii)(A)(2) of this section.

(iv) The services fee permitted by §453.2(b)(4)(iii)(C) (1) or (2) is the only funeral provider fee for services, facilities or unallocated overhead permitted by this part to be non-declinable, unless otherwise required by law.

(5) Statement of funeral goods and services selected.

(i) Give an itemized written statement for retention to each person who arranges a funeral or other disposition of human remains, at the conclusion of the discussion of arrangements. The statement must list at least the following information:

(A) The funeral goods and funeral services selected by that person and the prices to be paid for each of them;

(B) Specifically itemized cash advance items. (These prices must be given to the extent then known or reasonably ascertainable. If the prices are not known or reasonably ascertainable, a good faith estimate shall be given and a written statement of the actual charges shall be provided before the final bill is paid.); and

(C) The total cost of the goods and services selected.

(ii) The information required by this paragraph (b)(5) may be included on any contract, statement, or other document which the funeral provider would otherwise provide at the conclusion of discussion of arrangements.

(6) Other pricing methods. Funeral providers may give persons any other price information, in any other format, in addition to that required by §453.2(b)(2), (3), and (4) so long as the statement required by §453.2(b)(5) is given when required by the rule.

**453.3 Misrepresentations.**

(a) Embalming provisions.

(1) Deceptive acts or practices. In selling or offering to sell funeral goods or funeral services to the public, it is a deceptive act or practice for a funeral provider to:

(i) Represent that state or local law requires that a deceased person be embalmed when such is not the case;

(ii) Fail to disclose that embalming is not required by law except in certain special cases, if any.

(2) Preventive requirements. To prevent these deceptive acts or practices, as well as the unfair or deceptive acts or practices defined in §§453.4(b)(1) and 453.5(2), funeral providers must:

(i) Not represent that a deceased person is required to be embalmed for:

(A) Direct cremation;

(B) Immediate burial; or

(C) A closed casket funeral without viewing or visitation when refrigeration is available and when state or local law does not require embalming; and

(ii) Place the following disclosure on the general price list, required by §453.2(b)(4), in immediate conjunction with the price shown for embalming: "Except in certain special cases, embalming is not required by law. Embalming may be necessary, however, if you select certain funeral arrangements, such as a funeral with viewing. If you do not want embalming, you usually have the right to choose an arrangement that does not require you to pay for it, such as direct cremation or immediate burial." The phrase "except in certain special cases" need not be included in this disclosure if state or local law in the area(s) where the provider does business does not require embalming under any circumstances.

(b) Casket for cremation provisions

(1) Deceptive acts or practices. In selling or offering to sell funeral goods or funeral services to the public, it is a deceptive act or practice for a funeral provider to:

(i) Represent that state or local law requires a casket for direct cremations;

(ii) Represent that a casket is required for direct cremations.

(2) Preventive requirements. To prevent these deceptive acts or practices, as well as the unfair or deceptive acts or practices defined in §453.4(a)(1), funeral providers must place the following disclosure in immediate conjunction with the price range shown for direct cremations: "If you want to arrange a direct cremation, you can use an alternative container. Alternative containers encase the body and can be made of materials like fiberboard or composition materials (with or without an outside covering). The containers we provide are (specify containers)." This disclosure only has to be placed on the general price list if the funeral provider arranges direct cremations.

(c) Outer burial container provision

(1) Deceptive acts or practices. In selling or offering to sell funeral goods and funeral services to the public, it is a deceptive act or practice for a funeral provider to:

(i) Represent that state or local laws or regulations, or particular cemeteries, require outer burial containers when such is not the case;

(ii) Fail to disclose to persons arranging funerals that state law does not require the purchase of an outer burial container.

(2) Preventive requirement. To prevent these deceptive acts or practices, funeral providers must place the following disclosure on the outer burial container price list, required by §453.2(b)(3)(I), or, if the prices of outer burial containers are listed on the general price list, required by §453.2(b)(4), in immediate conjunction with those prices: "In most areas of the country, state or local law does not require that you buy a container to surround the casket in the grave. However, many cemeteries require that you have such a container so

that the grave will not sink in. Either a grave liner or a burial vault will satisfy these requirements." The phrase "in most areas of the country" need not be included in this disclosure if state or local law in the area(s) where the provider does business does not require a container to surround the casket in the grave.

(d) General provisions on legal and cemetery requirements

(1) Deceptive acts or practices. In selling or offering to sell funeral goods or funeral services to the public, it is a deceptive act or practice for funeral providers to represent that federal, state, or local laws, or particular cemeteries or crematories, require the purchase of any funeral goods or funeral services when such is not the case.

(2) Preventive requirements. To prevent these deceptive acts or practices, as well as the deceptive acts or practices identified in §§453.3(a)(1), 453.3(b)(1), and 453.3(c)(1), funeral providers must identify and briefly describe in writing on the statement of funeral goods and services selected (required by §453.2(b)(5)) any legal, cemetery, or crematory requirement which the funeral provider represents to persons as compelling the purchase of funeral goods or funeral services for the funeral which that person is arranging.

(e) Provisions on preservative and protective value claims. In selling or offering to sell funeral goods or funeral services to the public, it is a deceptive act or practice for a funeral provider to:

(1) Represent that funeral goods or funeral services will delay the natural decomposition of human remains for a long-term or indefinite time;

(2) Represent that funeral goods have protective features or will protect the body from gravesite substances, when such is not the case.

(f) Cash advance provisions

(1) Deceptive acts or practices. In selling or offering to sell funeral goods or funeral services to the public, it is a deceptive act or practice for a funeral provider to:

(i) Represent that the price charged for a cash advance item is the same as the cost to the funeral provider for the item when such is not the case;

(ii) Fail to disclose to persons arranging funerals that the price being charged for a cash advance item is not the same as the cost to the funeral provider for the item when such is the case.

(2) Preventive requirements. To prevent these deceptive acts or practices, funeral providers must place the following sentence in the itemized statement of funeral goods and services selected, in

immediate conjunction with the list of itemized cash advance items required by §453.2(b)(5)(i)(B): "We charge you for our services in obtaining: (specify cash advance items)," if the funeral provider makes a charge upon, or receives and retains a rebate, commission or trade or volume discount upon a case advance item.

**453.4 Required purchase of funeral goods or funeral services.**

(a) Casket for cremation provisions

(1) Unfair or deceptive acts or practices. In selling or offering to sell funeral goods or funeral services to the public, it is an unfair or deceptive act or practice for a funeral provider, or a crematory, to require that a casket be purchased for direct cremation.

(2) Preventive requirement. To prevent this unfair or deceptive act or practice, funeral providers must make an alternative container available for direct cremations, if they arrange direct cremations.

(b) Other required purchases of funeral goods or funeral services

(1) Unfair or deceptive acts or practices. In selling or offering to sell funeral goods or funeral services, it is an unfair or deceptive act or practice for a funeral provider to:

(i) Condition the furnishing of any funeral good or funeral service to a person arranging a funeral upon the purchase of any other funeral good or funeral service, except as required by law or as otherwise permitted by this part;

(ii) Charge any fee as a condition to furnishing any funeral goods or funeral services to a person arranging a funeral, other than the fees for: (1) Services of funeral director and staff, permitted by §453.2(b)(4)(iii)(C); (2) other funeral services and funeral goods selected by the purchaser; and (3) other funeral goods or services required to be purchased, as explained on the itemized statement in accordance with §453.3(d)(2).

(2) Preventive requirements.

(i) To prevent these unfair or deceptive acts or practices, funeral providers must:

(A) Place the following disclosure in the general price list, immediately above the prices required by §453.2(b)(4)(ii) and (iii): "The goods and services shown below are those we can provide to our customers. You may choose only the items you desire. If legal or other requirements mean you must buy any items you did not specifically ask for, we will explain the reason in writing on the statement we provide describing the funeral goods and services you selected." Provided, however, that if the charge for "services of funeral director and staff" cannot be declined by the purchaser, the statement shall include the sentence: "However, any funeral arrangements you select will include a charge for our basic services" between the second and third sentences of the statement specified above herein. The statement may include the phrase "and overhead" after the word "services" if the fee includes a charge for the recovery of unallocated funeral provider overhead;

(B) Place the following disclosure in the statement of funeral goods and services selected, required by §453.2(b)(5)(i): "Charges are only for those items that you selected or that are required. If we are required by law or by a cemetery or crematory to use any items, we will explain the reasons in writing below."

(ii) A funeral provider shall not violate this section by failing to comply with a request for a combination of goods or services which would be impossible, impractical, or excessively burdensome to provide.

## 453.5 Services provided without prior approval.

(a) Unfair or deceptive acts or practices. In selling or offering to sell funeral goods or funeral services to the public, it is an unfair or deceptive act or practice for any provider to embalm a deceased human body for a fee unless:

(1) State or local law or regulation requires embalming in the particular circumstances regardless of any funeral choice which the family might make; or

(2) Prior approval for embalming (expressly so described) has been obtained from a family member or other authorized person; or

(3) The funeral provider is unable to contact a family member or other authorized person after exercising due diligence, has no reason to believe the family does not want embalming performed, and obtains subsequent approval for embalming already performed (expressly so described). In seeking approval, the funeral provider must disclose that a fee will be charged if the family selects a funeral which requires embalming, such as a funeral with viewing, and that no fee will be charged if the family selects a service which does not require embalming, such as direct cremation or immediate burial.

(b) Preventive requirement. To prevent these unfair or deceptive acts or practices, funeral providers must include on the itemized statement of funeral goods and services selected, required by §453.2(b)(5), the statement: "If you selected a funeral that may require embalming, such as a funeral with viewing, you may have to pay for embalming. You do not have to pay for embalming you did not approve if you selected arrangements such as a direct cremation or immediate burial. If we charged for embalming, we will explain why below."

**453.6 Retention of documents.** To prevent the unfair or deceptive acts or practices specified in §453.2 and §453.3 of this rule, funeral providers must retain and make available for inspection by Commission officials true and accurate copies of the price lists specified in §§453.2(b)(2) through (4), as applicable, for at least one year after the date of their last distribution to customers, and a copy of each statement of funeral goods and services selected, as required by §453.2(b)(5) for at least one year from the date of the arrangements conference.

**453.7 Comprehension of disclosures.** To prevent the unfair or deceptive acts or practices specified in §453.2 through §453.5, funeral providers must make all disclosures required by those sections in a clear and conspicuous manner. Providers shall not include in the casket, outer burial container, and general price lists, required by §453.2(b)(2)-(4), any statement or information that alters or contradicts the information required by this Part to be included in those lists.

**453.8 Declaration of intent.**

(a) Except as otherwise provided in §453.2(a), it is a violation of this rule to engage in any unfair or deceptive acts or practices specified in this rule, or to fail to comply with any of the preventive requirements specified in this rule;

(b) The provisions of this rule are separate and severable from one another. If any provision is determined to be invalid, it is the Commission's intention that the remaining provisions shall continue in effect.

(c) This rule shall not apply to the business of insurance or to acts in the conduct thereof.

**453.9 State exemptions.** If, upon application to the Commission by an appropriate state agency, the Commission determines that:

(a) There is a state requirement in effect which applies to any transaction to which this rule applies; and

(b) That state requirement affords an overall level of protection to consumers which is as great as, or greater than, the protection afforded by this rule; then the Commission's rule will not be in effect in that state to the extent specified by the commission in its determination, for as long as the State administers and enforces effectively the state requirement.

# B State Rules
Summary of selected laws and regulations

In 1996 the ICFA surveyed cemetery laws and regulations by state. Although the responses were not as complete as desired, it is the best available compilation on the subject. The following pages are excerpted from that survey and are included in this book by the courtesy of the ICFA. No independent verification was made of the responses by ICFA or the author. Also, this is not intended to cover all laws and regulations that may apply within a state. Laws and regulations change frequently, so action should not be taken without researching current laws and regulations as well as consulting with an attorney when appropriate.

The following comments explain the column headings of the charts:

1.  "*" Responses obtained by ICFA from state regulatory agency. A blank indicates no response.

2.  "**" See notes at end of chapter.

3.  *For Profits Permitted.* May cemeteries be owned by for-profit organizations?

4.  *Property Taxes.* Are property taxes assessed on *undeveloped* property? *Developed* property? Sold interment property (*graves*)?

5.  *Can Sell.* Are cemeteries allowed to sell *monuments*? *Memorials*? *Vaults*?

6.  *Mortuary.* Can a cemetery *own/operate* a mortuary? Can a mortuary be built and operated *on cemetery grounds* (dedicated)?

7. *Reclaim "Abandoned" lots*: Is there a statutory provision for the cemetery taking back previously sold lots that have not been used? I have a philosophical objection to this, but as can be seen from the table, some states do allow this.

8. *Sell Caskets & Other Funeral Merchandise.* Can a cemetery sell caskets and other funeral merchandise without an additional license (e.g. funeral directors license)?

9. *Sales Personnel.*
   a) *Licensed*: is a license required?
   b) *As Real Estate Agent*: Are cemetery sales people licensed as real estate agents?
   c) *Solicitation Restriction*: Are there statutory restrictions on who, where, or how the salespeople can solicit?

10. *Preneed Contract Cancellation*: Does state law have a specific provision for cancellation of preneed contracts? This is in addition to the three day "cooling off" period mandated by the Federal Trade Commission.

11. *Endowment Care Trust*:
    a) *Lot, Crypt, Niche*: What is the minimum amount required to be put into the endowment care fund from each sale of these types of property.
    b) *New Cemetery*: How much must be put into an endowment care fund as part of the process of establishing a new cemetery?
    c) *"Care" Defined*: Does the law define what is included in the way of maintenance under the "care" in endowment care?

12. *Amount for Cemetery Merchandise.* The amount that must be put in trust from the preneed sale of cemetery merchandise.

13. *Amount for Cemetery Services.* The amount that must be put in trust from the preneed sale of cemetery services.

14. *Master Trust.* Does the state allow different sellers to combine their merchandise trusts into a "master trust?"

15. *Finance Charges.* Can the seller charge for a time payment sale of preneed merchandise or services?

16. *Constructive Delivery.* Can the seller make constructive delivery of the merchandise to avoid putting money in trust?

17. *Irrevocable Trusts.* Can the amount placed in trust from the sale of preneed services or merchandise be held in an irrevocable trust to protect it from creditors or to qualify for government assistance program?

18. *Excessive Earnings Withdrawal.* Can funds be withdrawn from the merchandise/service trust if the amount exceeds what is required under some specified formula?

19. *Interest Earnings Withdrawal.* Is the seller entitled to take the interest earnings from the trust fund as received?

20. *Restrictions on Trust Investments.* Does the state limit what the trust can use for investments?

21. *Can Cemetery Sell Funeral Insurance.* Can cemeteries sell funeral insurance without a funeral home license?

22. *Licensing Requirements.* What license(s) is required to sell funeral insurance?

23. *Restrictions on Selling Insurance.* General comments about restrictions on selling insurance.

24. *Preconstructed Property:*
    a) *Trust:* Must the proceeds of sales of property that hasn't been built be put in a trust?
    b) *Deadlines:* Is there a prescribed time period when the preconstructed property must be built after it is sold?
    c) *Alternative to Trust:* Is there a requirement for performance guarantee other than trusting or an alternative to trusting?

---

**CAUTION!**

This information is provided to show the range of state laws and regulations concerning cemeteries. It was developed from questionnaires sent in by respondents and no verification was made of accuracy. Other factors which may affect accuracy include details which are not shown and changes in state law or regulations. Current and complete information, including consultation with legal counsel, should be sought before taking any action regarding laws or regulations.

| State | For-profits Permitted | Property Tax | | | Can Sell | | | Mortuary | |
|---|---|---|---|---|---|---|---|---|---|
| | | Undeveloped | Developed | Graves | Monuments | Memorials | Vaults | Own/Operate | On Cemetery Grounds |
| AL | Yes | Yes | - | - | Yes | Yes | Yes | Yes | Yes |
| AK | ** | - | - | - | - | - | - | - | - |
| AR* | Yes | Yes | Yes | - | Yes | Yes | Yes | Yes | Yes |
| AZ* | Yes | - | - | Yes | Yes | Yes | Yes | Yes | Yes |
| CA* | n/a | - | - | - | Yes | Yes | Yes | Yes | Yes |
| CO | Yes | - | - | - | Yes | Yes | Yes | Yes | Yes |
| CT | No | No | No | No | Yes | Yes | Yes | Yes | No |
| DE* | - | - | - | - | Yes | Yes | Yes | - | - |
| DC | - | - | - | - | - | - | - | - | - |
| FL | Yes | Yes | Yes | Yes | Yes | Yes | Yes | Yes | Yes |
| GA | Yes | - | - | - | Yes | Yes | Yes | Yes | Yes |
| HI | Yes | Yes | - | - | Yes | Yes | Yes | Yes | Yes |
| ID* | Yes | Yes | | Yes | | Yes | Yes | Yes | Yes |
| IL* | Yes | - | - | - | Yes | Yes | Yes | Yes | Yes |
| IN | Yes | Yes | No | No | Yes | Yes | Yes | Yes | Yes |
| IA* | Yes | - | - | - | Yes | Yes | Yes | Yes | Yes |
| KS* | Yes | - | - | - | Yes | Yes | Yes | Yes | Yes |
| KY* | Yes | - | - | - | Yes | Yes | Yes | Yes | Yes |
| LA | Yes | - | - | - | Yes | Yes | Yes | Yes | Yes |
| MD* | Yes | Yes | Yes | Yes | Yes | Yes | Yes | No | - |
| MA | No | No | No | No | No | No | Yes | No | - |
| ME | No | No | No | No | Yes | Yes | Yes | No | - |
| MI* | Yes | Yes | - | - | Yes | Yes | Yes | No | - |
| MN | Yes | Yes | No | No | Yes | Yes | Yes | Yes | Yes |
| MS | - | - | - | - | - | - | - | - | - |
| MO | Yes | - | - | - | Yes | Yes | Yes | Yes | Yes |

**For general information only. Not to be used for compliance.**

| State | For-profits Permitted | Property Tax | | | Can Sell | | | Mortuary | |
| | | Undeveloped | Developed | Graves | Monuments | Memorials | Vaults | Own/Operate | On Cemetery Grounds |
|---|---|---|---|---|---|---|---|---|---|
| MT | Yes | Yes | - | - | Yes | Yes | Yes | Yes | Yes |
| NE* | Yes | - | - | - | Yes | Yes | Yes | Yes | Yes |
| NV | Yes | No | No | No | Yes | Yes | Yes | Yes | Yes |
| NH | Yes | No | No | No | Yes | Yes | Yes | Yes | No |
| NJ | No | No | No | No | No | No | No | No | No |
| NM* | Yes | Yes | Yes | Yes | Yes | Yes | Yes | Yes | Yes |
| NY* | No | - | - | - | No | Yes | No | No | No |
| NC* | Yes | Yes | Yes | No | Yes | Yes | Yes | Yes | Yes |
| ND | - | - | - | - | - | - | - | - | - |
| OH | Yes | Yes | Yes | - | Yes | Yes | Yes | No | - |
| OK* | Yes | - | - | - | Yes | Yes | Yes | Yes | Yes |
| OR* | Yes | Yes | No | No | Yes | Yes | Yes | Yes | Yes |
| PA* | Yes | - | - | - | Yes | Yes | Yes | Yes | Yes |
| RI | Yes | Yes | Yes | Yes | Yes | Yes | - | No | - |
| SC | Yes | | No | No | Yes | Yes | Yes | Yes | Yes |
| SD | - | - | - | - | - | - | - | - | - |
| TN | - | - | - | - | - | - | - | - | - |
| TX* | Yes | Yes | Yes | No | Yes | Yes | s/note | Yes | Yes |
| UT | Yes | Yes | Yes | - | Yes | Yes | Yes | Yes | Yes |
| VT* | - | - | - | - | Yes | Yes | Yes | Yes | Yes |
| VA | Yes | Yes | Yes | Yes | Yes | Yes | Yes | Yes | Yes |
| WA* | Yes | Yes | - | - | Yes | Yes | Yes | Yes | Yes |
| WV | Yes | No | No | No | Yes | Yes | Yes | Yes | Yes |
| WI* | Yes | - | - | - | Yes | Yes | Yes | No | - |
| WY | ** | Yes | Yes | - | Yes | Yes | Yes | Yes | Yes |

**For general information only. Not to be used for compliance.**

| State | Reclaim "Abandoned Lots" | Sell Caskets & Other Funeral Merchandise | Sales Personnel | | | Preneed Contract Cancellation |
| | | | Licensed | As Real Estate Agents | Solicitation Restriction | |
|---|---|---|---|---|---|---|
| AL | No | No | No | No | No | Yes |
| AK | - | - | - | - | - | - |
| AR* | No | Yes | No | - | No | Yes |
| AZ* | No | Yes | Yes | - | Yes | - |
| CA* | No | Yes | Yes | No | No | Yes |
| CO | No | Yes | No | - | Yes | Yes |
| CT | Yes | Yes | No | No | No | Yes |
| DE* | - | Yes | - | - | No | - |
| DC | - | - | - | - | - | - |
| FL | Yes | Yes | Yes | No | No | Yes |
| GA | Yes | No | No | - | No | Yes |
| HI | No | Yes | No | - | - | Yes |
| ID* | No | Yes | Yes | No | No | Yes |
| IL* | Yes** | Yes | No | - | Yes | Yes |
| IN | No | Yes | No | - | Yes | Yes |
| IA* | Yes | Yes | Yes** | - | No | Yes |
| KS* | No | Yes | No | No | Yes | Yes |
| KY* | Yes | No | No | No | No | Yes |
| LA | No | No | No | - | No | No |
| MD* | No | Yes | No | - | No | Yes |
| MA | Yes | No | No | - | - | Yes |
| ME | Yes | Yes | No | - | Yes | Yes |
| MI* | Yes | Yes | No | - | Yes | Yes |
| MN | Yes | - | Yes | - | none | Yes |
| MS | - | - | - | - | - | - |
| MO | No | Yes | No | No | No | Yes |

**For general information only. Not to be used for compliance.**

| State | Reclaim "Abandoned Lots" | Sell Caskets & Other Funeral Merchandise | Sales Personnel | | | Preneed Contract Cancellation |
|---|---|---|---|---|---|---|
| | | | Licensed | As Real Estate Agents | Solicitation Restriction | |
| MT | No | Yes | No | - | No | No |
| NE* | - | Yes | Yes | n/a | Yes | Yes |
| NV | Yes | Yes | Yes | No | Yes | Yes |
| NH | Yes | Yes | No | - | No | Yes |
| NJ | Yes | No | Yes | No | No | No |
| NM* | No | Yes | - | - | Yes | Yes |
| NY* | Yes | No | No | No | No | Yes |
| NC* | No | No | Yes | No | Yes | Yes |
| ND | - | - | - | - | - | - |
| OH | No | No | Yes | Yes | No | Yes |
| OK* | No | No | No | - | No | No |
| OR* | Yes | Yes | Yes | No | Yes | Yes |
| PA* | No | Yes | Yes | No | No | Yes |
| RI | Yes | - | No | - | No | Yes |
| SC | No | No | No | - | Yes | No |
| SD | - | - | - | - | - | - |
| TN | - | - | - | - | - | - |
| TX* | No | No | No | No | Yes** | Yes |
| UT | Yes | No | Yes | No | No | Yes |
| VT* | - | Yes | No | No | Yes | Yes |
| VA | No | No | No | No | No | Yes |
| WA* | Yes | No | No | No | Yes | Yes |
| WV | No | Yes | No | - | No | No |
| WI* | Yes | Yes | Yes | No | No | Yes |
| WY | No | Yes | Yes | - | No | Yes |

**For general information only. Not to be used for compliance.**

| | | Endowment Care Trust | | | | |
|---|---|---|---|---|---|---|
| State | Lot | Crypt | Niche | New Cemetery | Special Regulations | "Care" Defined |
| AL | None | None | None | None | None | No |
| AK | - | - | - | - | - | - |
| AR* | 20% | $40 | $40 | None | - | Yes |
| AZ* | 2.75sf | $120 | $36 | $25,000 | - | Yes |
| CA* | 2.25sf | $110 | $35 | $35,000 | - | No |
| CO | 15% | 10% | 10% | n/a | - | Yes |
| CT | None | $100 | 10% | None | Yes | No |
| DE* | - | - | - | - | - | - |
| DC | - | - | - | - | - | - |
| FL | 10% | 10% | 10% | $50,000 | Yes | Yes |
| GA | 10% | 5% | 5% | $10,000 | - | No |
| HI | $20 | $20 | $20 | No | - | No |
| ID* | $10/10% | $25 | $5 | $50,000 | Yes | Yes |
| IL* | 15% | 10% | 10% | $7,500** | Yes | Yes |
| IN | 15% | 8% | $10 | $25,000 | - | Yes |
| IA* | 20% | 20% | 20% | $25,000 | - | Yes |
| KS* | 15% | 0 | 0 | $35,000 | - | No |
| KY* | 20% | 5% | 10% | - | 20,000 | No |
| LA | 10% | 10% | 10% | $25,000 | - | No |
| MD* | 10% | - | - | $25,000 | Yes | No |
| MA | - | - | - | - | - | - |
| ME | - | 30% | 30% | - | - | Yes |
| MI* | 15% | 15% | 15% | $25,000 | - | No |
| MN | 20% | 10% | 10% | None | None | No |
| MS | - | - | - | - | - | - |
| MO | 15% | 10% | 10% | $25,000 | Yes | Yes |

**For general information only. Not to be used for compliance.**

| State | Endowment Care Trust | | | New Cem- etery | Special Regulations | "Care" Defined |
|---|---|---|---|---|---|---|
| | Lot | Crypt | Niche | | | |
| MT | 15% | - | - | None | No | No |
| NE* | - | - | - | - | - | - |
| NV | 5% | 5% | 5% | - | - | No |
| NH | No | No | No | None | - | Yes |
| NJ | 15% | 10% | 10% | $25,000 | - | - |
| NM* | 25% | 10% | 10% | $25,000 | Yes | No |
| NY* | 10% | 10% | 10% | n/a | No | No |
| NC* | $40 | $40 | $40 | $50,000 | - | No |
| ND | - | - | - | - | - | - |
| OH | 10% | 10% | 10% | $50,000 | - | No |
| OK* | 10% | 10% | 10% | No | - | Yes |
| OR* | 15% | $15 | $5 | - | Yes | Yes |
| PA* | 15% | 15% | 15% | $25,000 | Yes | No |
| RI | 20% | 20% | 20% | No | No | Yes |
| SC | 10% | 5% | 10% | $15,000 | Yes | Yes |
| SD | - | - | - | - | - | - |
| TN | - | - | - | - | - | - |
| TX* | 10%** | 5%** | 10%** | $50,000 | Yes | Yes |
| UT | - | - | - | $50,000 | Yes | No |
| VT* | - | - | - | - | - | - |
| VA | 10% | 10% | 10% | $25,000 | Yes | No |
| WA* | 10% | 10% | 10% | $25,000 | - | Yes |
| WV | 10% | 5% | 5% | $10,000 | - | Yes&No |
| WI* | 15% | 25% | 25% | - | - | No |
| WY | .90 s/f** | 20** | 20** | n/a | n/a | No |

**For general information only. Not to be used for compliance.**

| State | Amount for Cemetery Merchandise | Amount for Cemetery Services | Master Trust | Finance Charges | Constructive Delivery |
|---|---|---|---|---|---|
| AL | None | None | Yes | Yes | Yes |
| AK | -0- | -0- | Yes | Yes | n/a |
| AR | 100% | 100% | n/a | n/a | n/a |
| AZ* | ** | ** | No** | No | No |
| CA* | Unregulated | Unregulated | Yes | Yes | Yes |
| CO | 10% | 10% | No | Yes | Yes |
| CT | Not Limited | Not Limited | n/a | n/a | n/a |
| DE* | Unregulated | Unregulated | n/a | n/a | n/a |
| DC | - | - | - | - | - |
| FL | 110%W-30%F | 100% | Yes | Yes | Yes |
| GA | 35% S/Pr | 50 | No | Yes | Yes |
| IL* | 50% | 50% Deposit | Yes | Yes | Yes |
| IN | 100% | 100% | n/a | Yes | Yes |
| IA* | 125% W/sale | 80% Retail | Yes | Yes | Yes |
| KS* | 110%W/sale | 100% S/Price | No | n/a | Yes |
| KY* | 5,925,130 | 954,983 | Yes | Yes | Yes |
| LA* | 50% S/Price | 50% S/Price | No | Yes | Yes |
| MD* | 55% Contract | 55% Contract | Yes | No | Yes |
| MA | Not Limited | Not Limited | n/a | n/a | n/a |
| ME | 100% Purch. | 100% Trusted | Yes | No | No |
| MI* | 130% Cost | 100% | No | Yes | n/a |
| MN | 100% | 100% | Yes | Yes | None |
| MS | - | - | - | - | - |
| MO* | 80% | 80% | Yes | Yes | No |
| MT | W/sale Cost | 100% | Yes | No | Yes |

**For general information only. Not to be used for compliance.**

| State | Amount for Cemetery Merchandise | Amount for Cemetery Services | Master Trust | Finance Charges | Constructive Delivery |
|---|---|---|---|---|---|
| NE* | 85% Deposit | 85% Deposit | Yes | Yes | No |
| NV | 60% | 60% | n/a | Yes | Yes |
| NH | n/a | n/a | n/a | Yes | n/a |
| NJ | 100% | 100% | Yes | No | n/a |
| NM | -0- | -0- | Yes | Yes | No |
| NY* | n/a | n/a | No | Yes | No |
| NC* | 60% Retail | 60% Retail | Yes | Yes | Yes |
| ND | - | - | - | - | - |
| OH | 60% for Vault | None | n/a | Yes | Yes |
| OK* | 110% W/sale | n/a | n/a | n/a | Yes |
| OR* | Formula | 100% | Yes | n/a | Yes |
| PA* | 70% | 70% | Yes | n/a | n/a |
| RI | n/a | n/a | n/a | n/a | n/a |
| SC* | n/a | n/a | n/a | n/a | n/a |
| SD | - | - | - | - | - |
| TN* | n/a | n/a | n/a | n/a | n/a |
| TX* | n/a | n/a | Yes | Yes | n/a |
| UT | 100% | 100% | No | No | Yes |
| VT* | n/a | n/a | n/a | n/a | n/a |
| VA | n/a | n/a | n/a | n/a | n/a |
| WA* | 50% Trusting | 50% Trusting | Yes | Yes | Yes |
| WV | 40% of Retail | 40% of Retail | Yes | Yes | Yes |
| WI* | 40% Princ** | None | No | n/a | No |
| WY | 100% | 100% | Yes | No | n/a |

**For general information only. Not to be used for compliance.**

| State | Irrevocable Trusts | Excessive Earnings Withdrawal | Interest Earnings Withdrawal | Restrictions on Trust Investments |
|---|---|---|---|---|
| AL | Yes | Yes | Yes | No |
| AK | No | No | No | No |
| AR | n/a | n/a | n/a | No |
| AZ* | No | No | No | n/a |
| CA* | Yes | n/a | Yes | Yes |
| CO | Yes | No | Yes | Yes |
| CT | n/a | n/a | n/a | n/a |
| DE* | n/a | n/a | n/a | n/a |
| DC | - | - | - | - |
| FL | Yes | No | No | Yes |
| GA | Yes | Yes | Yes | Yes |
| HI | Yes | Yes | Yes | Yes |
| ID | Yes | Yes | No | No |
| IL* | Yes | Yes | Yes 25% | Yes |
| IN | Yes | Yes | Yes | Yes |
| IA* | Yes | Yes | Yes** | Yes |
| KS* | No | Yes | No | No |
| KY* | Yes | No | No | Yes |
| LA* | Yes | No | No | Yes |
| MD* | No | No | No | Yes |
| MA | n/a | n/a | n/a | n/a |
| ME | No | No | No | Yes |
| MI* | No | Yes | Yes | Yes |
| MN | Yes | No | No | Yes |
| MS | - | - | - | - |
| MO* | Yes | Yes | Yes | Yes |

**For general information only. Not to be used for compliance.**

| State | Irrevocable Trusts | Excessive Earnings Withdrawal | Interest Earnings Withdrawal | Restrictions on Trust Investments |
|-------|--------------------|-------------------------------|------------------------------|-----------------------------------|
| MT | No | No | No | Yes |
| NE* | Yes | Yes | Yes | Yes |
| NV | Yes | Yes | Yes | Yes |
| NH | Yes | n/a | n/a | No |
| NJ | Yes | No | No | Yes |
| NM | Yes | Yes | Yes | n/a |
| NY* | Yes | No | Yes | Yes |
| NC* | No | Yes | Yes | Yes |
| ND | - | - | - | - |
| OH | Yes | No | No | Yes |
| OK* | n/a | Yes | Yes | Yes |
| OR* | n/a | No | Yes | Yes |
| PA* | n/a | No | n/a | Yes |
| RI | n/a | n/a | n/a | No |
| SC* | n/a | n/a | n/a | n/a |
| SD | - | - | - | - |
| TN* | n/a | n/a | n/a | n/a |
| TX* | Yes | n/a | n/a | No** |
| UT | Yes | Yes | Yes | Yes |
| VT* | n/a | n/a | n/a | n/a |
| VA | n/a | n/a | n/a | - |
| WA* | n/a | No | No | Yes |
| WV | Yes | Yes | Yes | Yes |
| WI* | No | No | No | Yes |
| WY | Yes | n/a | No** | Yes |

**For general information only. Not to be used for compliance.**

| State | Can Cemetery Sell Funeral Insurance | Licensing Requirements | Restrictions on Selling Insurance |
|-------|------|------|------|
| AL | Yes | Life Insurance Agent License Required | n/a |
| AK | n/a | n/a | n/a |
| AR | No | n/a | n/a |
| AZ | Yes** | n/a | n/a |
| CA | Yes | Business & Professions Code 9700 | Person must be a Licensed Agent |
| CO | Yes | Must be Licensed Pre-Need Insurance Rep | Must Comply with Statutes and Regulations |
| CT | No | Licensed with Insurance Department | n/a |
| DE | No | Life Insurance Agent | Licensed Life Insurance Agent |
| DC | - | - | - |
| FL | No | n/a | n/a |
| GA | No | n/a | n/a |
| HI | Yes | Many | Many |
| ID | Yes | Licensed | License Life Insurance Agent |
| IL | Yes | Must be Licensed with Dept. of Insurance | Seller or Provider Cannot be Beneficiary |
| IN | Yes | Must Have Life Insurance Licensing | n/a |
| IA | Yes | Licensed Insurance Agent | Advertising Disclosure Rule - NAIC Mode |
| KS | n/a | n/a | n/a |
| KY | Yes | Licensed by the Department of Linsurance | n/a |
| LA | Yes | n/a | n/a |

**For general information only. Not to be used for compliance.**

| State | Can Cemetery Sell Funeral Insurance | Licensing Requirements | Restrictions on Selling Insurance |
|---|---|---|---|
| MD | No | Only Licensed Insurance Agent | Yes |
| MA | - | - | - |
| ME | No | - | - |
| MI | Yes | Limited Life Insurance License Required | Must Associate w/ Funeral Service Provider |
| MN | Yes | Yes | Not be Employee or Interest in Cem/Home |
| MS | - | - | - |
| MO | Yes | Must be Registered with Board as Sellers | Must be Licensed to Sell Insurance |
| MT | No | State License | n/a |
| NE | Yes | Meet State Requirements | Same as Agent or Agency License within State |
| NV | Yes | License | None |
| NH | Yes | Insurance Comm. | None |
| NJ | No | Yes** | Yes** |
| NM | n/a | n/a | n/a |
| NY | No | No | n/a |
| NC | n/a | n/a | n/a |
| ND | - | - | - |
| OH | Yes | Ohio License | License (Insurance, Health, etc.) |
| OK | Yes | Insurance License/ Permit from State Embalmers Brd. | Licensed by Insurance Commission |
| OR | Yes | Must be Licensed by Department of Insurance | n/a |

**For general information only. Not to be used for compliance.**

| State | Can Cemetery Sell Funeral Insurance | Licensing Requirements | Restrictions on Selling Insurance |
|-------|------|------------------------|-----------------------------------|
| PA | Yes | Yes | Must be Licensed by Ins. Commission |
| RI | No | n/a | n/a |
| SC | No | n/a | Licensed FD Employed by Licensed FH |
| SD | - | - | - |
| TN | n/a | n/a | n/a |
| TX | Yes | Pre-Need License | Agent Licensed by Ins. Commission |
| UT | No | n/a | n/a |
| VT | Yes | Pass Insurance Test | Only for Burial Insurance |
| VA | - | - | - |
| WA | No | Agents Licensed by Commissioner's Office | n/a |
| WV | Yes | Standard Life Isurance Agent's License | n/a |
| WI | No | n/a | n/a |
| WY | Yes | Licensed Agent - Insurance Rep | None |

**For general information only. Not to be used for compliance.**

| State | Trust | Deadlines | Alternatives to Trust | State | Trust | Deadlines | Alternatives to Trust |
|---|---|---|---|---|---|---|---|
| | Preconstructed Property | | | | Preconstructed Property | | |
| AL | No | No | Yes | MT | Yes | n/a | Yes |
| AK | - | - | - | NE* | Yes | No | Yes |
| AR* | Yes | No | Yes | NV | Yes | No | No |
| AZ* | - | - | - | NH | No | No | No |
| CA* | No | No | No | NJ | No | No | No |
| CO | No | No | No | NM* | Yes | No | No |
| CT | - | - | - | NY* | No | No | No |
| DE* | - | - | - | NC* | Yes | Yes | Yes |
| DC | - | - | - | ND | - | - | - |
| FL | Yes | Yes | Yes | OH | No | Yes | - |
| GA | Yes | - | - | OK* | No | No | No |
| HI | No | No | No | OR* | Yes | Yes | No |
| ID* | 50% | No | Yes | )PA* | - | - | - |
| IL* | Yes | Yes | Yes | RI | Yes | Yes | Yes |
| IN | No | No | No | SC | Yes | Yes | No |
| IA* | Yes | No | No | SD | - | - | - |
| KS* | Yes | - | - | TN | - | - | - |
| KY* | Yes | Yes | Yes | TX* | No | No | No |
| LA | Yes | Yes | No | UT | Yes | No | Yes |
| MD* | No | No | No | VT* | - | - | - |
| MA | - | - | - | VA | Yes | Yes | Yes |
| ME | No | No | Yes | WA* | Yes | - | No |
| MI* | Yes | Yes | - | WV | Yes | Yes | No |
| MN | No | No | Yes | WI* | Yes | Yes | Yes |
| MS | - | - | - | WY | Yes | No | No |
| MO | No | No | No | | | | |

**For general information only. Not to be used for compliance.**

# Notes:

## Alaska

No Licensing in Alaska

## Arizona

1. Merchandise and Services Trust—Amount for Cemetery Merchandise and Services
2. No Law or Regulation on the Sales of Pre-Need Cemetery Goods or Services
3. Merchandise and Services Trust—Master Trust Cemetery
4. Endowed Care Cemeteries. Master Trust Cemetery—32-2194.26 Requires Minimum Deposit (Initial) 32-2194.28 Deposit Required From Sales. No Trust for Cemeteries for Cemetery Merchandise. 32-2194.30 Prudent Man—Investment of Funds
5. Insurance Vehicles—Can Cemetery Sell Funeral Insurance if Licensed by Department of Insurance

## Connecticut

1. Merchandise and Services Trust
2. Irrevocable Funeral Trust (Title 19 Limit is $4800)
3. Revocable Funeral Trust—No Limit

## Illinois

1. Reclaim Abandon Lots On Very Limited Basis
2. Endowment Care Trust—New Cemeteries $25,000 Based on Population

## Iowa

1. Salesmen Licensed, if Pre-Need Sales
2. Merchandise and Services Trust—Interest Earnings: Can Withdraw ½ of $ Earned over the Rate of Inflation

## New Jersey

1. Insurance Vehicles—Licensing Requirements
2. Yes, but New Jersey Practitioner's License also Required
3. Insurance Vehicles—Restrictions on Selling Insurance
4. Yes, but New Jersey Insurance Practitioner's License also Required

**For general information only. Not to be used for compliance.**

## Texas
1. Cemeteries—Vault
2. Can Only Sell At-Need, Not Pre-Need Without Pre-Need Permit
3. Chart 1—Cemeteries—Solicitation Restriction
4. Not in Cemetery Statute, but in Other Laws
5. Chart 1—Cemeteries—Lot
6. Of Sales Price or $1.50 Per Square Foot, Whichever is Greater
7. Chart 1—Cemeteries—Crypt
8. Of Sales Price or $90 For Each Crypt, Whichever is Greater
9. Chart 1—Cemeteries—Niche
10. Of Sales Price or $30 Per Niche, Whichever is Greater
11. Merchandise and Services Trust—Restrictions on Trust Investments
12. Only Prudent Man Rule

## Wisconsin
1. Merchandise and Services Trust—Amount for Cemetery Merchandise
2. If Sold as Pre-Need

## Wyoming
1. Chart 1—Cemeteries—Permitted W.S. 35-8-103
2. Chart 1—Cemeteries—Lot W.S. 35-8-103
3. Chart 1—Cemeteries—Crypt W.S. 35-8-404
4. Chart 1—Cemeteries—Niche W.S. 35-8-404
5. Merchandise and Services Trust—Interest Earnings Withdrawal Cemetery Interest and Income Must Be Applied To Perpetual Care Unless it is a Pre-Need Trust for Goods and Services

**For general information only. Not to be used for compliance.**

# C Glossary

This glossary includes funeral related terms as well as cemetery terms because cemeteries often work with funeral directors, operate mortuaries, or may expand into the mortuary business. Also, see the Federal Trade Commission's Funeral Trade Rule in Appendix A.

**alternative container** A non-metal receptacle without ornamentation or interior lining which is designed to hold human remains and is made of cardboard, pressed-wood, composition materials (with or without an outside covering), or pouches of canvas or other materials.

**American Cemetery Association (ACA)** *See* International Cemetery and Funeral Association.

**ashes** *See* cremated remains.

**at need** At time of death, including immediately following or when impending.

**at need solicitation** Any uninvited contact by a seller for the purpose of selling merchandise or services to the family of one whose death is impending or has just occurred. Illegal in some jurisdictions.

**before need** *See* preneed.

**below ground crypt** *See* lawn crypt.

**burial** *See* entombment, interment, and inurnment. **syn.** inhumation.

**burial permit** A legal document issued by a local authority authorizing final disposition of human remains.

**cash advance** Any item of service or merchandise described to a purchaser as a "cash advance," "accommodation," "cash disbursement," or similar term. A cash advance item is also any item obtained from a third party and paid for by the seller on the purchaser's behalf. Cash advance items may include, but are not limited to, cemetery or crematory services, pallbearers, public transportation, clergy honoraria, flowers, musicians or singers, nurses, obituary notices, gratuities, and death certificates.

**casket** A rigid container for the interment of human remains. May be made of wood, metal, or like material and are ornamented and lined with fabric. Wooden models include cloth covered soft woods and hardwoods finished like fine furniture. Metal caskets are most commonly made of steel, copper, or bronze. Additionally, metal caskets may be "protective" or "sealing" because they have a gasket around the lid. The FTC Funeral Trade Rule and some states have specific requirements regarding representations about sealing caskets.

**cemetery** 1 A place dedicated to and used, or intended to be used, for the final disposition and memorialization of human remains. 2 A place for burial of dead human remains.

**cemetery authority** Any person, partnership, or corporation that owns or controls a cemetery or conducts cemetery business.

**cenotaph** A memorial in honor of a deceased person who is interred elsewhere.

**coffin** A container for burial of human remains, usually applied to a hexagonal shaped container. *Also see* **casket**.

**columbarium** *pl.* **-ia, iums** A structure, room, or space in a building or structure used, or intended to be used, for the inurnment of cremated remains.

**cremated remains** The bone fragments remaining after the cremation process which may include the residue of any foreign materials that were cremated with the human remains. Usually processed, after removal of metalic parts of caskets and prosthetics, by crushing or grinding to achieve a uniform consistency.

**cremated remains container** A receptacle in which cremated remains are placed after cremation.

**cremation** The irreversible process of reducing human remains to bone fragments through intense heat and evaporation in a specifically designed furnace or retort which may include any other mechanical or thermal process whereby the bone fragments are pulverized or otherwise further reduced in size or volume. Cremation is a process and is not final disposition. (Note: some states don't agree with this and hold that cremation is a form of disposition.)

**cremation container** An enclosed receptacle which is combustible, rigid, and leak-resistant, and is designed to hold human remains prior to cremation; includes non-metallic caskets.

**crematory** A structure containing a furnace or retort used or intended to be used for the cremation of human remains.

**crypt** A concrete enclosure for interment. Mausoleum crypts are generally above ground and in buildings. Crypts in garden mausoleums also are usually above ground but are open to the outside rather than being in an enclosed building. Crypts also may be installed in large groups underground in lawn sections—*See* lawn crypt. Lawn crypts do not require the use of an additional outer burial container. Lawn crypts are sometimes also are referred to as garden crypts.

**death certificate** A legal document containing vital statistics pertaining to the life and death of the deceased. Must be accepted and filed with the proper agency before a burial permit is issued.

**deed** A document conveying a right of interment in specific cemetery property. Usually doesn't convey any fee ownership.

**direct cremation** Disposition of human remains by cremation without formal viewing, visitation, or ceremony with the body present.

**direct disposition** Any final disposition of human remains without formal viewing, visitation, or ceremony with the body present.

**disinterment** Removing human remains that have been interred. *Also see* interment.

**embalmer** A person authorized by law to engage in embalming.

**embalming** A procedure where human remains are chemically treated by injection and/or topical application for temporary preservation, including, but not limited to, the act of disinfecting, preserving, and restoring the human remains to a natural life-like appearance. The preservation is intended to allow for adequate time to plan a funeral service and for friends and family to travel from out-of-town, rather than for any long-term protection from decomposition.

**endowment care** The maintenance, repair, and care of all places in the cemetery, subject to the rules and regulations of the cemetery authority. May also be known as endowed care, perpetual care, improvement care, permanent care, etc.

**endowment care fund** An irrevocable trust fund set aside by law with a trustee, with the earnings therefrom to provide for the long-term care of the cemetery. Sometimes be referred to as a "Perpetual Care Fund."

**entombment** The act of placing human remains in a crypt.

**final disposition** The lawful disposal of human remains whether by interment, burial at sea, scattering, etc.

**FTC Trade Rule** In 1982, the Federal Trade Commission promulgated a set of regulations requiring disclosure of price and other information by mortuaries and other sellers of funeral services and merchandise (*See* Appendix A).

**funeral director** A person who manages a mortuary. In many states, this person is also an embalmer. This definition varies according to individual state laws and regulations.

**funeral** The ceremony held commemorating the deceased with the remains present.

**funeral establishment** *See* mortuary.

**funeral home** *See* mortuary.

**garden crypt** *See* lawn crypt.

**garden mausoleum** An outdoor mausoleum. Sometimes called "wall crypts" because of the configuration of the crypts and to avoid confusion with indoor mausolea. *Also see* mausoleum.

**grave space** A space of ground in a cemetery that is used or intended to be used for ground burial.

**guaranteed price prepaid contract** A contract with a fixed price for services or merchandise purchased before death. *Also see* nonguaranteed price prepaid contract.

**immediate burial** Disposition of human remains by burial without formal viewing, visitation, or ceremony with the body present, except for a graveside service.

**interment** **1** Final disposition by burial in ground, entombment in a mausoleum, or placement of cremated remains in a niche (inurnment). **2** The process of making an interment, including all administrative, clerical, legal, and mechanical services performed by the cemetery authority in conjunction with the opening of an interment space and closing of the interment space after the remains have been placed in the space.

**interment right** The right to inter human remains in a particular interment space in the cemetery.

**interment right owner** The person or persons who lawfully possess an interment right. There is a presumption of ownership in favor of the person listed as the owner in the records of the cemetery. *syn.* property owner.

**interment space** A space intended for the final disposition of human remains, including, but not limited to, a grave space, mausoleum crypt, garden crypt, columbarium, and lawn crypt.

**International Cemetery And Funeral Association (ICFA)** The largest cemetery trade association. Formerly called the American Cemetery Association. Previous to that name change, the National Association of Cemeteries merged with the American Cemetery Association.

**inurnment** The act of putting cremated remains in an urn and placing the urn in a niche.

**lawn crypt** A pre-placed enclosed chamber, which is usually constructed of reinforced concrete, poured in place or precast unit installed in quantity, either side by side or multiple depth, and covered by earth or sod and also may be known as a garden crypt (not the above ground type), below ground crypt, or turf-top crypt.

**marker** *See* memorial.

**mausoleum** *pl.* **-leums, -lea.** A chamber or structure used, or intended to be used, for entombment. A building that houses crypts for burial. A community mausoleum is for many families, and a private mausoleum is generally sold for the use of a single family. Some vendors sell what they call private or family mausoleums with only a few spaces. Many of these are more correctly called sarcophagi.

**memorial** The physical identification of an interment space. Generally has at least the name, date of birth, and date of death of the deceased and may include an epitaph or commemoration of the life, deeds, or career of the deceased person. These may be in the form of bronze or granite tablets flush with the ground, upright monuments, individual cut out bronze letters applied to the front of a mausoleum crypt, statuary, benches, or other artwork or architectural features. Other terms that might be used are memorial tablet (flush bronze memorial), marker, headstone, crypt plate, or garden plaque. *Also see* cenotaph.

**memorialization** The existence of a memorial or the process of erecting a memorial.

**memorial-park** A cemetery which has adopted a park like style and abolished the use of upright memorials. As envisioned by Hubert Eaton who coined the term, a memorial-park has "sweeping lawns" and must also be inspirational, "...a place that uplifts and educates a community." Some cemeteries continue to allow upright memorials but call themselves memorial-parks because they have some sections where upright memorials are not allowed.

**memorial service** A ceremony commemorating the deceased without the remains present.

**memorial society** A membership organization which distributes information about funerals. May promote methods of prearrangement, changes to funeral laws, and offer referrals to specific funeral homes. Generally, not regulated.

**merchandise** Any personal property offered or sold by any seller for use in connection with the funeral, final disposition, memorialization, or interment of human remains.

**monument** An upright memorial, including what used to be called a tombstone, also includes large structures like obelisks, usually made from granite.

**mortuary** A place of business used in the care, planning, and preparation for final disposition or transportation of human remains. Operations may include arranging and conducting funerals, sales of services and funeral merchandise, and embalming.

**National Association of Cemeteries (NAC)** *See* International Cemetery and Funeral Association.

**niche** A space within a columbarium used or intended to be used for inurnment of cremated remains.

**non-guaranteed price prepaid contract** A prepaid contract where the seller reserves the right to charge additional fees in the future in addition to the price stated in the prepaid contract. *Also see* guaranteed price prepaid contract.

**opening and closing** *See* interment.

**outer burial container** A container which is designed for placement in the grave space around the casket, including, but not limited to, containers commonly known as burial vaults, grave boxes, and grave liners.

**perpetual care** Generally replaced by the term "endowment care." *See* endowment care.

**Potter's Fields** A cemetery for paupers. The term comes from Matthew 27:7 when the chief priests determined what to do with the thirty pieces of silver returned by Judas: "So they took counsel, and bought with them the potter's field, to bury strangers in."

**predeveloped** Designated areas or buildings within a cemetery that have been mapped and planned for future construction, but are not yet completed.

**prearrangement** Making plans for a funeral or interment prior to death or impending death. A broad term which can encompass both preplanning and prepaid purchases.

**prefinancing** *See* prepaid purchase and prepaid contract.

**preneed** Prior to death or prior to an impending death. Not at need.

**prepaid contract** A written contract to purchase merchandise or services from the seller on a preneed basis. *Also see* guaranteed price prepaid contract and non-guaranteed price prepaid contract.

**prepaid purchase** Purchasing cemetery or funeral commodities or services preneed. Purchase may be for a lump sum or on an installment contract. Not necessarily a price guarantee but often perceived to include one. *Also see* guaranteed price prepaid contract and non-guaranteed price prepaid contract.

**preplanning** Making and recording the preneed decisions for interment or funeral services. Does not necessarily include a preneed purchase. *Also see* prepaid purchase and prearrangement.

**private mausoleum** A mausoleum for one family. *See* mausoleum and sarcophagus.

**processing cremated remains** The grinding or pulverizing of the bone fragments remaining from a cremation to achieve a more uniform consistency. *Also see* cremation.

**property owner** *See* interment right holder.

**residue** Cremated remains which are imbedded in cracks and uneven spaces of the cremation chamber or in the cremated remains container and cannot be removed through reasonable manual contact with sweeping or scraping equipment.

**rules and regulations** Rules adopted by a cemetery to govern uses, care, control, and management as well as other restrictions deemed necessary by the governing board for protection of the cemetery.

**sarcophagus** *pl.* **-gi.** A structure of marble or stone, or covered with marble or stone, for entombment of one or more casketed human remains. May be indoors.

**services** Any services which may be used to care for and prepare human remains for burial, cremation, or other final disposition and to arrange, supervise, or conduct the funeral ceremony or the final disposition of human remains.

**special care** Any care provided, or to be provided, in excess of endowment care in accordance with the specific directions of any donor of funds for such purposes. Funds for special care may be held in a trust fund similar to an endowment care fund.

**tombstone** *See* monument.

**traditional cemetery** A cemetery which allows or requires traditional upright memorials. *See* memorial-park.

**undertaker** *See* funeral director.

**urn** A receptacle for cremated remains. Should not be confused with an alternative container or cremation container.

**vault** *See* outer burial container.

**wall crypt** *See* garden mausoleum.

# Bibliography

Bowen, William G., *Inside the Boardroom: Governance By Directors and Trustees*, New York: John Wiley & Sons, 1994.

Burk, Margaret and Gary Hudson, *Final Curtain*, Santa Ana, California: Seven Locks Press, 1996.

Burek, Deborah, ed., *Cemeteries of the U.S.: A guide to contact information for U.S. cemeteries and their records*, Detroit: Gale Research, 1994.

Davey, Richard, *A History of Mourning*, London, England: Jay's, 1889.

De Pree, Max, *Leading Without Power*: Finding hope in serving the community, San Francisco: Jossey–Bass, Inc., 1997.

Deacy, William, *Memorial Today For Tomorrow*, Tate, Georgia: Georgia Marble Co., 1928.

Eaton, Hubert, *The Comemoral: The Cemetery of the Future*, Los Angeles: Interment Association of California, 1954.

Fulton, Robert, *Death and Identity*, New York: John Wiley & Sons, Inc., 1965.

Furth, Jane, and Sheree R. Curry, "Going for the Geezers," *Fortune*, December 25, 1995.

Hancock, Ralph, *The Forest Lawn Story*, Los Angeles: Angelus Press, 1964.

Habenstein, Robert W., and William M. Lamers, *Funeral Customs The World Over*, Milwaukee: Bulfin Printers, 1960.

———*The History of American Funeral Directing*, Milwaukee: Bulfin Printers, 1955.

Harris, Marlyn, "The Final Payment," *Money*, September 1997.

Herzberg, Frederick, *Work and the Nature of Man*, Cleveland: World Publishing, 1966.

Horn, Miriam, "The Deathcare Business," *U.S. News & World Report*, March 23, 1998, vol. 124, no. 11.

Irion, Paul E., *The Funeral: Vestige or Value?*, Nashville: Abingdon Press, 1966.

"Industry Reacts to '60 Minutes' Segment—Same Old Story," *American Funeral Director*, vol. 121, no. 3 (March 1998).

Klupar, G. J., *Modern Cemetery Management*, Catholic Cemeteries of the Archdiocese of Chicago, 1962.

Kubler-Ross, Elisabeth, M.D., *On Death and Dying*, New York: Macmillan Company, 1969.

Larson, Erik, "Fight to the Death: A battle between rival funeral-home dynasties puts the spotlight on a vast but quiet transformation in the way we bury our dead," *Time*, vol. 148, no. 26 (December 9, 1996).

Lowrie, Walter, *Classical Cemeteries as Works of Art*, Gloucester Art, 1984.

Lynch, Thomas, *The Undertaking: Life Studies From the Dismal Trade*, New York: Penguin Books, 1997.

Mann, A. T., *Sacred Architecture*, Shaftsbury, Dorset: Element Books, Ltd., 1993.

Marion, John Francis, *Famous and Curious Cemeteries*, New York: Crown, 1977.

Meyer, Richard E., ed., *Ethnicity and the American Cemetery*, Bowling Green, Ohio: Bowling Green State University Popular Press, 1993.

Meyer, Richard E. and S. Bronner, eds., *Cemeteries and Gravemarkers: Voices of American Culture*, Ann Arbor, Michigan: UMI Research Press, 1989.

Mitford, Jessica, *The American Way of Death*, New York: Simon and Schuster, 1963.

Newman, Juduth, "At Your Disposal: The funeral industry prepares for boom times," *Harpers Magazine*, November 1997.

Roberts, Darryl J., *Profits of Death: An insider exposes the death care industries / Learn how to cut funeral costs in half!*, Chandler, Arizona: Five Star Publications, 1997.

Robinson, W., F.L.S., *God's Acre Beautiful or The Cemeteries of the Future*, London: John Murray, 1883.

Salkever, Alex, "Making a Killing," *Hawaii Business*, March 1998.

Saporito, Thomas J., "Pitfalls in the CEO Selection Process," *Director's Monthly*, National Association of Corporate Directors, Vol. 22, No. 1, January 1998.

Schmall, V. L., and C. Pratt, *When Death Comes*, Oregon State University Extension Service, rev. 1993.

Sloan, David Charles, *The Last Great Necessity: Cemeteries in American History*, Baltimore: The Johns Hopkins University Press, 1991.

Smith, Ronald G. E., *The Death Care Industries in the United States*, Jefferson, North Carolina: McFarland & Company, 1996.

Sonnenfeld, Jeffrey A., *The Hero's Farewell: What happens when CEOs retire*, Oxford: Oxford University Press, 1988.

St. Johns, Adela Rogers, *First Step Up Toward Heaven*, Englewood Cliffs: Prentice Hall, 1959.

Strangstad, Lynette, *A Graveyard Preservation Primer*, Walnut Creek, California: Alta Mira Press, 1995.

Tarnes, Richard, *The Passion of the Western Mind: Understanding the Ideas That Have Shaped Our World View*, New York: Ballantine Books, 1991.

# Index

# About the Author

John Llewellyn is CEO of Forest Lawn Memorial-Parks and Mortuaries in Southern California and a third generation cemeterian. Forest Lawn is widely recognized as a leader within the industry and is responsible for innovations such as the memorial-park plan and mortuaries within cemeteries as well as being a pioneer in the preneed sales field.

As an active leader in the cemetery industry, he is a past-president and director of the International Cemetery and Funeral Association and the Interment Association of California and is a director of the California Mortuary Alliance and Western Cemetery Alliance. He also holds California licenses as a Cemetery Broker and Funeral Director.

John has served as a director of many non-profit and for-profit organizations—ranging in size from small start-up operations to one with several billion dollars in assets. He has chaired the Braille Institute of America, Los Angeles Convention and Visitors Bureau, Los Angeles Area Council–Boy Scouts of America, and Economic Round Table. He has served as a director of Beneficial Standard Life Insurance Company, California Chamber of Commerce, Claremont Graduate University, Employers Group, and many other organizations as well as several corporations related to Forest Lawn.

A graduate of the University of Redlands with a major in Economics, John earned an MBA from the University of Southern California.

John and his wife, Linda, live in Pasadena, California, with their daughter and two Russian Blue cats.

# Order Form

## *A Cemetery Should Be Forever*

Name

Company

Address

City        State        Zip

_____ copies @ $19.95 USD   _____

Sales Tax   _____

Shipping   _____

Total Enclosed   _____

**Sales tax:** Add appropriate sales tax for books shipped to a California or Ohio address.

**Shipping** (CHECK BOX FOR SHIPPING METHOD):

❏ U.S. Standard: $5.00 for the first book plus $2.00 for each additional book.

❏ U.S. Second Day Air: $9.00 for the first book plus $2.00 for each additional book. Add an additional $13.00 for AK, HI, PR, or American Samoa.

❏ International Standard: $6.00 for the first book plus $3.00 for each additional book.

**Send check with order to:** (DO NOT SEND CASH)

Tropico Press
P.O. Box 1151
Glendale, CA 91205

Also available at **www.TropicoPress.com**

Prices subject to change without notice.